Ius Gentium: Comparative Perspectives on Law and Justice

Volume 126

Ius Gentium is a book series which discusses the central questions of law and justice from a comparative perspective. The books in this series collect the contrasting and overlapping perspectives of lawyers, judges, philosophers and scholars of law from the world's many different jurisdictions for the purposes of comparison, harmonisation, and the progressive development of law and legal institutions. Each volume makes a new comparative study of an important area of law. This book series continues the work of the well-known journal of the same name and provides the basis for a better understanding of all areas of legal science.

The *Ius Gentium* series provides a valuable resource for lawyers, judges, legislators, scholars, and both graduate students and researchers in globalisation, comparative law, legal theory and legal practice. The series has a special focus on the development of international legal standards and transnational legal cooperation.

Boldizsár Artúr Szentgáli-Tóth

The Past, Present, and Future of Legislation with Supermajority

Springer

Boldizsár Artúr Szentgáli-Tóth
HUN-REN Centre for Social Sciences
Institute for Legal Studies
Budapest, Budapest, Hungary

ISSN 1534-6781 ISSN 2214-9902 (electronic)
Ius Gentium: Comparative Perspectives on Law and Justice
ISBN 978-3-031-99323-7 ISBN 978-3-031-99324-4 (eBook)
https://doi.org/10.1007/978-3-031-99324-4

This Springer imprint is published by the registered company Springer Nature Switzerland AG
The registered company address is: Gewerbestrasse 11, 6330 Cham, Switzerland

Acknowledgements

I would like to express my gratitude to those without whom this book would not have been possible. First of all, I would like to thank my family for their persistent and unconditional love. I am grateful to my colleagues who have helped me in my professional growth, and also to my friends who provided invaluable support in challenging times. I would like to extend special thanks to those who provided professional advice or feedback on language accuracy, which helped in the finalization of this volume. Please note that I take full responsibility for any errors.

Competing Interests The author has no competing interests to declare that are relevant to the content of this manuscript.

Contents

Chapter 1
Aims and Methods

1.1 Introduction: The Definition of Supermajority Law

In more than fifty countries all around the world, supermajority law appears in almost all branches of law. For example, it affects[1] the status, organization, and competences of the main constitutional actors, the protection of fundamental rights, and, rarely, also public policy matters.[2] I have prepared a publicly available online table which provides a full and global overview from the topical coverage of supermajority law.[3]

Parliaments primarily enact legislation with a simple majority, which means the majority of the deputies present in a particular parliamentary sitting should be the minimum quorum met. These laws are referred to as ordinary laws vis-à-vis supermajority laws, whose enactment is subject to elevated parliamentary consent.

In most cases, this supermajority means the absolute majority or two-thirds majority of all parliamentary representatives. Sporadically, other prescribed levels of elevated majority might also appear, such as the four-sevenths majority in Chile or the three-fifths majority in Rwanda or Slovakia. The supermajority mechanism works differently in unicameral and bicameral parliaments: bicameral parliaments prefer weaker forms of supermajority, like the absolute majority, while countries with unicameral parliaments usually operate with more demanding versions of elevated parliamentary consent.

Moreover, besides the demand for broad parliamentary consent, further safeguards might also be implemented into the concept of supermajority legislation. The most frequent element could be the mandatory or potential prior constitutional

[1] https://airtable.com/appiQMCks9chv0vEo/shrvTQWgBL6uFAc77.

[2] Szentgáli-Tóth (2022).

[3] https://airtable.com/appiQMCks9chv0vEo/shrvTQWgBL6uFAc77.

B. A. Szentgáli-Tóth, *The Past, Present, and Future of Legislation with Supermajority*, Ius Gentium: Comparative Perspectives on Law and Justice 126,
https://doi.org/10.1007/978-3-031-99324-4_1

review after the enactment but before the promulgation of supermajority laws. This means that once the parliament adopts a supermajority law, it is sent to the constitutional court, which would assess the constitutionality of the adopted supermajority law. The supermajority law cannot be promulgated unless the constitutional court has confirmed by its ruling its conformity with the constitution. This prior constitutional review could be mandatory, as in France and in Francophone countries, as well as in Venezuela. The optional version also exists in Portugal, where certain authorized constitutional actors could turn to the Constitutional Tribunal within a constitutionally determined deadline, requesting the constitutional review of the enacted supermajority law before its promulgation by the president of the republic.

However, apart from supermajority and prior constitutional review, other potential procedural safeguards might also be introduced. As Figs. 5.1 and 5.2 illustrates, several models of supermajority law exist around the world; these may be distinguished based on the procedural rules attached to the supermajority legislative process.

Furthermore, the exact rank of supermajority law, somewhere between the constitution and ordinary statutes, has remained a highly dubious matter wherever this concept has been introduced. Therefore, the classification of supermajority law concepts shall also reflect on this matter. The constitution may establish the hierarchy between supermajority and ordinary laws; however, without such clarifications, constitutional courts and legal scholars should assess whether the stricter procedural requirements for the enactment of supermajority laws correlate with their supremacy over ordinary laws.

Besides this, the scope of supermajority legislation provided by the constitution also makes a significant difference between supermajority law concepts. Heightened parliamentary consent should cover, at least in principle, the most important legislative fields. Since the significance of legislative subjects obviously depends on subjective value judgments, the enumeration of supermajority legislative fields varies considerably from country to country. Figure 9.1 shows those legislative fields that shall be regulated by supermajority legislation in at least 15 countries.

Based on these assumptions, supermajority law might be defined as a constitutionally prescribed subcategory of laws with quasi-constitutional character, which covers at least theoretically the most crucial legislative fields and is subject to stricter procedural safeguards than the requirements of the ordinary legislative process.[4] This indicative definition reflects on the three main distinctive features of supermajority law: its special legal rank; the unique procedural rules attached to this concept; and the scope of its applicability. The constitutional rank of supermajority law should fall somewhere between the constitution and ordinary law; the procedural rules for enacting or amending supermajority law should be stricter vis-à-vis ordinary laws, while the scope of applicability should cover some significant fields of legislation provided by the constitution.

---

[4] Camby (1998), pp. 1686–1698; Jakab and Szilágyi (2014), pp. 96–110; Avril and Gicquel (2014), pp. 267–307.

One may recognize supermajority laws based on these three features. Among others, French "lois organiques," Spanish "leyes orgánicas," Portuguese "leis orgânicas," Italian "leggi costituzionali," Romanian "legi organice," Croatian "organski zakoni," and Hungarian "sarkalatos törvények" also fall within this broad category, which represents an excellent example of the long, partly intentional, partly incidental migration of a constitutional idea. The various denominations of supermajority laws will be clarified in Sect. 1.6.

During the period of cumulative crises, when a number of evolving military, political, economic, health, and environmental issues increase the fragmentation of society, consensus-building and all of its instruments should be granted more weight than ever before, as only widely supported, carefully negotiated solutions could meaningfully contribute to the effective tackling of current challenges. Considering all of its disadvantages, supermajority legislation can be exploited during such negotiation processes. Therefore, the elaboration on and deeper understanding of this instrument further serves more inclusive and reliable decision-making processes for the sake of long-term sustainability.

1.2 Questions Raised During the Research

Supermajority laws are often discussed in constitutional scholarship, but their assessment always focuses on one particular aspect. My purpose is to provide a broad overview of the legal issues related to supermajority legislation and the main alternatives regarding how the following challenges may be tackled.

- Firstly, On the one hand, the legal rank of supermajority law should be assessed: the hierarchy between ordinary- and supermajority laws or the lack of it decide, whether ordinary laws could contradict supermajority laws.[5] On the other hand, the relationship between the constitution and supermajority laws might also raise significant uncertainty; numerous arguments could support the quasi-constitutional character of supermajority laws.
- Secondly, the procedural details of the supermajority legislative process should be taken into account: which level of majority is required for the enactment of these laws; whether prior constitutional review is involved is involved in the supermajority law concept;
- Thirdly, the scope of supermajority should be scrutinized: whether the status, organisation and competences of the main constitutional actors are covered by supermajority laws; whether fundamental rights would fall under the stricter legislative process; and whether public policy matters such as the pension- or tax system may appear amongst the supermajority legislative fields.

[5] Camby (1998), p. 1688.

Some of these questions have already been raised by several authors. As a new avenue in my research, I put the issue in a broader context than anybody else has, and therefore, the horizons of the assessment cover more important aspects. I do not state, and I should not state, that this book provides a full overview of supermajority legislation: in reality, merely fragments are outlined from such a legal instrument. More could be and should be written in the future to understand the issue more deeply.

The scientific assessment of supermajority legislation dates back to its appearance in constitutional systems. The origins of this framework are found in the Middle Ages. Since supermajority laws are often surrounded by serious legal and political debates, several prestigious constitutional lawyers in France, Spain, Hungary, and several other jurisdictions have formed an opinion on this legal instrument. As will be demonstrated later, the considerations of these authors remarkably influenced my opinion on supermajority legislation. Apart from the existing points of reference in the literature, extensive constitutional case law also deals with these matters;[6] constitutional practice considers a wide range of relevant issues.

The adoption of new constitutions always enriches the debate around supermajority law in those countries where this legal instrument exists. Several authors still argue either for the negligence of this concept or at least for the diminution of its scope.[7] French scholarship provides the most extensive and detailed reflections, including the contributions of Jean-Pierre Camby,[8] Pierre Avril,[9] and Michel Debré,[10] regarding organic law. Among contemporary authors, the works of Michel Troper[11] are also worth contemplating.

In Spain, during the almost five decades since organic laws have existed, more experts[12] have shared their thoughts on this matter, while the relevant practice of the Spanish Constitutional Tribunal has also added several valuable elements.[13]

Supermajority legislation has not been introduced in Germany; however, legislative supermajority as a potential alternative has been regularly discussed in the German literature and legal discourse, especially in the field of financial and criminal law.[14]

Some Latin American constitutions also mention organic law, while the constitutional case law, as well as the relevant literature from that continent, and also reflect

[6] Küpper (2014), pp. 2–5.

[7] As an example, please see the commentary on the previous Constitution of Hungary published shortly before the enactment of the Fundamental Law, which also contested the implementation of supermajority laws. Jakab (2011), pp. 76–77.

[8] Camby (1989), p. 1401.

[9] Avril and Gicquel (2014), pp. 267–307.

[10] Debré (1959), pp. 7–29.

[11] Troper (2006), p. 43.

[12] To set an example: Serramalera (2004), pp. 15–17.

[13] For instance: Chofre Sirvent (1994), pp. 99–202.

[14] Hufeld et al. (2016), pp. 96–102; Vormbaum (2018), pp. 53–63; Waldhoff (2016).

the uncertainties around this legal instrument.[15] Although supermajority legislation is not preferred in common law systems, opinions can also be found in English-language literature.

Even though supermajority laws have raised the interest of numerous prestigious scholars, a complex and contextual analysis of this legal instrument has not yet been provided. Those authors who covered this topic restricted their reflections to the current practical challenges and did not attempt to thoroughly understand the theoretical and dogmatic background of supermajority law. Consequently, the experts who touched upon supermajority legislation concentrated on narrower aspects and did not take into account the broader context. In this volume, I aim to cover as many relevant aspects as possible. Supermajority laws should be assessed as comprehensively as possible to elaborate on the multifaceted puzzle around the advantages and disadvantages of currently existing models and the possible directions of further development.

1.3 Main Hypotheses

My analysis is based on three main hypotheses correlating with the procedural rules, the legal rank and the scope of supermajority laws. The justification of these assumptions, as well as the enumeration of the counterarguments forms the primary purposes of my work. The three primary starting points are the following:

- Firstly, I posit that supermajority shall be distinguished from ordinary laws as a separate constitutional concept and a category of legal sources with a legal rank falling clearly under the constitution, but over ordinary laws. Strong arguments support that, for certain crucial legislative subject matters, special safeguards might be reasonable, but direct constitutional protection would impose too severe restrictions on the ordinary legislative power. On these grounds, I cannot agree with the views arguing for the abolishment of the whole concept of supermajority law.

My second assumption states that due to several short-comings, the current procedural frameworks of supermajority law could not maximize its efficiency as a constitutional instrument. Other tools might better highlight the role of supermajority laws as safeguards vis-á-vis their currently mostly restrictive character.

- Thirdly, the current concept of supermajority law covers an overbroad range of statutes. Therefore, I argue for the necessity of narrowing the supermajority legislation to counterbalance the distortive effects of this framework. Crucial

[15] As an example please see: Sepúlveda (2006), pp. 100–112; Peña (2005), p. 7; Supreme Court of Venezuela, Constitutional Chamber, no. 2573. October 16, 2002; Supreme Court of Venezuela, Constitutional Chamber, no. 34, January 26. 2004; Supreme Court of Venezuela, no. 229, February 14. 2007.

advantages and disadvantages would obviously arise from extensive supermajority legislation. However, in my view, the arguments against this idea hold more weight. Supermajority legislation may be justified in the regulation of certain key institutions of the state, where the consent of the constitutional and political actors should be meaningful. By contrast, beyond this scope, supermajority legislation might hinder the construction of a well-functioning parliamentary democracy that safeguards constitutional stability.

In light of these three considerations, more legitimate alternative directions can be identified to further develop the existing main models: the scope of this legal instrument might be diminished; mandatory a priori review might be established; while the reconsideration of the legislative process; or the elaboration of precise contours for the hierarchy of norms might also be necessary. My general proposals stem from these ideas; although the country-specific implementation would still obviously significantly vary depending on historical traditions, on the currently applicable model of supermajority legislation and on the broader constitutional and social context where the proposed constitutional reform would be implemented.

1.4 The Methodology of the Research

The research comprised four main steps. Firstly, I studied each national constitution of the world and selected those that have implemented a certain form of supermajority law. The outcome of this phase is summarized in Fig. 1.1, which shows the geographical spread of supermajority law, and also in Figs. 5.1 and 5.2, which illustrate the various models of supermajority law distinguished on the basis of applicable procedural rules and the uni- or bicameral parliaments of the different countries.

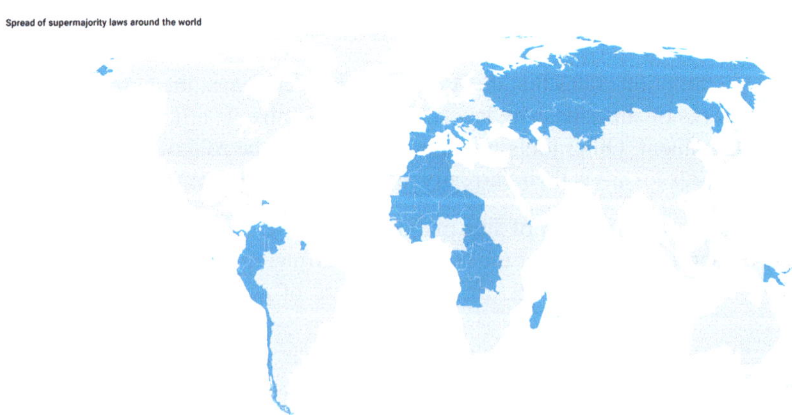

Fig. 1.1 Spread of supermajority laws around the world, Source: desk research of the author

Secondly, I have analyzed the structure of each supermajority law concept, which resulted in the identification of three distinctive features: the legal rank, the procedural rules, and the scope of supermajority law. These three characteristics might be used to distinguish supermajority laws from other similar legal concepts. The legal rank should fall somewhere between the constitution and ordinary laws; the procedural rules should be stricter vis-à-vis the ordinary legislative process; and the scope should include a subcategory of significant legislative fields determined by the constitution.

If these three criteria are met, one can classify a legal concept as supermajority law and may compare it with other alternative versions of the same legal instrument. As Figs. 5.1 and 5.2 shows, under the coverage of the three aforementioned categories, several alternative models have been developed, operating with diverse procedural rules, different denominations (Fig. 1.2), and multiple scopes of application (Fig. 9.1).

Constitutional scholarship exploited the broad comparative perspectives on supermajority law only in a limited manner; therefore, after having identified the three aforementioned distinctive characteristics, Chap. 2 will demonstrate the specificities of various supermajority law concepts around the world from these three respects and also from a historical perspective. This analysis outlines a broad comparative overview of the diversity of supermajority law concepts that has not been elaborated on by constitutional scholarship so far.

Then, as the third main step, my assessment will turn to the arguments justifying the existence of supermajority laws. Two sets of sources have been used for the identification of the five main arguments. On the one hand, this structure of the volume relies on the academic scholarship briefly mentioned in Sect. 1.2. Although the comparative analysis in Chap. 2 has been extended to all countries operating with supermajority law, most academic references come from France, Spain, and Hungary, since most doctrinal analyses and legal practices focusing on

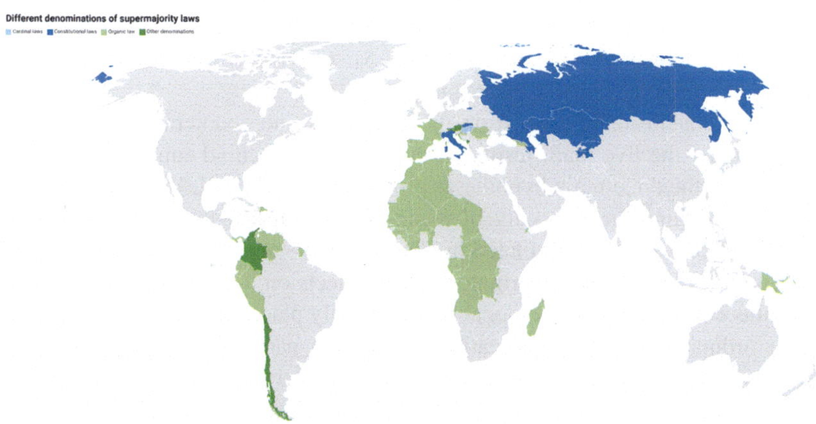

Fig. 1.2 Different denominations of supermajority laws, Source: desk research of the author

supermajority law have been available from these countries. However, the relevant academic discourse and constitutional case law of other countries have also been involved in the assessment of the five justifying arguments, as long as the availability of the sources and the language barriers made it possible.

On the other hand, I relied on the three aforementioned defining elements of supermajority law and used them for the separation and detailed conceptualization of the five main justifying arguments in Chaps. 3–7. The first two of these arguments are linked to the legal rank of supermajority laws and investigate the special position of supermajority laws between the constitution and ordinary laws. One of them highlights the quasi-constitutional character of supermajority laws and describes these norms as extensions of the constitution. The second potential approach considers supermajority law as a paramount instrument serving the stability of the constitution.

The third justifying argument gives greater weight to the procedural rules attached to the supermajority legislative process and focuses on the political impact of these additional requirements for the enactment of certain significant laws.

The fourth and fifth justifying considerations derive from the constitutionally prescribed scope of supermajority law. If any form of supermajority is required for regulating the status, competences, and organization of the main constitutional actors, this would impact the separation of powers considerably. Moreover, if certain fundamental rights are also included among the fields of supermajority legislation, the role of this concept in the protection of fundamental rights may also underline their implementation into national constitutions.

In Chaps. 3–7, a complex overview is targeted within the frameworks of each justifying argument: the significance of these concepts is estimated with the help of contrasting numerous considerations supporting or weakening their relevance. Although several arguments mentioned in this assessment clearly contradict this outcome, the complete analysis favors the main elements of the proposed alternative model of supermajority law (Chap. 9): the exact legal rank of supermajority law under the constitution but above ordinary laws (Chaps. 3 and 4); the requirement of an absolute parliamentary majority for the enactment of supermajority laws with additional supplementary safeguards (Chap. 5); and the considerably narrowed scope of supermajority law (Chaps. 6 and 7).

The main conclusions drawn from the arguments and counterarguments to be presented under the five main justifying considerations behind supermajority law would support the three main hypotheses provided under Sect. 1.3. These hypotheses would underline the necessity of reconsidering supermajority law concepts; exact suggestions will be formulated in Chaps. 8 and 9 for this purpose. The suggested alternative model of supermajority law reflects on the three distinctive features of this concept: it proposes legal rank explicitly placed under the constitution but over ordinary laws; the application of absolute parliamentary majority as a weaker form of supermajority with some supplementary elements; and a significantly narrowed scope of supermajority legislation.

In Chaps. 3 and 4, the factors of uncertainty will be presented, which requires the clarification of supermajority law's position under the constitution, but above ordinary laws in the hierarchy of legal sources (detailed in Sect. 8.2). Chapter 5 will demonstrate how the various procedural elements of supermajority law concepts contribute to the distortion of the political discourse; these unwanted effects of supermajority laws lead to the elaboration of the suggestion of an absolute parliamentary majority as supermajority (Sect. 8.3) and the introduction of mandatory prior constitutional review after the enactment, but before the promulgation of these laws (Sect. 8.4). Finally, Chaps. 6 and 7 take into account the fundamental rights and the institutional aspects of supermajority law and give the reasons behind the proposed narrower scope of supermajority law to be detailed under Sect. 8.5.

The topic of supermajority law is considered a relatively well-researched area; therefore, this volume also relies on the relevant literature from recent decades. My work will nevertheless fill a significant gap, as nobody has examined supermajority legislation systematically, from a broader perspective with the goal of publishing a monograph about this concept. This does not mean that the interdisciplinary character of supermajority law is a completely new insight: some aspects of supermajority legislation have been researched deeply, for instance, the comparative approach has already been highlighted by several academic contributions.[16] This book attempts to reconcile the different narratives, the formulation of some crucial theses from supermajority legislation, and substantiate them from several angles.

My book will analyze the dogmatic background and theoretical framework of supermajority law, and based on this, I will draw conclusions on the alleged perspectives of supermajority legislation. After considering this basic concept, I will generally discuss the legal relationship between the constitution, supermajority and ordinary laws. In other cases, my assumptions will be supported by specific examples from different countries. Since my primary topic focuses on supermajority law as a legal instrument, and supermajority legislation as a widespread phenomenon around the world, I will not take into account the regulatory structure of each supermajority legislative field. For example, whether the ideal scope of supermajority law might vary from field to field. The responsible research of such issues would not only require knowledge of the supermajority law as a concept itself, but also specialized expertise in the particular fields of supermajority legislation. Therefore, these dilemmas should be conceptualized by interdisciplinary research groups in the future.

The final purpose of researching supermajority law is to create a test for constitutional courts as a point of reference to decide, in which circle supermajority is required from the legislation in the light of the constitutionally stipulated orientations. Such construction would considerably serve the accountability of the legal practice. To establish such a well-founded test, it is necessary to review the main theoretical issues concerning supermajority legislation. In this volume, I would like to contribute to the first step of this challenging route: the elaboration of the dogmatic framework at the broader sense. I hope that after having detailed the theoretical setting, at a later stage, research groups comprised of experts from

[16] An overview from this please see: Szentgáli-Tóth (2023), pp. 171–197.

different backgrounds may be able to examine these issues from a more pragmatic perspective as well.

This book fosters the development of a test in constitutional literature and practice within a foreseeable timeframe. This test aims to open up new perspectives on the history of supermajority legislation. It is motivated by the fact that several important questions regarding supermajority laws have not been addressed. As a result, there are many areas that have not been thoroughly explored, presenting significant challenges for legal researchers. One such area is the comparative aspect.[17] Therefore, the comparative approach still holds considerable potential in this field of legal research.

I do not cover the potential role of supermajority in the decision-making mechanisms of international organisations, especially the European Union, for various reasons. The special majority requirements set by the founding treaties of the European Union for certain decisions of the European Council probably constitute the most researched aspect of supermajority.[18] First, instead of the decision-making of a sovereign state, supermajority in international organizations is applied for the voting of supranational bodies entitled to conclude compromises amongst the member states.[19] Second, as a clear consequence, elevated majorities might be required from multiple aspects considering the political and economic weight, as well as the territory and the population of each member state.[20] Third, due to the inherently different background of supermajority at the supranational level, the historical development of this legal instrument,[21] the procedural rules,[22] the scope and the legal rank[23] of supermajority cannot be compared to the national versions of supermajority legislation. Consequently, I delimit this volume to the emergence of supermajority legislation at the national level however, one should keep in mind that several theoretical considerations might also contribute to the better understanding of supranational supermajority regimes.

Supermajority required for legislation should clearly be distinguished from the elevated level of prescribed consent for constitutional amendments.[24] The supermajority necessary for constitutional amendments serves the stability of the constitution.[25] In contrast, the supermajority legislation only serves as one, probably not the most important, function attached to the stability of the constitution.

---

[17] Troper and Chagnollaud (2012), pp. 328–346.

[18] A separate volume has been devoted to this issue, providing a broad compilation of several contributions from related matters: Cichocki and Życzkowski (2011).

[19] Ion (2023), pp. 39–57.

[20] Peters (2020), pp. 370–387.

[21] Hahm et al. (2020), pp. 599–623.

[22] Warntjen (2017), pp. 673–687.

[23] Nováky (2021), p. 239.

[24] Albert (2023), pp. 9–10.

[25] Albert (2023), p. 12.

The relationship between supermajority legislation and the constitution needs further noteworthy clarification. While legal practice often classifies supermajority laws as statutes, strong arguments also support the constitutional or quasi-constitutional character of these norms. However, despite the clear link between quasi-constitutional and supermajority legislation, the two categories should be separated clearly.[26] Quasi-constitutional laws almost confer constitutional authority on certain statutes regardless of the applicable procedural rules, while supermajority legislation describes the establishment of a special statutory subcategory that can be placed somewhere between ordinary laws and the constitution and is distinguished by special procedural requirements. A law might either be quasi-constitutional and supermajority law at the same time, but in most cases, the two slightly overlapping classifications can result in different outcomes and theoretical consequences as will be demonstrated below.

The discourse around various supermajority requirements prescribed for passing certain parliamentary decisions has also been closely linked to supermajority legislation;[27] but another important distinction is once more necessary. As Schwartzberg describes,[28] the discussion on supermajority also concerns elevated consent requirements provided for constitution-making; constitutional amendments and legislation. Adapted to the scope of supermajority legislation, this book will only cover the legislative aspect of this branch of the literature in detail, because supermajority legislation means from this perspective the imposition of supermajority requirements for the enactment of certain pieces of legislation. Schwartzberg identifies three justifications of supermajority rules: consensus-building; constitutional stability and the protection of minorities.[29] Whereas, due to the specific legislative context, I will operate with five main justificatory arguments in this volume, partly overlapping with those highlighted by Schwartzberg.

1.5 The Essence of the Interdisciplinary Approach

The assessment of supermajority laws shall not be limited to selected aspects or to one particular scientific discipline. A careful overview of the complex puzzle can be provided with proper consideration of the main overlapping functions performed by supermajority law.[30] My work has been shaped by this approach: I focus on the different functions of supermajority legislation from various scientific viewpoints. When researching a category of legal sources, the approach of constitutional law should take precedence. However, it is also noteworthy that, similar to other legal

[26] MacDonnell (2016).

[27] Schermers and Blokker (2011), pp. 561–563.

[28] Schwartzberg (2013), p. 44.

[29] Schwartzberg (2013), pp. 25–27.

[30] 4/1997. (I. 22.) AB decision, ABH 1997, 41–45.

instruments, supermajority law is not independent from its legal, political, and social context in which it is intended to operate. Besides strictly legal considerations, a historical, social, political, and comparative approach is also deemed necessary to thoroughly examine supermajority law. I aim to provide new answers to the raised questions with the combined evaluation of the mentioned factors.

It is therefore necessary, in this early stage, to outline what comprises the approach of various disciplines, which form the basis/foundation of my argumentation. Supermajority law constitutes an ultimately legal category; therefore, most issues should be answered primarily by the discipline of constitutional law. As legal sources, supermajority laws reshape the relationship between the constitution and ordinary laws, supermajority laws may be seen as a bridge between these two hierarchical levels of norms.[31] Constitutional law shall elaborate on the category of supermajority law as a legal source; its constitutional background; the extent of the relevant constitutional authorizations and the potential hierarchy between supermajority- and ordinary law. The primary sources of constitutional law for these assessments are provided by the relevant constitutional provisions; by the texts of supermajority laws themselves; and by the case law attached to this legal concept. Even if the case law does not usually constitute a coherent logic, judicial bodies with different composition often overrule formerly established approaches.[32]

Some further paramount issues of constitutional law might also be worth contemplating: which fields of constitutional law shall be covered by supermajority legislation? Which principles and considerations determine the distinction between supermajority and ordinary subject matters? What does the supermajority requirement mean for institutional fields, and for acts on fundamental rights?

In political science, the impact of legislative supermajority on public discourse forms the most important element. Due to the supermajority requirement, the government will not have sufficient support in parliament, so the consent or at least the cooperation of certain opposition parliamentarians will be necessary to pass a supermajority law. This may compel the parties to engage in constructive dialogue, which could prove beneficial in the case of a well-established political culture. The opposition may exploit this negotiating position, potentially leading to a boycott of supermajority legislation. This could ultimately prevent the amendment of supermajority laws in the long run, resulting in a rigid regulatory landscape.

The issue of political responsibility behind supermajority legislative decisions is still to be clarified, since not only the support of the governmental side, but also the consent of certain oppositional actors should be an important component of a supermajority. It remains dubious who shall undertake the political responsibility for these decisions.

The context of a supermajority requirement can be inherently different when a parliamentary supermajority stands behind the government. In this case, such as in Hungary in the 2010s and 2020s, supermajority laws might be amended

[31] Jakab and Cserne (2001), pp. 40–49.

[32] Jakab and Cserne (2001), pp. 40–49.

unilaterally, and their modification might be excluded in the long term. Due to the broad consent requirement, it will be more difficult to amend supermajority laws adopted with this elevated level of parliamentary support. The governmental side with a legislative supermajority may eliminate the opposition from the political process and further might be able to limit the margin of movement of future governments with the incorporation of key policies into supermajority laws.

Supermajority also reconsiders the issue of minority governance and the vote of no-confidence and influences the system of checks and balances.[33] As a significant factor in the political role of a supermajority, the electoral system has to be considered, as this will determine whether parliamentary supermajority would realistically be targeted during the elections under a particular constitutional regime.

The comparative/international dimension of the issue has received greater attention during the last few years, especially in light of the latest developments in the law of the European Union. However, the overall assessment of the main models has not yet been achieved. One argument could be that the foreign models of supermajority law have had a greater impact in the countries where this concept has been introduced, compared to the local historical points of reference.[34] The French, Spanish, Austrian, and Hungarian models are usually mentioned as the most significant.

The approach of decision theory is closely related to that of political science, while the more formalistic decision theory is more strongly linked to legal considerations. This field of science analyzes who makes important decisions and the mechanisms they use, as well as how the decision-making process can be better supported by organizational schemes. It also examines how social, political, legal, and economic phenomena influence decision-making.[35] The government should draft proposals that are supported not only by pro-government parliamentarians, but also by certain oppositional groups. This amount to a two-fold characteristic of supermajority law: it may mathematize the political discourse, but it could carry a risk factor as the pro- and counter-governmental leaders should develop unusual behaviors as a result of these circumstances. This happens due to the different level of required majority for certain acts, and that these matters of legislation are deemed to be the most important for all interested stakeholders. As a consequence, the regulation of these matters needs distinguished care, especially in the light of additional difficulties in amending adopted supermajority laws in the future.

A further issue arose in the sociology of law and decision theory: how supermajority laws influence the attitudes of citizens and political leaders, and whether the aforementioned consequences are relevant for the practice. If leaders and ordinary citizens do not consciously rely on supermajority laws, the elevated level of required majority could easily be degraded to a technical precondition of legislation.

---

[33] Persson et al. (1997), pp. 1163–1165.

[34] Szentgáli-Tóth (2023), p. 171.

[35] Steele and Stefánsson (2020).

1.6 Issues of Terminology: Different Denominations of Supermajority Law

The complex terminology linked to supermajority legislation must also be clarified. Multiple formulations have been used, whose meanings are similar, but their exact emphases are slightly different. Therefore, these terminologies can easily cause serious misunderstandings. Figure 1.2 attempts to facilitate the proper distinctions of these denominations with the illustration of their geographical spread.

Although not used by any constitution, the term supermajority law' implies legal instruments that cover a special category of laws with a legal rank somewhere under the constitution and over ordinary laws; subject to a supermajority requirement; and with a scope of applicability determined by the constitution. The first common characteristics of these concepts are that stricter procedural rules are laid down to enact them (supermajority, mandatory a priori constitutional review, and other additional safeguards for the legislative process). Secondly, all supermajority law concepts fall somewhere between the constitution and ordinary laws as regards their legal rank. Thirdly, the scope of supermajority law is determined at least in principle by the legislative fields with paramount importance, which obviously means an inherently subjective standard. Moreover, the list of supermajority legislative fields shall be enumerated by the relevant constitutional provisions.

Further denominations refer to the supermajority law concepts of each national constitutional system, and these special formulations will be used when the sample of particular countries is highlighted. In most of the countries concerned, this legal instrument is known as "organic law". It will be clear from the exact context to which country the different terms of organic law refer. The French Constitution also uses the wording of organic law or "institutional act" mirroring the priority of institutional matters amongst French organic legislative fields.[36] The category of organic law also exists in Croatia, Georgia, Moldova, Portugal, Romania, Spain, and also in a number of African- and Latin-American countries, as well as in Papua New Guinea. By contrast, the term of constitutional law has been incorporated into the constitutions of Azerbaijan, Italy, Kazakhstan, Kyrgyzstan, Russia, Slovakia, and Tajikistan.

In Hungary, supermajority laws, introduced in 1989 during the democratic transition, were called as "constitutional laws", similar to the simultaneous appearance of constitutional laws in other post-communist countries in the region. Hungarian constitutional laws have shifted as a result of the so-called "MDF-SZDSZ Compromise" (the two strongest Hungarian political parties of that period) to two-thirds laws.

The historically known term[37] "cardinal law" reappeared with a specific meaning with the adoption of the Fundamental Law of Hungary in 2011 to cover legislation

[36] Art. 46 (3) of the Constitution of France (October 4, 1958).

[37] Kilényi (1989), pp. 18–32.

with a supermajority.[38] The forms of "two-thirds law" and "cardinal law" will be used exclusively in the Hungarian context in this volume, and they will refer to the respective concept of Hungarian supermajority laws.

1.7 The Structure of This Volume

After the introductory section, my volume continues with a chapter outlining the different national models of supermajority law. In the comparative chapter (Chap. 2), the three main waves of modern supermajority law, the spread, and the primary models of supermajority laws will be conceptualized. These samples represent different directions of the development of the same legal instrument; therefore, it is important to make a comparative analysis between them also taking into consideration their interdependence.

The next five major chapters enumerate those crucial arguments of justification usually mentioned in the literature focusing on supermajority laws. The deeper understanding of the main concepts also provides the opportunity to highlight each function behind the different interpretation of supermajority law's role in the constitutional framework.

From the perspective of constitutional law and the legal rank of supermajority law, one of the justifications considers supermajority laws as the expansion of the constitution (Chap. 3). According to this argument, due to the limited length of the constitution, not all essential rules should be incorporated into the constitutional text itself; quasi-constitutional rules may include these details under almost the same level of protection. In this system supermajority laws fall within the broader constitutional concept, they stand above ordinary laws in the hierarchy of norms. Consequently, supermajority laws might be invoked during the constitutional review of ordinary acts, and ordinary statutes shall not contradict substantially with supermajority laws.

The best example for this approach has been provided by Hungary during 1989–1990, when the category of constitutional law was established. These acts were enacted with two-thirds consent from all parliamentarians, and the wording proves that they possessed practically the same legal force as the constitutional provisions. We shall not consider them as constitutional amendments, as the text of the constitution remained untouched; however, their quasi-constitutional character had been beyond doubt. According to the Constitutional Court, the primary function of constitutional laws was to provide quasi-constitutional status for the statutory regulation on the primary institutions of the state, and on fundamental rights, to highlight the significance of these matters.[39] The idea of expanding the constitution may be a proper instrument to improve the flexibility of the constitution and to establish

[38] Bán-Forgács (2023).

[39] 1/1999. (II. 24.) AB decision, ABH 1999, 25.

additional safeguards. It is also noteworthy that such a solution may weaken the position of the constitution above the legal norm's hierarchy, and it may relativize the distinction between the constitution and legal norms below it.

Supermajority laws also contribute to the stability of the constitutional system (Chap. 4), owing to the stricter procedural regime; as these laws are less accessible for amendments than their ordinary counterparts.[40] This idea underlines the meaningful weight of supermajority legislative matters, so additional safeguards can be crucial for the amendments of these acts. However, this argument may not be convincing, because the list of supermajority legislative matters does not fully correlate with the social importance of these laws. Moreover, special importance constitutes an inherently subjective standard. Nevertheless, a separate legal category beyond the constitution and ordinary laws undoubtedly means protection for the constitution in at least three respects.

- First, the constitution only contains the most crucial norms: other essential rules are stipulated by supermajority laws.
- Second, due to the supermajority requirement, the regulation on the primary institutions of the state and on fundamental rights requires broad consent from parliamentary representatives. The players of the political and constitutional debates will probably accept the constitutional framework when they are involved in the enactment of its detailed rules. Therefore, the political discussion will focus not on the constitutional design itself but on the current social and economic issues.
- Third, the constitution merely provides the framework; the details will be fleshed out by supermajority laws. In case of minor amendments, supermajority laws will be sufficient. The constitution could preserve its stability and the number of constitutional amendments would be remarkably fewer than in countries without supermajority. The relevance of this statement depends on the exact rules on amending the constitution in the particular country.

If supermajority laws are seen primarily as political instruments, (Chap. 5) the procedural rules will determine the exact impact of this legal concept, and the evolving relationship between the political stakeholders should be scrutinized.[41] Generally, parliamentarism grants a broad margin of movement to the current parliamentary majority to fulfill its ambitions the political responsibility is conferred upon this legislative majority. By contrast, the opposition aims at controlling the government during the parliamentary debates via other tools of pressure. The government and the opposition may not have completely different viewpoints on a particular issue, but when this occurs, the opposition attempts to prevent the implementation of governmental policies.

Regarding supermajority laws, these mechanisms function inherently differently. The governmental side without a supermajority indispensably needs oppositional

[40] Gohin (2019), pp. 682–683.

[41] Szentgáli-Tóth (2022).

votes, and the content of the bills has to be negotiated with the opposition. This is compounded by the assumption that supermajority laws have more weight than ordinary ones, so it would be advisable to regularly communicate amongst the main political actors during the preparation of such bills.

Therefore, not only is the amendment procedure of supermajority laws more complex, but the preparation of such bills also requires a higher level of carefulness. A series of political negotiations precludes frequent amendments of supermajority laws, in an ideal situation; one may expect more carefully tailored legislation from this. In reality, the amendments of supermajority laws often depend on political compromises. In this chapter, I will focus on the consent-building function: how the implementation of this concept modifies the inherent logic of parliamentarism, whether the consideration of professional standards and the inclusivity of the political process are supported or undermined by the supermajority requirement.

According to a different interpretation focusing on its topical coverage, supermajority laws might be important safeguards of fundamental rights (Chap. 6); these may complement the system of safeguards for this purpose.[42] This approach gained more popularity in those countries where the Spanish sample is followed.[43]

The function of supermajority law as a tool of fundamental right protection derives from the context of the implementation, often surrounded by a democratic transition and the fall of a former dictatorship. These moments rely on the experience in the recent past where fundamental rights were violated, and society tries to prevent the repeat of such incidents through strong safeguards. It might be dangerous to provide an unlimited margin of decision for the government to enact statutes on fundamental rights, as the crimes of totalitarian regimes were the result of their unrestricted power. For this reason, the opposition has a legitimate expectation to participate in the preparation of such amendments. In a stable democracy where the respect for fundamental rights is safeguarded by the courts, the constitutional court, ombudspersons, further authorities, and NGOs, the role of supermajority law as a safeguard may be considered less significant. The analysis always depends on the context in the specific country. Another risk factor is the overbroad interpretation of the role of supermajority law as a safeguard, as almost all legal norms pertain to fundamental rights. Consequently, ordinary laws would ultimately vanish from the legal system.

Finally, supermajority laws have a remarkable impact on the separation of powers in at least three respects (Chap. 7).

Supermajority laws influence the relationship between the government and the constitutional court, as the constitutional court may decide whether the distinction between supermajority and ordinary laws meets the constitutional standards. This opens up a new formal aspect of constitutional review, extending the margin of movement by the constitutional court, and also strengthens its dependence on the political environment. These tendencies are more impactful when the constitutional

---

[42] 14/B/2002. (V. 27.) AB decision, ABH 2003, 1476.

[43] JCC no. 185/1995.

court reviews the constitutionality of each supermajority law before its entry into force, as in France.

- The aforementioned factors may also considerably influence the position of the government and the parliament, especially the parliamentary opposition.
- The interdependence between the current and future governments is the third aspect regarding the impact on the separation of powers, as an adopted supermajority law can obstruct a future government from obtaining the necessary parliamentary majority to amend or repeal it. This effect might be more plausible when a supermajority is attached to matters of public policy, such as the fundamental rules of the tax or pension system.

After having analyzed my primary arguments, I outline my proposals on reconsidering the current supermajority law concepts reflecting on their three main distinctive characters (Chap. 8).

Firstly, supermajority and ordinary laws would be clearly separated; an act would exclusively include supermajority or ordinary provisions. The constitution should explicitly stipulate that supermajority laws are below the constitution but above ordinary laws in the hierarchy of norms.

Secondly, the elaboration on a special legislative procedure for supermajority laws might be necessary. Stricter requirements of social participation would be provided, and a separate permanent parliamentary commission would be set up to hear each proposal to enact or amend supermajority laws. Furthermore, a mandatory prior constitutional review might also be a worthy idea for further consideration: each supermajority law should be sent before its entry into force to the constitutional court for constitutional review; this would strengthen the constitutional control of the most crucial laws.

In the practice of constitutional courts, a test should be created to provide a coherent standard regarding which provisions of legislative subject matters should be covered by the supermajority requirement, and which possess less relevance and may be amended by a simple majority. A further—but in my view not fruitful—idea would be the spread of bicameral parliamentarism, as supermajority laws should be passed through at least two filters. This recommendation may lead to the reconsideration of the whole constitutional system, and I do not go into its details in my book. My volume concludes with the summary of the research's main outcomes (Chap. 9).

Thirdly, the scope of supermajority law would be significantly reduced to a narrow field of acts covering the key institutions of the state. In my view, the new concept of supermajority law would operate with 6–8 legislative subject matters.

Furthermore, my intent with the publication of this volume is to demonstrate how important it is to find a proper balance between the theoretical and practical points of view when examining a legal issue. During the assessment of supermajority laws, most authors solely focus on their characteristics experienced in practice. Therefore, the theory and dogmatics of supermajority laws have been less discussed. This is probably caused by the political significance of supermajority laws: legal and constitutional arguments are often played down by political ambitions. The presence of supermajority law is explained mostly by political necessity. Supermajority laws function in various and constantly changing constitutional configurations. Therefore, in each chapter, after providing the theoretical setting, I demonstrate my assumptions with practical examples from different countries.

Finally, it should be highlighted that I do not wish to close the professional discourse on any matter related to supermajority laws. By contrast, my goal is to contribute to the invigoration of the professional dialogue and to add new elements to the thinking on supermajority law. My proposals detailed in the last two chapters, might be worthy of consideration during a constitution-making process, obviously depending on the particular circumstances in the given country. After the introductory notes, the detailed analysis of supermajority law begins with the history and the main models of this legal instrument.

References

Albert R (ed) (2023) The architecture of constitutional amendments. Bloomsbury Publishing

Avril P, Gicquel J (2014) Droit parlamentaire. Dalloz, Paris

Bán-Forgács N (2023) Procedural Constitution-Making: Lessons Learnt from Hungary. In: Željko, Mirjanić (szerk.) Međународни научни скуп „изазови и перспективе развоја правних система у XXI вијеку": зборник радова, година III, бањa лука, број 3 (2023), том I / International Scientific Conference "Challenges and perspectives of the development of legal systems in the xxi century" Conference Proceedings, Year III, Banja Luka, No. 3

Camby JP (1989) La loi organique dans la Constitution de 1958. RDP, Paris

Camby JP (1998) Quarante ans de lois organiques. Revue de droit publique 5–6:1686–1698

Chofre Sirvent JF (1994) Significado y función de las leyes orgánicas. Tecnos, Madrid

Cichocki MA, Życzkowski K (eds) (2011) Institutional design and voting power in the European Union, 1st edn. Routledge, London

Debré M (1959) La nouvelle Constitution. Revue française de science politique 9(1):7–29

Gohin O (2019) Droit constitutionnel, 4[é] Lexis Nexis, Paris

Hahm H et al (2020) Institutional reform and public attitudes toward EU decision making. EJPR 59(3):599–623

Hufeld U et al (2016) Entwicklungslinien der Finanzverfassung. Lehmanns Media, Berlin

Ion OA (2023) Assessing the fairness of the EU Council supermajority voting. A voting power critical perspective of the liberal intergovernmentalist accounts. EJGE 12(1):39–57

Jakab A (2011) Az új Alaptörvény keletkezése és gyakorlati következményei. HVG-ORAC, Budapest

Jakab A, Cserne P (2001) A kétharmados törvények helye a magyar jogforrási hierarchiában. Fundamentum 5(2):40–49

Jakab A, Szilágyi E (2014) Sarkalatos törvények a magyar jogrendben. Új Magyar Közigazgatás 7(3):97–103

Kilényi G (1989) (ed) Az Alkotmány alapelvei. Alkotmányjogi Füzetek 1. ÉGSZI, Budapest

Küpper H (2014) A kétharmados/sarkalatos törvények jelensége a magyar jogrendszerben. MTA Law Working Papers 46:2–5

MacDonnell V (2016) A theory of quasi-constitutional legislation. Osgoode Hall Law J 53(2):508–539

Nováky N (2021) Qualified majority voting in EU foreign policy: make it so. Eur View 20(2):117–249

Peña HG (2005) Los Tipos Normativos en la Constitución de 1999. Tribunal Supremo de Justicia, Caracas
Persson T et al (1997) Separation of powers and political accountability. Quart JE 112(4):1163–1165
Peters D (2020) Justifying inequality as equality: germany and the reform of voting weights in the council of the European Union. Glob Soc 34(3):370–387
Schermers HG, Blokker NM (2011) International institutional law: Unity within diversity. Fifth Revised (ed) Martinus Nijhoff Publishers, Leiden
Schwartzberg M (2013) Prelude: acclamation and aggregation in the ancient world - the origin of supermajority rules. Counting the many: the origins and limits of supermajority rule. CUP, Cambridge
Sepúlveda R (2006) Las leyes orgánicas constitucionales: el inicio de una nueva constitucionalidad en méxico. Editorial Porrúa, México
Serramalera M (2004) La ley Organica ámbito material y posición en el systema de fuentes. Atelier Libros Juridicos, Barcelona
Steele K, Stefánsson HO (2020) Decision theory. The Stanford Encyclopedia of Philosophy. (Winter 2020 Edition), Zalta EN (ed) Stanford Encyclopedia of Philosophy. Stanford University 8
Szentgáli-Tóth B (2022) Organic/cardinal laws. In: Grote R et al (eds) Max Planck Encyclopedia of Comparative Constitutional Law. (MPECCoL). OUP, Oxford. Paper e302
Szentgáli-Tóth B (2023) The Legal transplant during the democratic transition: the regional migration of a constitutional idea: The spread of supermajority law in the central and East-European regions. Studia Prawnicze 227(1):171–197
Troper M (2006) La V Republique et la separation des pouvoirs. Droits 43(1):33–44
Troper M, Chagnollaud D (eds) (2012) Traite international de droit constitutionnel. Dalloz, Paris
Vormbaum T (2018) Strafgesetze als Verfassungsgesetze. In memoriam Knut Amelung. Juristen Zeitung 73(2):53–63
Waldhoff C (2016) Der positiver und negativer Verfassungsvorbehalt. Nomos, Baden-Baden
Warntjen A (2017) Do votes matter? Voting weights and the success probability of member state requests in the Council of the European Union. JEI 39(6):673–687

Part I
The Role of Legislative Supermajority: A Comparative International Overview

Chapter 2
The Role of Legislative Supermajority: A Comparative International Overview

2.1 International Comparison

2.1.1 The Spread of Supermajority Laws Around the World

Turning to the historical references, the modern development of supermajority laws began in 1958 with the Constitution of the Fifth French Republic.[1] After the decolonisation of Africa, under French influence, a number of African countries[2] belonging to the Francophone legal family adopted this solution. Currently, twenty-four African countries have supermajority laws in their constitutions.[3] The second wave of the spreading of supermajority laws is linked to the fall of the Spanish and

[1] Art. 46 of the Constitution of France (October 4, 1958).

[2] David (1964), p. 630.

[3] Art. 145 of the Constitution of Algeria (November 1, 2020); Art. 166 (2) (b) and 169 (2) of the Constitution of Angola (January 21, 2010); Art. 97 of the Constitution of Benin (December 2, 1990); Art. 155 of the Constitution of Burkina Faso (June 2, 1991); Art. 175 of the Constitution of Burundi (February 28, 2005); Art. 139 of the Constitution of Chad (December 29, 2023); Art. 66 of the Constitution of Djibouti (September 4, 1992); Art. 104 of the Constitution of Equatorial Guinea (November 16, 1991); Art. 71 of the Constitution of Côte d'Ivoire (November 8, 2016); Art. 97 of the Constitution of Gabon (November 16, 2024); Art. 91 of the Constitution of Guinea (March 22, 2020); Art. 26 of the Constitution of Comoros (December 23, 2001); Art. 124 of the Constitution of Democratic Republic of Congo (February 18, 2006); Art. 151 of the Constitution of Republic of Congo (October 25, 2015); Art. 67 of the Constitution of Mauritania (July 12, 1991); Art. 126, 131, 134, 138 and 143 of the Constitution of Central African Republic (August 30, 2023); Art. 124 of the Constitution of Mali (July 22, 2023); Art. 78 of the Constitution of Senegal (January 7, 2001); Art. 31 of the Constitution of Togo (May 6, 2024); Art. 75 of the Constitution of Tunisia (July 25, 2022); Art. 73 (3) and 86 (2) (b) of the Constitution of Cape Verde (September 5, 1980).

B. A. Szentgáli-Tóth, *The Past, Present, and Future of Legislation with Supermajority*, Ius Gentium: Comparative Perspectives on Law and Justice 126,
https://doi.org/10.1007/978-3-031-99324-4_2

Portuguese dictatorships.[4] Supermajority law was incorporated into the constitutions of both countries and was later followed by other Latin American states such as the Dominican Republic, Ecuador, Panama, Peru, and Venezuela.[5] Finally, as a third wave, this legal instrument became part of the Hungarian, Romanian, and Moldovan[6] constitutional systems following the democratic transition. Other countries of the region also adopted similar constructions to supermajority laws, as will be illustrated later.

Supermajority legislation spread around the world in three waves during the second half of the twentieth century. First, this concept was incorporated into the French constitutional regime de Gaulle, the main framer of the Fifth French Republic, aimed at protecting the key institutions of the state and ensuring greater stability of the constitutional order.[7] After decolonization, several African countries also decided to include this framework in their constitutions.[8]

Two decades later, in the second half of the 1970s, during the democratic transition in Spain and Portugal, the necessity of a supermajority law has again been put forward and led to the introduction of organic laws in these countries.[9] Similar to France, Spain, and Portugal formerly possessed a number of colonies, and as a result, organic laws have filtered into several Latin-American systems.[10]

In Central and Eastern Europe, supermajority laws gained considerable exposure after the democratic transition in the wake of the fall of the communist regimes. Following the French example, Romania[11] and Moldova[12] introduced this concept, while in Hungary the role of historical traditions has also been significant. Croatia, Montenegro, and Slovakia should be mentioned as well, where supermajority law exists.

Moreover, additional former Soviet member states such as Azerbaijan, Georgia, Kazakhstan, Kyrgyzstan, Russia, and Tajikistan have adopted organic/constitutional laws after their democratic transition. The comparative approach promises the assessment of the relevant literature and case law from different countries, opening up further perspectives for the professional dialogue on these issues. The analogies between the different countries should be treated as limited concepts for two reasons. On the one hand, significant differences can be detected between the two-thirds and the absolute majority models of supermajority law, and the applicability of my conclusions mostly depends on this distinction. On the other hand, most

[4] Art. 169 (2) of the Constitution of Portugal (April 2, 1976).

[5] Art. 133 of the Constitution of Ecuador (September 28, 2008); Art. 203 of the Constitution of Venezuela (December 20, 1999).

[6] Art. 72 (1), (3) and (4) of the Constitution of Moldova (July 29, 1994).

[7] Blacher (2012), pp. 11–23.

[8] Art. 145 of the Constitution of Algeria (November 1, 2020); Art. 78 of the Constitution of Senegal (January 7, 2001); Art. 75 of the Constitution of Tunisia (July 25, 2022).

[9] Comella (2013), pp. 4–34.

[10] Art. 203 of the Constitution of Venezuela (December 20, 1999); Art. 133 of the Constitution of Ecuador (September 28, 2008).

[11] Art. 73 of the Constitution of Romania (December 8, 1991).

[12] Art. 72 (3) of the Constitution of Moldova (July 29, 1994).

countries that have implemented supermajority laws operate with semi-presidential systems, while the weight of parliamentary structures is also worth contemplating. These differences will be highlighted later, but one should keep in mind that these factors do not concern the basic functions of supermajority law, which are almost the same despite the diverse constitutional landscape.

2.1.2 Organic Law in France

The concept of supermajority law has already existed in France during the constitutional development of the last two centuries.[13] It was the first country to explicitly incorporate supermajority laws into its constitutional system in 1958. The incorporation of the organic law into the constitution cannot be understood without the historical background: it proved to be a suitable tool for weakening the role of the legislature and changing the contours of the separation of powers. The fall of the French Third Republic was followed by the joint reign of terror by the Vichy regime and the occupying German army, and the adoption of the new constitution in 1946 led to the establishment of the Fourth Republic. During these years, France faced an almost permanent political crisis, with successive governments failing to deal with pressing social and economic problems, particularly with the wars in Indochina and Algeria, and rapidly losing the confidence of the legislature. The vote of confidence in parliament allowed the government to be dismissed by a simple majority of those present, and the fragmented party structure and the weakening position of the head of state and the head of government shifted the balance of powers towards the parliament.[14]

The parliamentary framework was constantly shifting, and governments changed every few months, depending on the negotiations between political parties. The internal flaws of the political system were exacerbated by the ongoing colonial conflicts. After World War II ended, France was involved in a protracted war with local forces fighting for independence in Indochina, and after their withdrawal from the region, armed action had to be taken to maintain French rule in Algeria. Algeria was closely linked to mainland France, and French public opinion was not ready to accept the secession of the North African country. At the same time, French governments were unable to control the military situation; therefore, the distance between the army and the government was widened.

In this extremely tense situation, the political elite turned to General de Gaulle, the leader of the French resistance against the Germans during World War II, who received the mandate to establish a new constitutional system. De Gaulle, a soldier and a believer in the centralization of power, played a key role in carrying out his

---

[13] Camby (1998), p. 1686.

[14] Giles (1991).

task and considered at least four arguments when he advocated for weakening the legislature.[15]

- First, stable governments were not established during the French Fourth Republic, and governments usually remained in office for less than a year.[16] It had been generally believed that the frequent changes of government were caused by the weakness of the executive, resulting in an overbroad legislative position. De Gaulle and his entourage therefore sought to reduce the dominant role of Parliament and to redesign the system of checks and balances in favour of the executive. Parliament no longer had unlimited power to decide on the organization of the state, while the executive had been given additional competences.[17]
- Second, laws of major importance have often been amended during the Fourth Republic to suit the needs of the current parliamentary majority. The composition of the legislature changed rapidly; nothing guaranteed the stability of the legal/constitutional environment. In order to rationalize parliamentarism·[18] certain subjects were removed from the scope of parliamentary decision making, thus protecting the basic rules of the state organization against momentary political ambitions.[19]
- Third, the Constitution of the Fifth Republic originally focused on outlining the institutions of the state, and the French Constitution still does not contain a catalogue of fundamental rights.[20] Hence, the French organic laws are primarily concerned with institutional issues of the state; fundamental rights do not form part of this concept. The drafters of the new constitutional order only wished to provide an additional guarantee for the fundamental institutions of the State and were not interested in other areas, such as fundamental rights.
- Fourth, the unconscious fear of the return of the dictatorship France experienced during World War II might have played a significant role as well. Organic laws not only protected the democratic establishment from instability but also aimed to prevent a potentially attempted autocratic takeover. The organic laws served to strengthen control over parliament and give additional powers to the executive, particularly for the president of the republic, so that a more predictable yet stable political system based on democratic foundations could be safeguarded. Let us not forget that, at that time, authoritarian regimes ruled in most European countries. Moreover, the dictatorship has been directly experienced in France during the Second World War. Moreover, the distant Communist threat had to be reckoned with too, as adjacent to France two strong nationalist dictatorships had been constructed in Spain and Portugal.

[15] Szentgáli-Tóth (2020a), p. 212.

[16] Debré (1959), p. 7.

[17] Blacher (2012), pp. 11–23.

[18] Ardant and Mathieu (2014), pp. 344–345.

[19] Mélin-Soucramanien and Pactet (2021), pp. 655–656.

[20] Troper (2008), pp. 1–34.

The initial model of the organic law was later shaped by several constitutional amendments, but the essential features of the system set up in 1958 are still in place today. As an example of smaller revisions, the organic law on the status of the Senate can only be adopted with identical terms by the two chambers. This clause ensures that the rules governing the status of the Senate cannot ultimately be adopted by the National Assembly without the consent of the Senate. This compromise resulted in a complex political constellation. EU citizens who are not French nationals living in France could vote in local elections, but not in the election of members of the Senate.[21]

One final implicit constitutional amendment is worth mentioning: the establishment of the concept of the constitutional block. The constitutional block was gradually developed by the French Constitutional Council since the early 1970s and provides that the sources of law mentioned in the preamble to the French Constitution are considered by the Constitutional Council to be part of the Constitution in the broader sense. Thus, the Preamble of the Constitution of 1791 and 1946, the Declaration of Human and Civil Rights, certain major laws of the French Third Republic and the Charter of the Environment possess constitutional force.[22] As will be demonstrated later, the involvement of organic laws in the constitutional block provides valuable arguments to potentially reconsider the rank of organic laws in the order of legal sources. As another crucial consequence, the constitutional block now includes rules protecting fundamental rights, so that the Constitutional Council can consider fundamental rights when reviewing the constitutionality of organic laws.

The parliament consists of two chambers both in France and Spain; an absolute majority is required in each of these chambers for the enactment or amendment of an organic law.[23] In France, before the promulgation of organic laws, these acts should be sent mandatorily to the Constitutional Council for constitutional review.[24] In Spain, this requirement shall be applied only for the status of autonomous communities.[25]

Despite their clear constitutional background, the Constitutional Council has clarified that organic laws do not fall within the constitutional framework, or in the constitutional bloc.[26] The Constitutional Council has significantly improved its practice during the recent decades and its approach is based on two considerations.

First, the Council has recognized the different legal character of organic and ordinary statutes but has refused to create any clear hierarchy between them.[27] This

[21] The constitutional amendment in France was promulgated on June 25, 1992.

[22] Granger (2011), pp. 1–18.

[23] Art. 46 (3) of the Constitution of France (October 4, 1958); Art. 81 (2) of the Constitution of Spain (January 4, 1978).

[24] Art. 46 (5) of the Constitution of France (October 4, 1958).

[25] Chofre Sirvent (1994), pp. 215–224.

[26] La décision du CC, n° 84-177 DC du 30 août 1984.

[27] Camby (1998), p. 1690.

approach was also confirmed by the French Government[28] and the academic literature.[29] Both the competence of the organic as well as the ordinary legislature enjoys the same level of constitutional protection, and is prohibited from any interference in the other domain.[30] "From 1958, the term of organic law has been descriptive rather than normative."[31] In other words, the relationship between organic and ordinary statutes has been outlined by the principle of competence instead of the principle of hierarchy. The principle of competence emphasizes that ordinary and supermajority laws have the same rank within the hierarchy of norms but separate domains of subject matters. By contrast, the principle of hierarchy means that supermajority law has supreme effect over ordinary law.[32] Despite the consistent rejection of organic law's supremacy over ordinary law, the French framework has been controversial; for instance, the prohibition of explicit or even implicit amendment of organic law by an ordinary statute refers to some sort of hierarchical order.[33]

Although an organic law could refine and complete the constitutionally prescribed scope of statutes,[34] this authorization does not constitute an extra constitutional power to outline the scope of organic law; hence this catalogue shall be in conformity with constitutional provisions and principles. Organic laws fall outside of the constitutional bloc;[35] nevertheless, the contradiction with an organic law has the same impact as a conflict with a constitutional provision.[36] Furthermore, the rules of the procedure of the two assemblies [37] as well as other parliamentary acts[38] shall also comply with organic laws.

Second, the French practice crucially distinguishes within the category of organic law: some sort of hierarchy exists even amongst institutional acts.[39] This legal framework does not constitute a unified legal concept; some subgroups of organic law demand special treatment.[40] Certain ordinances (legislative acts adopted by the

[28] Documents pour servir àl'histoire de l'élaboration de la Constitution, (Documents from the history of the drafting of the Constitution) volume III, 350.

[29] Luchaire and Conac (1987), pp. 179–207.

[30] N° 87-234, DC du 7 janvier 1988, Rec. 2.

[31] Avril and Gicquel (2014), p. 274.

[32] Noel (2021), p. 204.

[33] La décision n° 96-386, DC du 30 décembre 1996.

[34] Art. 34 of the Constitution of France (October 4, 1958), last clause.

[35] Verpeaux and Bonnard (2007), p. 101.

[36] La décision du Cc, n°60-8 DC du 11 aout 1960.

[37] Le Pourhiet 2007, Cited above 379; La décision en 2006-537 DC, 22 juin 2006; la décision en 99-419 DC du 9 novembre 1999.

[38] Art. 40 (5) of the Rules of Procedure of the French National Assembly.

[39] Szentgáli-Tóth (2020c), p. 69.

[40] Camby (1998), p. 1695.

executive on the basis of parliamentary authorization)[41] are not allowed only in the field of ordinary law but also within the domain of certain organic laws.[42]

In light of legal practice, the organic law on public finances and social security has a supreme effect over other organic laws[43] and has a quasi-constitutional character.[44] The theoretical background of this distinction has not yet been crystallized; generally, it is supported by some constitutional references.[45] The Constitution further requires enactment with identical terms by both houses for the organic laws related to the status and composition of the Senate.[46] This classification opens up a matter of constitutional interpretation: which organic law is related to the Senate and which is not. The Constitutional Council interpreted this concept fairly restrictively, considering only the direct impact on the Senate in this regard.[47] For instance, the number of senators shall not be determined by identical terms, while the composition of the electoral colleges of the second chamber shall be regulated under this requirement.[48] These examples demonstrate that the Constitution provides the basis of the diversification within organic laws; but the Constitutional Council shall clarify the details.

In France, most of the organic laws cover institutional fields: inter alia, the functioning of the Parliament,[49] the status of the members of the judiciary,[50] the status of the Constitutional Council,[51] the functioning of the Economic, Social and Environmental Council,[52] the powers and actions of the Defender of Rights.[53] The limitation of sovereignty of France also falls under the scope of organic law. The most conspicuous phenomenon here is the almost exclusive dominance of the institutional aspect. Since fundamental rights were not included in the original framework of the Constitution of the Fifth Republic, they are almost ineligible to fall within the scope of organic law. Since 1958, the scope of organic law has been slightly extended by constitutional amendments. For instance, in 2008, the defender of rights was included in the organic domain.[54]

---

[41] Ardant and Mathieu (2014), pp. 417–419.

[42] Droit constitutionnel et science politique, XVe édition, 379; also for instance: Organic ordonance of October 24, 1958.

[43] Braibant (1996), p. 323.

[44] N° 98-401, DC du 10 juin 1998.

[45] Chabrier and Haudrechy (2020), p. 89.

[46] Art. 88-3 of the Constitution of France (October 4, 1958).

[47] N° 85-195, DC du 10 juillet 1985.

[48] Blacher (2021), p. 146.

[49] Art. 25 sec. 1 of the Constitution of France (October 4, 1958).

[50] Art. 64 sec. 3 of the Constitution of France (October 4, 1958).

[51] Art. 63 of the Constitution of France (October 4, 1958).

[52] Art. 71 of the Constitution of France (October 4, 1958).

[53] Art. 71-1 sec. 3 of the Constitution of France (October 4, 1958).

[54] https://www.conseil-constitutionnel.fr/les-revisions-constitutionnelles/loi-constitutionnelle-n-2008-724-du-23-juillet-2008.

The organic legislative character within the practice of the Constitutional Council is related to particular provisions and subject matters rather than specific laws that regulate organic subject matters.[55] Consequently, several statutes contain both organic and ordinary provisions. Therefore, in case of legal doubt, the Constitutional Council must determine the scope of ordinary and organic law, even within the same legal text. Moreover, organic law not only describes a technical circle of laws, but it also enjoys strong constitutional protection, with the help of the notion of organic character.[56] Each law shall explicitly state its character; organic laws may contain ordinary provisions, but these provisions shall be clearly separated.[57] In contrast, organic provisions shall not be included within ordinary laws.[58] This ambiguity demonstrates that, despite the primary role of the competence principle, certain hierarchical elements are not absent from the relationship between organic and ordinary laws in France.[59]

2.1.3 *Organic Law in Spain*

In Spain, organic laws originated from the 1978 Constitution during the democratic transition following the fall of Franco. Despite the strong French influence, the constitutional process differed significantly because Spain lacked a meaningful democratic tradition; the first two Spanish republics proved short-lived, and democratic forces were unable to defend their positions against autocratic tendencies.[60] Although this happened to the first two French republics, the novelty and the global historical significance of the events that took place at the end of the eighteenth century, in 1830 and in 1848 made the French republican tradition a model of liberalism throughout Europe.

Spain joined the democratization process after a considerable delay, in the last third of the 19th century. The First Spanish Republic ended with the restoration of the monarchy, while the second republican attempt in the 1930s led to the bloody events of the Spanish Civil War. Spain's historical experience has thus encouraged those in charge of the political process to seek means of stability after the death of Franco. The period of democratic transition was marked by a high degree of uncertainty. Initially, it was not clear whether the new king would maintain the previous system of government of a 'soft dictatorship' or whether he would be willing to take the lead in the democratic process because John Charles I had succeeded to the Spanish throne as a result of Franco's wishes in his will. In the first years of his

[55] Camby (1998), p. 1690.

[56] n° 84-177 DC du 30 août 1984.

[57] 75-62 DC du 28 janvier 1976, 87-228 DC du 26 juin 1987, 88-242 DC du 10 mars 1988.

[58] 86-217 DC du 18 septembre 1986.

[59] Szentgáli-Tóth (2019), p. 65.

[60] Comella (2013), pp. 4–34.

reign, the new king only took tentative steps towards a democratic political system. In this situation, the participants in the constitutional process sought solutions that could strengthen the self-defense of democracy. Organic laws were therefore seen as an important safeguard for democracy in the Spanish constitutional process.

Due to the fragmented party system and ethnic diversity,[61] the Spanish political landscape was extremely heterogeneous, and the imposition of a broad consensus was deemed essential to the establishment of a stable constitutional framework. Similar to the democratic transition in the former socialist countries, political parties were formed without direct precedent, and the balance of power and popularity among them was not clear. In Spain, the dictatorship temporarily pushed regional identities into the background, but they resurfaced with renewed force in the 1970s. The conflict between the government in Madrid and the main autonomous provinces (Catalonia and Basque Country) escalated during the civil war when the autonomous provinces rallied behind the republican government that recognized their autonomy. After Franco's death, Catalan and Basque autonomy and independence aspirations intensified, and the supermajority requirement was seen as an instrument of keeping the territorial integrity of the country.

Despite the strong French influence,[62] the special atmosphere of the democratic transition, fear of dictatorial tendencies, and the demands of autonomous regions, Spanish organic laws regulate with a broader scope than the French.

The dominant considerations are similar in Spain as in France: organic laws as legal sources are provided by the Constitution,[63] and by the organic law from the constitutional court.[64] As a result, Spanish organic laws are subject to constitutional review.[65] Although some hierarchical elements have been acknowledged between organic and ordinary laws,[66] the principle of competence is highlighted vis-á-vis the principle of hierarchy. Organic law does not describe a separate constitutional category.[67] Some hierarchical aspects are also relevant, as organic laws are considered during the constitutional review of ordinary statutes.[68] Nevertheless, the constitutional character of supermajority laws has been consistently rejected;[69] organic laws shall comply with constitutional provisions.[70] The Spanish approach is more pragmatic than the French, and consequently, supermajority and ordinary provisions have not been distinguished within the same statute as harshly. The intervention in the ordinary domain shall still be prevented; therefore, the Constitutional Tribunal

[61] Bonime-Blanc (2010), pp. 417–432.

[62] Troper and Chagnollaud (2012), p. 344.

[63] Art. 9 (3) of the Constitution of Spain (January 4, 1978).

[64] 2/1979 Organic law from the Constitutional Court of Spain, Art. 27 (2) and 28 (2).

[65] Troper and Chagnollaud (2012), p. 344.

[66] Troper and Chagnollaud (2012), pp. 344–345.

[67] JCC no. 236-2007.

[68] Troper and Chagnollaud (2012), pp. 344–345.

[69] Prakke et al. (2004), p. 743.

[70] JCC no. 53 of 1985.

strikes out ordinary and organic provisions infringing on the constitutionally prescribed distribution of regulatory competences, respectively.[71] Although organic laws are incorporated within the constitutional block in Spain, they are considered as infra-constitutional sources of law, and their legal value falls clearly between the constitutional and the statutory level.[72]

The scope of Spanish organic laws differs significantly from the French approach. A separate constitutional article determines the two primary areas of organic law: the statutes of the autonomous communities, and fundamental rights and freedoms.[73] Several additional articles of the Spanish Constitution prescribe organic law on further institutional matters: for instance, the organization of military forces,[74] the succession of the throne,[75] the referendum,[76] or the organization of the judiciary,[77] and the functioning and organization of the Constitutional Tribunal.[78] Accordingly, the scope of Spanish Organic Law covers two fields: fundamental rights, and the most important institutions, as the Spanish Constitutional Tribunal has identified. The institutional framework is based on the statutes of autonomous communities; however, other fields are also crucial.

An organic law has also covered the accession of Spain to the European Union,[79] and an organic law shall also be passed for the limitation of the sovereignty of Spain in favor of international organizations.[80] It should be noted here that the limitation on sovereignty constitutes a supermajority subject matter in almost all countries even if the concept of supermajority law has not been implemented in that country.[81] Going back to Spain, one may find some sort of balance between the fundamental right and the institutional aspect of organic law. Supermajority law covers a wider circle of laws than in France.[82]

Regarding the extent of organic legislation, the Spanish Constitutional Tribunal has specified that fundamental rights subject to a supermajority are exclusively those regulated by articles 15–29 of the Spanish Constitution.[83] As the Spanish Constitution outlines the scope of organic law in very broad terms, the Constitutional

---

[71] JCC no. 236 of 2007.

[72] Troper and Chagnollaud (2012), p. 346.

[73] Art. 81-1 of the Constitution of Spain (January 4, 1978).

[74] Art. 8 of the Constitution of Spain (January 4, 1978).

[75] Art. 57 (5) of the Constitution of Spain (January 4, 1978).

[76] Art. 93 of the Constitution of Spain (January 4, 1978).

[77] Art. 122 (1) of the Constitution of Spain (January 4, 1978).

[78] Art. 65 of the Constitution of Spain (January 4, 1978).

[79] Iliopoulos-Strangas (2007), p. 153.

[80] Art. 104 par. 1 of the Constitution of Spain (January 4, 1978).

[81] Art. 93. of the Constitution of Norway; Art. 90 (1) of the Constitution of Poland (April 2, 1997).

[82] Szentgáli-Tóth (2020a), pp. 210–228.

[83] SJCC 76/1983, of 5 August, LC 2; 160/1987, of 27 October LC 2).

Tribunal must provide a rational interpretation in this regard. The practice of the Spanish Constitutional Tribunal refers to the reserved constitutional domain for organic law[84] instead of the organic character or essential content of a subject. If an ordinary law were to intervene in the organic domain, it would be struck down by the Constitutional Tribunal.

2.1.4 The Various Hungarian Models of Supermajority Law

Parts of the historical Constitution of Hungary until 1944 were not incorporated into written rules, but were enriched by a kind of constitutional custom. Accordingly, the Hungarian historical constitution lacked a unified written constitutional text.[85] Instead, a narrow set of laws were placed on the top of the legal system adopted under the same procedural rules as ordinary laws. These were referred to as the 'cardinal laws' and were effectively part of the Constitution in the broader sense. It is therefore essential to emphasize that these laws were not enacted by Parliament as cardinal laws, but were subsequently given this character by a more or less general social consensus.[86]

The communist Constitution of 1949 did not attach any importance to the use of supermajority voting in lawmaking and only required a two-thirds majority for the drafting and amendment of the Constitution,[87] although this was not strictly enforced in practice. The need for a two-thirds rule arose from the historical circumstances of 1989 and, as in other countries it came as a result of a particular political situation. However, this would certainly not have been sufficient, as international examples, in particular the French organic laws and the Austrian constitutional system, and domestic legal precedents, also played a significant role.[88]

Serious fears were articulated around the communist party or its descendant potentially winning an overwhelming majority of votes in the forthcoming free elections, as the former state party was the only one with a nationally established organization, a broad membership, and the financial backing necessary for its preparations. Therefore, the opposition had to gain meaningful weight in the legislature on as wide range of laws as possible, to limit the overwhelming power of the majority, even at the expense of governability. In accordance with this political vision, the

---

[84] JCC no. 236-2007.

[85] Mezey (2011), p. 39.

[86] Hóman and Szekfű (1928), p. 170; Toldy (1861); Marczali (1907), p. 110; Hajnóczy (1791), pp. 236–240; Fényes (1843), p. 1; Széchenyi (1864).

[87] Pursuant to Art. 15 (3) of the Constitution of the Hungarian People's Republic, a two-thirds majority of the votes of the Parliamentarians was required to amend the Constitution. (Official Gazette, 20 VIII 1949).

[88] Kilényi (1989).

Constitution was amended in October 1989, specifying areas regulated by a constitutional law adopted by a two-thirds majority of all parliamentarians.

The final concept and the form of the implementation of constitutional laws showed that the category of constitutional law became a politically highly influenced legal instrument, since the scope of constitutional laws at that time differed from the later "two-thirds laws" in two respects. First, in the case of constitutional law, the majority required was not two-thirds of the total number of deputies present but two-thirds of all parliamentarians, so that constitutional laws in 1989 were stricter than the later versions of supermajority law in this respect. Furthermore, the scope of constitutional laws at that time did not coincide with the current scope of cardinal laws. For instance all regulations affecting fundamental rights and obligations should also be included in constitutional laws. This would have meant a degree of constraint on the government that would have seriously compromised the functioning of the system in practice, as a supermajority was required for the enactment of most laws.

Many participants in the political life of three decades ago agreed that the system of constitutional laws established in October 1989 was unsustainable in the long term, as it threatened the very foundations of the governability of the country.[89] The turn of events in the 1990 elections, when the newly-formed democratic parties won a majority of seats and were able to form a government, also encouraged a reconsideration of the situation. In addition, the Constitutional Court, beginning its work in January 1990, addressed the issue of constitutional laws and pointed out the serious constitutional consequences of maintaining this arrangement.[90] The pact concluded between the major parties of the country resulted in the replacement of constitutional laws with the category of 'two-thirds laws'[91] and the rewriting of supermajority legislative subjects. Act XL of 1990 was enacted in the wake of the Pact and amended the Constitution[92] to require supermajority voting for some thirty pieces of legislation.

Two-thirds laws established at that time remained in force with minor amendments until 2011, thus Act XL of 1990 demonstrably established a workable model with all of its shortcomings. The altered concept of two-thirds legislation was completed by the Constitutional Court, ruling that only the essential guarantees of supermajority subjects need to be adopted by a two-thirds majority, while minor legal provisions and detailed rules can be included in ordinary laws.[93] The 1990 constitutional amendment did not radically change the scope of two-thirds

[89] Szentgáli-Tóth (2017), pp. 770–779.

[90] 4/1990. (III. 4.) AB decision, ABH 1990, 28–30.

[91] So-called two-thirds laws were first introduced into the Hungarian legal system by the amendment to the Constitution that entered into force on October 23, 1989. (Until then, such a majority was only required for the adoption and amendment of the Constitution.) In: Soltész (2010), p. 107.

[92] According to the explanatory memorandum to the constitutional amendment, the category of constitutional law had to be abolished in order to "establish a stable parliamentary system" and "ensure the stable functioning of government". 66/1997. (XII. 29.) AB decision, ABH 1997, 397.

[93] 4/1993. (II. 12.) AB decision, ABH 1993, 48.

legislation, but it did correct the previous system in two respects. First, it removed the open-ended nature of the list of subjects covered by the two-thirds requirement and replaced the overly broad clause on fundamental rights with a specific list of human rights that require a supermajority. This amendment has made the scope of two-thirds legislation manageable with twenty-six covered subjects. The other far-reaching novelty was the requirement of a two-thirds majority of all MEPs present for the enactment of almost all supermajority laws, except for the two-thirds law about the flag and the coat of arms of Hungary, which is still subject to the two-thirds consent of all parliamentarians. This was later expanded in 2002 with the signing of international treaties defining the exercise of shared competence in preparation for EU accession.

The concept of the two-thirds law did not focus on the relationship of these laws to the Constitution but on their rank vis-á-vis ordinary statutes, as the Constitutional Court has pointed out.[94]

The two decades before 2011 can be considered a calmer period for two-thirds legislation, during which Hungary experienced the functioning of this construction in parliamentary practice for more than twenty years. Amendments to two-thirds laws have been relatively rare, and no major overhauls have taken place. The nature of supermajority voting meant that some thirty laws became the subject of political bargaining, and any amendments could only be pushed through if they could win support from the opposition. This resulted in increased stability, but in more than one case the lack of adequate consensus has preserved inadequately drafted legislation that could not keep pace with rapidly changing circumstances, as was the case, for example, with the remuneration of members of parliament. In addition, some subjects were considered to require a two-thirds majority, despite the Constitution not explicitly providing this. These included the law on the election of MEPs and the law on the status of local government representatives. Consequently, despite the relative stability of the regulatory framework, the two-thirds arena has slowly expanded during this period.

The previous Constitution of Hungary did not contain a uniform definition of two-thirds laws, and provided for this form of majority separately for each two-thirds subject. In contrast, Article T (4) of the Fundamental Law now reads as follows: 'A cardinal law is a law which requires the vote of two-thirds of the members of Parliament present to be passed and amended.' This formulation reshapes discussions about supermajority by creating a specific concept to indicate the laws concerned. In addition, the scope of the legislation to be included has been made more uniform. With the exception of the ratification of international treaties, legislation with the stronger form of supermajority, the so-called large two-thirds majority, has been abolished.[95] The Hungarian Constitutional Court has clarified that a two-thirds majority only binds the legislator when setting the regulatory direction of a specific subject matter, while a simple majority may be sufficient to adopt a rule on detailed

[94] 66/1997. (XII. 29.) AB decision, ABH 1997, 397.

[95] Art. E (4) of the Fundamental Law of Hungary (April 25, 2011).

issues or on less essential guarantees of the subject matter.[96] Once a rule has been raised to the two-thirds level, it can no longer be amended by a simple parliamentary majority.[97]

The cardinal law should be sharply distinguished from the two-thirds and the constitutional laws, as in contrast to the constitutional and political connotations of supermajority law, the cardinal law highlights the controversial reinstatement of historical traditions, but does not orient towards the current aspects of supermajority voting.[98] It is not the law itself that is cardinal, but the subject matter it regulates, and thus the designation of the cardinal law itself is inaccurate, since not laws but certain legal provisions are given increased protection. In practice, cardinality does not refer to whole laws, but to subject areas and the legal provisions which are specifically named in the cardinality clauses within the framework of the Fundamental Law. This practice amplified an already existing trend: since the 1990s, certain chapters of seemingly ordinary laws were in practice considered as subject to two-thirds parliamentary consent.[99]

Unlike the previous Constitution, the Fundamental Law only defines the framework for the application of supermajority voting. The actual scope of the cardinal provisions has been delineated by the cardinal clauses enacted in each cardinal law.[100] The amendment of the cardinality clauses may be challenged before the Constitutional Court on the basis of an appropriate plea. As that, as in the past, the Constitutional Court has continued to have the final say on the scope of the cardinal law in the event of a dispute.[101] The previous practice on the operation of simple majority for the adoption of detailed rules relating to a cardinal provision has also been maintained.[102]

The Constitutional Court has also dealt with the rank of two-thirds laws in the hierarchy of legal sources in several cases.[103] Its consistent position outlines that the two-thirds laws do not constitute a separate category of legal sources and that all laws should be treated as equal in this respect, an approach that many experts do not consider to be justified. The Fundamental Law does not satisfactorily settle this issue, although strong arguments support that the relationship between the cardinal laws and the ordinary statutes is determined by competence rather than a hierarchical principle.[104] The Constitutional Court seems to have maintained the doctrinally objectionable principle of formal equality even after the entry into force of the

[96] 4/1993. (II. 12.) AB decision, ABH 1993, 48.

[97] 1/1999. (II. 24.) AB decision, ABH 1999, 25; 55/2010. (V. 5.) AB decision, ABH 2010, 366.

[98] Könczöl (2020), pp. 161–174.

[99] Jakab and Szilágyi (2014), pp. 96–102.

[100] Gárdos-Orosz and Bán-Forgács (2024), p. 9.

[101] 13/2013. (VI. 17.) AB decision, ABH 2013, 440.

[102] 24/2016. (XII. 12.) AB decision, ABH 2016, 560.

[103] 4/1993. (II. 12.) AB decision, ABH 1993, 48; 53/1995. (IX. 15.) AB decision, ABH 1995, 238; 3/1997. (I. 22.) AB decision, ABH 1997, 33; 1/1999. (II. 24.) AB decision, ABH 1999, 25; 27/2008. (III. 12.) AB decision, ABH 2008, 289.

[104] Szentgáli-Tóth (2020b), p. 53.

Fundamental Law, for example by applying the principle of lex posterior derogate legi priori between a cardinal and an ordinary law regulating an ordinary subject matter.[105] In summary, one can argue that despite the reform attempts, the Fundamental Law mostly continued the approach of the previous Constitution when it replaced two-thirds laws with cardinal ones.[106]

The codification of the Fundamental Law has not resulted in a change of supermajority's scope in terms of quantity alone, as two-thirds majority has been required by the Fundamental Law for thirty-four legislative subjects. This means the scope of supermajority legislation in Hungary remained very extensive, even by international comparison. The shift is noticeable in other respects as well: while two-thirds laws were primarily considered as instruments for stabilizing the essence of fundamental rights and the key features of the state organization, the Fundamental Law relegates the former to the background leaving the institutional aspect as the dominant one.[107] This might be evaluated as a step towards the French model from the Spanish example, although the reform was not inspired by such intentions.

In addition, certain public policy issues have been included in the list of legislation requiring supermajority voting: the protection of families,[108] the acquisition of field lands,[109] the basic principles of the tax system and the pension system[110] shall be included in cardinal laws. The tax and pension systems are segments of society usually subject to profound restructuring after each successive government. Regarding the tax system, I would further like to draw attention to the fact that supermajority should be read in conjunction with Article 37 (4) of the Fundamental Law.[111] This results in the Constitutional Court only exercising its review power to a limited extent in relation to the cardinal laws concerning public finances within the foreseeable future, as long as the government debt exceeds half of the total gross domestic product.[112] This situation points to a shortcoming foreshadowing the safeguarding role of the Hungarian model of cardinal law. If a supermajority requirement is conferred upon certain provisions, but without the real possibility of

[105] 43/2012. (XII. 20.) AB decision, OJ 2012, 296.

[106] Varju et al. (2016), p. 27.

[107] Mazza (2013), pp. 140–155.

[108] Art. L (3) of the Fundamental Law of Hungary (April 25, 2011).

[109] Art. P (2) of the Fundamental Law of Hungary (April 25, 2011).

[110] Art. 40 of the Fundamental Law of Hungary (April 25, 2011).

[111] Art. 37 (4) of the Fundamental Law of Hungary (April 25, 2011): as long as the public debt exceeds half of the total gross domestic product, the Constitutional Court may, in accordance with Art. 24. The Constitutional Court may review the conformity of the laws on the central budget, on the implementation of the central budget, on central taxes, on fees and contributions, on customs duties and on the central conditions of local taxes with the Fundamental Law only in connection with the right to life and human dignity, the right to the protection of personal data, the right to freedom of thought, conscience and religion or the rights related to Hungarian citizenship, and may annul them for infringement of these rights. The Constitutional Court may also annul laws in this field without restriction if the procedural requirements of the Fundamental Law concerning the drafting and promulgation of the law have not been fulfilled.

[112] 40/2012. (XII. 6.) AB decision, OJ 2012, 229.

constitutional review, supermajority legislation will mostly function as a distortive factor with severe threat rather than a safeguard.[113]

2.1.5 *Supermajority Law in Austria*

The Austrian framework does not use the concept of supermajority law, but it does include several elements of it in its constitutional regime. The Austrian constitutional evolution has a unique historical background due to its partial legal continuity with the former Austrian empire. Additionally, despite its proximity to Central and Eastern Europe and the presence of the Soviet military between 1945–1955, Austria did not establish a communist system and therefore was not part of the constitution-making wave in Central and Eastern Europe. As a result, the supermajority legislative majority did not support the peaceful political transition in Austria, but rather completed the historically developed and inherently fragmented constitutional framework. Due to these differences, the Austrian experience does not constitute a separate model of Central-European supermajority law; this was rather a close point of reference for those lawyers and politicians who argued for the introduction of supermajority laws.[114] Nevertheless, the Austrian statutory norms with quasi-constitutional force play a crucial role in the protection of fundamental rights, and this inspired the Central and Eastern-European constitution-drafters to consider legislation with supermajority as a potential safeguard of fundamental rights and human dignity.

Although Austria lacks the explicit concept of a supermajority law, the constitution's multi-layered and fragmented structure nevertheless distinguishes between provisions that have constitutional status and simple statutory provisions. The Austrian federal constitution consists of a number of federal laws, such as the Basic Law of 1867,[115] and the Federal Constitution Act of 1920. International treaties at the constitutional level (such as the European Convention on Human Rights) and individual constitutional provisions in ordinary laws also fall into this category. The latter is illustrated by Article 1 of the Data Protection Act, which is considered a constitutional provision, while Article 2 of the Data Protection Act is treated as an ordinary statutory provision.[116] Constitutional amendments do not necessarily have to be inserted into the existing constitutional text, which is why the constitution is constantly fragmenting and becoming increasingly opaque. During the grand coalition periods, it became common practice for a two-thirds parliamentary majority to

[113] Szentgáli-Tóth (2014).

[114] Szentgáli-Tóth (2022), pp. 3–18.

[115] The Austrian Basic Law of December 21, 1867 on the general rights of citizens of the kingdoms and countries represented in the Imperial Council (Staatsgrundgesetz vom December 21, 1867 über die allgemeine Rechte der Staatsbürger für die im Reichsrathe represented Königreiche und Länder).

[116] Jakab (2010), p. 142.

unilaterally amend the constitution, not by amending the federal constitution, but by elevating the provision of the law in question to constitutional status.[117] It is no coincidence that the Austrian idea of "unconstitutional constitutional law" exists and that the constitutional court is empowered to review the substance of constitutional amendments.[118] It will be explained in more detail how the Austrian example puts the theory of constitutional extension into practice.

2.1.6 *Constitutional Law in Azerbaijan*

As a successor state of the Soviet Union, Azerbaijan implemented a sophisticated version of supermajority law with two different levels of supermajority. During the first years of its independence, Azerbaijan faced turbulent tensions with Armenia. These were the first chapters of the still ongoing Azeri-Armenian conflict for control over Karabakh. Moreover, attempted coups d'état during these years also surrounded the transition process, which forced constitution-drafters to consider safeguards for constitutional endurance.

As a result, the current Constitution of Azerbaijan provides for three different majorities required for various fields of legislation. The Milli Majlis, the Parliament of Azerbaijan, comprises 125 parliamentarians. Therefore, 63 supporting votes are needed for the adoption of an ordinary law. It should be noted that in Azerbaijan, an absolute majority is required for ordinary legislation. In several countries; this level of consent represents an elevated level of parliamentary majority reserved for the adoption of supermajority laws.

Apart from ordinary legislation to be passed with an absolute majority of all deputies,[119] two forms of supermajority law have been established. First, the Constitution of Azerbaijan stipulates that 83 favorable votes should be cast for the regulation of presidential elections,[120] the elections of parliamentarians,[121] the legal status of the deputies,[122] and also referendums.[123] Second, 95 votes would be required for the adoption of constitutional laws, including constitutional amendments and some additional pieces of legislation. The Azerbaijan Constitution fascinatingly operates with a concrete number of deputies instead of determined proportions of the representatives present. Furthermore, we can experience an additional model in which the distinction between the constitutional and the supermajority legislative level has not been elaborated in detail. Certain constitutional laws form part of the

[117] Wiederin (2007), pp. 389–449.

[118] VfSlg 11.756 (1988); VfSlg 11.829 (1988); VfSlg 11.916 (1988); VfGH 11.10.2001, G 12/00.

[119] Art. 94 (1) and (2) of the Constitution of Azerbaijan (November 12, 1995).

[120] Art. 94 (1) point 2 of the Constitution of Azerbaijan (November 12, 1995).

[121] Art. 94 (1) point 3 of the Constitution of Azerbaijan (November 12, 1995).

[122] Art. 94 (1) point 3 of the Constitution of Azerbaijan (November 12, 1995).

[123] Art. 94 (1) point 4 of the Constitution of Azerbaijan (November 12, 1995).

constitutional framework[124] and amend the main text of the Constitution.[125] While for instance, a separate constitutional law with quasi-constitutional character should regulate the national symbols, such as the hymn, the flag and the coat of arms of Azerbaijan.[126] National symbols as an outstanding legislative field can be recalled from the Hungarian example, also covered by the so-called large two-thirds requirement.

Regarding constitutional laws, a further procedural requirement has been established: the Milli Majlis should enact these laws in two readings, and at least 6 months should pass between the readings of these bills. The president of the republic shall sign the adopted constitutional law after both readings, but it would only enter into effect after the second reading.[127]

The supermajority law in Azerbaijan has also been connected to the presidential veto. If the president sends an ordinary law back to the Milli Majlis for reconsideration, the Milli Majlis can override the presidential veto with the agreement of 83 deputies. If there is such a broad agreement, the president must sign and enact the law. Additionally, if a supermajority law, which requires the consent of 83 deputies, is vetoed by the president, the Milli Majlis can ignore the veto if 95 parliamentarians vote to adopt the bill again. However, the Milli Majlis cannot overturn a presidential veto against a constitutional law. Constitutional laws should not be enacted without the consent of the president.[128]

2.1.7 Organic Law in Croatia

In Croatia, the crucial motivation for the implementation of organic law came from outside the Central-European region. The basic principles of the Croatian Constitution, the catalogue of fundamental rights, and the safeguards for their protection stem from the German constitutional tradition,[129] while the organizational framework is primarily based on the French constitutional design.[130] The introduction of organic law and the establishment of a special subcategory of law are clear examples of French influence. However, Croatian organic laws exist within a unicameral parliamentary system, while France utilizes a semi-presidential framework with bicameral legislation. Noticeably, the original Croatian Constitution stipulated a bicameral parliament after regaining independence, but this was abolished in

[124] Art. 156 (1) of the Constitution of Azerbaijan (November 12, 1995).
[125] Art. 156 (5) of the Constitution of Azerbaijan (November 12, 1995).
[126] Art. 23 (3) of the Constitution of Azerbaijan (November 12, 1995).
[127] Art. 156 (2)-(4) of the Constitution of Azerbaijan (November 12, 1995).
[128] Art. 110 (2) of the Constitution of Azerbaijan (November 12, 1995).
[129] Baric (2016).
[130] Lang et al. (2019), pp. 1155–1160.

1998.[131] Historical reasons might also explain why organic law was considered as a potential guarantee of inclusive legislation in Croatia. Similar to Romania, the democratic transition was surrounded by violent incidents and the long war against Serbia, so this experience highlighted the potential safeguards of a stable constitutional order.

Croatia has combined the two-thirds and the absolute majority models. The Constitution prescribes that the organic law on the rights of national and ethnic minorities may be enacted or amended with only two-thirds consent of the parliamentarians,[132] while for other organic laws, the absolute majority is required.[133] After the constitutional amendment in May 1990, the Hungarian Constitution also stipulated a two-thirds majority of the deputies present for the amendment of supermajority laws, except for the act on the national flag and the national coat of arms, which was subject to a two-thirds majority of all parliamentarians.[134] In addition, the aforementioned distinction of the status of autonomous communities amongst Spanish organic laws may have also had an impact on the Croatian framework.

Croatia represents a different model from Romania and Moldova as regards the scope of supermajority law; these constitutions do not include a complete list of the organic fields of legislation, only some general clauses are provided within the scope of supermajority law. In contrast, the Croatian Constitution stipulates: "Laws (organic laws) which elaborate on the constitutionally defined human rights and fundamental freedoms, the electoral system, the organization, authority and operation of government bodies and the organization and authority of local and regional self-government shall be passed by the Croatian Parliament by a majority vote of all representatives."[135]

The reference to the constitutionally provided fundamental rights and freedoms, and to the organization of the governmental bodies, leaves this list open-ended. It would be the Parliament's task, and on the final instance of the Constitutional Court's interpretation, to determine which statutes or statutory provisions fall within the coverage of organic law.

2.1.8 *Organic Law in Georgia*

The historical background of Georgian constitution-making shows certain similarities with the Spanish example, but important differences between the two countries should also be taken into account. The other country, which may be comparable to

---

[131] Lang et al. (2019), p. 1154.

[132] Art. 82 (1) of the Constitution of Croatia (December 22, 1990).

[133] Art. 82 (2) of the Constitution of Croatia (December 22, 1990).

[134] Art. 75 (3) of Act XX. from 1949 on the Constitution of Republic of Hungary (August 20, 1949).

[135] Art. 82 (1) of the Constitution of Croatia (December 22, 1990).

Georgia, is Moldova. The most striking characteristic of Georgian society was its fragmentation: the tensions between different political groups of interests, and movements of the national ethnic minorities threatened the peaceful transition and the territorial integrity of the country. Violent incidents took place in 1992, and for some months, a temporary military government led the country. South Ossetia and Abkhazia further targeted full independence, or at least the extension of their autonomy. Due to these factors of uncertainties, all relevant stakeholders expressed their willingness to enact the final constitution of the country, and to conclude the transition peacefully. Organic law was seen as a proper instrument for the promotion of these aims.[136]

Similarly to Romania, Georgia introduced the absolute majority system in a bicameral structure, but with additional safeguards.[137] If the president submits a veto against the adopted organic law, the Parliament may uphold the earlier version with only three-fifth majority consent of the deputies.[138] Interesting to note that a similar solution existed only in Tunisia until 2022.[139] The Georgian Constitution contains one further element, worthy of consideration in other countries. It often raises meaningful questions about how to calculate the fulfillment of the two-thirds requirement, and what exactly should be understood under the term "all deputies"? This may be problematic in case of temporary vacancies due to the resignation or death of certain parliamentarians. The counting of abstentions might also be questionable, as we have seen in the recent practice of the European Parliament.[140] The Constitution of Georgia expressly provides that supermajority should be calculated on the basis of the deputies on the current nominal list.[141] Therefore, the calculation does not derive from the constitutionally prescribed number of the representatives, but on those mandates filled at the reference moment.

As regard the scope, the Georgian model falls closer to the French and the current Hungarian solutions: organic law and the subsequent safeguards are outlined by the Constitution.[142] The Constitution expressly provides the acts to be adopted as organic on a case-by-case basis. A special temporary rule was also drafted that all organic laws should be passed until no later than the end of the second year after the enactment of the Constitution.[143]

[136] Aladashvili (2005).
[137] Art. 66 (2) of the Constitution of Georgia (August 24, 1995).
[138] Art. 68 (4) of the Constitution of Georgia (August 24, 1995).
[139] Art. 81 (5) of the Constitution of Tunisia (January 26, 2014).
[140] www.lawoforderblog.com/2018/03/4-things-most-people-get-wrong-about-abstentions/.
[141] Aladashvili (2005).
[142] Art. 66 (2) of the Constitution of Georgia (August 24, 1995).
[143] Art. 106 (3) of the Constitution of Georgia (August 24, 1995).

2.1.9 Constitutional Law in Italy

Constitutional laws have been introduced in Italy earlier than organic law in its current form in France: the constitutional law category was established by the republican Constitution of Italy in 1947 as part of the establishment of the post-war democratic framework in the country.[144]

Italian constitutional laws are treated as near equivalents to constitutional amendments: both categories are subject to the same procedural rules. Constitutional laws have equal rank at the top of the legal pyramid, alongside the main text of the Constitution itself. A constitutional law may prevail over a constitutional provision if the constitutional law has been enacted later.[145] The ordinary legislative procedure requires a simple majority in both chambers of the Italian Parliament. In contrast, constitutional laws must be passed twice, and the second reading cannot be scheduled within three months of the first vote on the bill.[146] During the second parliamentary discussion on the bill, the draft bill shall not be amended; the entire text should be passed or rejected. If the bill receives an absolute majority in both chambers, it should be published in the Official Gazette, and one fifth of the members of either parliamentary chamber or 500,000 electors or five regional councils may initiate a constitutional referendum from the enacted bill within three months. In case of a lack of such a request, the adopted constitutional law shall be promulgated once the deadline has been terminated. Should any authorized actor initiate a referendum, a constitutional plebiscite must be organized without any validity threshold.[147] Should a two-thirds majority of both parliamentary chambers support the bill of the constitutional law upon the second reading, the adopted bill may immediately be promulgated without considering the holding of a referendum.[148]

Regarding the scope of Italian constitutional laws, despite the identical procedure, constitutional amendments and additional constitutional laws can be distinguished.[149] Besides constitutional amendments, a narrow set of institutional fields are concerned: the composition of both parliamentary chambers and the election of parliamentarians;[150] the right to submit parliamentary initiatives;[151] ministerial offences;[152] the fundamental principles of public finances;[153] the status and competences of the Constitutional Court;[154] the status of the borders of the regions as

---

[144] Bin and Pitruzella (2008), p. 322.

[145] Bin and Pitruzella (2008), p. 325.

[146] Art. 138 (1) of the Constitution of Italy (December 22, 1947).

[147] Art. 138 (2) of the Constitution of Italy (December 22, 1947).

[148] Art. 138 (3) of the Constitution of Italy (December 22, 1947).

[149] Bin and Pitruzella (2008), p. 326.

[150] Art. 48 (3) of the Constitution of Italy (December 22, 1947).

[151] Art. 71 (1) of the Constitution of Italy (December 22, 1947).

[152] Art. 96 of the Constitution of Italy (December 22, 1947).

[153] Art. 81 (6) of the Constitution of Italy (December 22, 1947).

[154] Art. 137 (1) of the Constitution of Italy (December 22, 1947).

administrative units; as well as the autonomous regions of Sicily, Sardinia, Aosta Valley, Trentino-South Tyrol and Friuli-Venezia Giulia are sanctioned by constitutional laws.[155]

2.1.10 Constitutional Law in Kazakhstan

Kazakhstan follows the Eastern-European strand of supermajority legislation, however, similarly to Russia, with a bicameral system. In contrast to Western-European bicameralism operating with absolute majority requirements, a two-thirds majority has been required in both Kazakh chambers, either in the Mazhilis as the lower chamber or in the Senate. This result in a relatively rigid legislative framework, where the enactment of supermajority legislation depends on the willingness of three constitutional actors: the president of the republic, the Senate, and the Mazhilis.

Ordinary laws are passed by the absolute majority of both parliamentary chambers in Kazakhstan;[156] however, supermajority laws (referred to as constitutional laws by the Kazakh Constitution) should be adopted by a two-thirds majority in both houses.[157] Constitutional laws are discussed first by the Mazhilis, then, moving forward in the adoption process, it is sent to the Senate. If the Senate supports the bill with a two-thirds majority within 60 days, the draft constitutional law is forwarded to the president of the republic, who shall sign the constitutional law within 10 days. Then, it is promulgated. If the Senate does not vote with a two-thirds majority for the constitutional law, the Mazhilis shall discuss the bill again; if the Mazhilis confirms its two-thirds support, the objections of the Senate shall be disregarded.[158]

If the Senate passes the constitutional law but proposes amendments to its text by a two-thirds majority, the Mazhilis will discuss these proposals and might enact the amended version of the constitutional law by a two-thirds majority. Then, the bill will be sent to the president of the republic. If the Mazhilis disagrees with the proposed amendments, the two houses will set up a conciliation committee to conclude a compromise through negotiations.[159]

The president of the republic shall sign the forwarded constitutional laws within 10 days unless he/she wishes to veto the adopted constitutional law and will return it to the two chambers with his/her objections. In this case, both

---

[155] Art. 116 (1) of the Constitution of Italy (December 22, 1947).

[156] Art. 61 (4) of the Constitution of Kazakhstan (August 30, 1995).

[157] Art. 62 (4) of the Constitution of Kazakhstan (August 30, 1995).

[158] Art. 61 (5) of the Constitution of Kazakhstan (August 30, 1995).

[159] Art. 61 (5-1) of the Constitution of Kazakhstan (August 30, 1995.

chambers shall vote for the adopted bill with a three-quarters majority to override the presidential veto. If both chambers remain silent until one month, the bill is deemed to be adopted or rejected in compliance with the wording of the presidential message.[160]

Regarding the scope of Kazakhstani constitutional laws, institutional issues are emphasized: the national elections,[161] status and competences of the president of the republic;[162] the election[163] and status of parliamentarians and the organization for both chambers;[164] the status, organization and competences of the government,[165] the Constitutional Court[166] as well as the judiciary.[167] Elevated majority is also required for the statutory regulation of state symbols[168] and the administrative regime of the capital, Astana.[169]

Interesting to note, that from the Central-Asian region, apart from Kazakhstan, Kyrgyzstan[170] and Tajikistan[171] have also implemented constitutional laws subject to the approval of a two-thirds parliamentary majority.

2.1.11 *Organic Law in Moldova*

In Moldova, two special circumstances determined the priorities of the constitution-drafters. On the one hand, Moldova followed the Romanian example in several respects; this meant an important inspiration for the implementation of supermajority law.[172] On the other hand, society has been deeply divided in Moldova, with the Romanian and Russian communities have inherently different visions for the future of the country. Furthermore, the autonomous status of Gagauzia has a special status, which shall be provided by an organic law.

Moldova relied mostly on the Romanian model when the procedural safeguards of organic law were outlined, but the absolute majority requirement should be interpreted in a unicameral system,[173] so it has significantly less weight than in Romania.

---

[160] Art. 54 (2) point 1 of the Constitution of Kazakhstan (August 30, 1995).

[161] Art. 41 (1) of the Constitution of Kazakhstan (August 30, 1995).

[162] Art. 46 (4) of the Constitution of Kazakhstan (August 30, 1995).

[163] Art. 50 (2) - (3) and 51 (5) of the Constitution of Kazakhstan (August 30, 1995).

[164] Art. 49 (4) of the Constitution of Kazakhstan (August 30, 1995).

[165] Art. 64 (4) of the Constitution of Kazakhstan (August 30, 1995).

[166] Art. 71 (6) of the Constitution of Kazakhstan (August 30, 1995).

[167] Art. 75 (4); 79 (3) and 82 (3) of the Constitution of Kazakhstan (August 30, 1995).

[168] Art. 9 of the Constitution of Kazakhstan (August 30, 1995).

[169] Art. 3-1 of the Constitution of Kazakhstan (August 30, 1995).

[170] Art. 86 (5) of the Constitution of Kyrgyzstan (April 11, 2021).

[171] Art. 61 of the Constitution of Tajikistan (November 6, 1994).

[172] Carnat (2005), pp. 129–130.

[173] Art. 74 (1) of the Constitution of Moldova (July 29, 1994).

A special exception should be highlighted, inspired by certain elements of the French and Spanish systems. The organic law on the status of the Autonomous Community of Gagauzia should be adopted by at least a three-fifths majority in the Parliament, instead of the generally applied absolute majority requirement for organic laws.[174] The French Constitutional Council identified a hierarchy between organic laws themselves first: the organic law on public finances has been vested with quasi-constitutional force.[175] A closer analogy can be mentioned from Spain, where only the organic laws on the statutes of the autonomous communities should be subject to mandatory a priori constitutional review.

The circle of organic laws in Moldova may not be determined solely on the grounds of the Constitution itself.[176] Similar to Romania, article 72 (3) provides an extensive list of organic legislative fields, but other constitutional articles also stipulate supermajority requirements for certain issues.[177] The Parliament may also adopt organic laws on matters, not classified by the Constitution as an organic legislative field, but the application of the stricter procedural regime may be justified.[178] This margin of movement for the Parliament forms not only a theoretical competence: on the grounds of this authorization, the Parliament adopted organic laws on the public prosecutor, on the organization of the armed forces, on the status of the judiciary, on lawyers, and on the security forces, among others.[179]

These characteristics of the Moldovan constitutional system mean that besides the Constitution, the Moldovan constitutional framework is based on organic laws. Unlike other countries, supermajority law constitutes the ordinary way of legislation. Since Moldovan organic laws are applied broadly due to the aforementioned reasons, a greater number of supermajority laws have been enacted than elsewhere. This background explains why the necessity of organic law has not been contested in Moldova; organic laws stand undoubtedly over ordinary laws. Organic law is considered primarily as a safeguard. These norms are seen as the extensions of the Constitution, while the procedural regime provides sufficient flexibility in case of reform attempts.[180] In Moldova, only the substantial constitutionality of organic laws may be challenged; dogmatic debates on this topic have not been conducted.[181]

---

[174] Art. 111 (7) of the Constitution of Moldova (July 29, 1994).

[175] N° 98-401, DC du 10 juin 1998.

[176] Carnat (2005), pp. 114–115; 129–130; Art. 73 (3) point R) of the Constitution of Moldova (July 29, 1994).

[177] Art. 72 (3) point P) of the Constitution of Moldova (July 29, 1994).

[178] Art. 72 (3) point R) of the Constitution of Moldova (July 29, 1994).

[179] Roper (2008), p. 119.

[180] Roper (2008), p. 121.

[181] For instance, ruling 2013/36. of the Constitutional Court of Moldova (December 05, 2013).

2.1.12 Supermajority Law in Montenegro

Montenegro reclaimed its full independence in 2006, and its constitution entered into force in 2007, more than a decade later than most democratic constitutions of the region. Three levels of supermajority legislation are distinguished in Montenegro, but otherwise, the relevant constitutional provisions are very similar to the Croatian concept of organic law. However, the Constitution of Montenegro has not constituted a separate category of organic law; it merely enumerates those fields of legislation where different forms of elevated parliamentary majority should be conferred.

Montenegro has established a procedural regime similar to the Croatian approach, but with more sophisticated content. Supermajority laws are divided into three different classes: most of them require adoption with an absolute majority of parliamentary members, while the act on political rights and properties of foreigners should be enacted with a two-thirds majority of deputies. Finally, a third category is also established by the Constitution of Montenegro: the rights of national minorities and the use of Montenegrin armed forces abroad should be supported in the first vote by at least two-thirds of parliamentarians, and in the second vote, by at least a majority of all deputies.[182]

The Montenegrin Constitution also refers to the fundamental rights and freedoms provided by the Constitution,[183] and more specifically supermajority legislative matters are enumerated as well.[184] This regulatory method resembles the Hungarian solution applied during the 1989 constitutional revision: it operates with a very broad reference to the fundamental rights and duties, and with the exhaustive enumeration of the institutional matters.

2.1.13 Organic Law in Portugal

Organic law has similar roots in Portugal as in Spain, but in Portugal, the monarchy was abolished before World War I. However, the republican form of government did not prove to be stable internal struggles and anti-democratic movements intensified. In the mid-1930s, José Antonio Salazar seized power, formally maintaining a democratic framework, and led Portugal for more than three decades under a Franco-like soft dictatorship. After Salazar's death, Portugal began to democratize, partly in parallel with, if not ahead of, developments in Spain. During the last years of Salazar's rule, a state of emergency was introduced in the colonies, as the Portuguese elite refused to give in to independence aspirations. The Portuguese finally withdrew from the colonies after the fall of the nationalist dictatorship, but the recent

---

[182] Art. 91 of the Constitution of Montenegro (October 19, 2007).

[183] Drašković (2015), p. 26.

[184] Art. 91 of the Constitution of Montenegro (October 19, 2007).

memory of the authoritarian society and the armed conflicts remained vivid in the minds of the constitution-drafters.[185]

Portuguese organic laws enjoy supremacy over ordinary laws but fall clearly under the Constitution in the hierarchy of legal norms.[186] Regarding the procedural requirements, two elements distinguish the organic legislative procedure from the ordinary one. First, for the enactment of an organic law, two parliamentary readings are required.[187] After the second reading, an absolute majority shall support the bill, or two-thirds of the parliamentarians present if this number exceeds the absolute parliamentary majority.[188] Second, similar to France and Spain, a special form of prior constitutional review has been implemented in Portugal regarding organic laws. It resembles the French approach, where all enacted organic laws might be subject to prior constitutional review. However, in Portugal, this is only an option rather than a duty. The speaker of the Parliament informs the president of the republic, the prime minister, and the parliamentary groups as potential initiators for the enactment of the organic bill.[189] The informed constitutional actors have 8 days to initiate a prior constitutional review of the organic law, until the termination of this deadline; the law shall not be promulgated by the president of the republic.[190] On behalf of parliamentarians, at least one fifth of the members of the National Assembly could initiate the prior constitutional review of an organic law. If such a motion has not been submitted to the Constitutional Court by the authorized actors before the aforementioned deadline, the president of the republic shall promulgate the organic law. If prior constitutional review has been requested, the Constitutional Court should decide the matter within 25 days.[191]

Regarding the scope of Portuguese organic laws, a narrow range of institutional matters is covered: parliamentary and municipal elections;[192] referendums;[193] the status and competences of the Constitutional Court;[194] national defense and the armed forces;[195] as well as the detailed rules on the state of emergency[196] are provided as organic legislative subject matters.

---

[185] Cristas (2007), pp. 75–89.

[186] Art. 115 (2) of the Constitution of Portugal (April 25, 1976).

[187] Art. 167 (4) of the Constitution of Portugal (April 25, 1976).

[188] Art. 139 (3) and 167 (5) of the Constitution of Portugal (April 25, 1976).

[189] Art. 278 (4) and (5) of the Constitution of Portugal (April 25, 1976).

[190] Art. 278 (6) and (7) of the Constitution of Portugal (April 25, 1976).

[191] Art. 278 (8) of the Constitution of Portugal (April 25, 1976).

[192] Art. 167 point a) and Art. 169 (2) of the Constitution of Portugal (April 25, 1976).

[193] Art. 167 point b) and Art. 169 (2) of the Constitution of Portugal (April 25, 1976).

[194] Art. 167 point c) and art. 169 (2) of the Constitution of Portugal (April 25, 1976).

[195] Art. 167 point d) and Art. 169 (2) of the Constitution of Portugal (April 25, 1976).

[196] Art. 167 point e) and Art. 169 (2) of the Constitution of Portugal (April 25, 1976).

2.1.14 Organic Law in Romania

The Romanian history of organic laws originates from the 1832 laws of Wallachia and Moldavia, which functioned as quasi-constitutional norms, although these documents did not serve as the constitutions of their respective countries.[197] Romanian society also learned from the revolution of 1989, resulting in exceptional care from the drafters of the new constitution, who considered organic law as a potential long-term safeguard of the democratic transition. French constitutional development was traditionally monitored closely by Romanian scholars and politicians: in the light of the established framework, this served as an essential source of inspiration for the Romanian model of supermajority law.[198]

The Romanian legislative branch operates with the absolute majority system in a bicameral framework: the majority of either all deputies or all senators should support the supermajority bill for its enactment.[199] This procedural safeguard originated in the French Constitution, but the Romanian approach does not include those further safeguards that had been added to the absolute majority requirement in France, such as the mandatory a priori constitutional review of organic laws, which does not appear in the legal systems of any Central or Eastern-European country.[200] This can be explained through the use of a priori constitutional review as a primary competence of the French Constitutional Council, whereas in most of the European countries, the German constitutional tradition was considered more attractive. By contrast, in Africa, where the French model produced a stronger impact, and the local traditions played a less important role, mandatory a priori constitutional review has been transplanted by a huge number of countries.[201]

Similar to the Spanish solution,[202] article 72 (3) of the Romanian Constitution outlines most organic legislative matters, but several other constitutional provisions require a supermajority for the regulation of certain issues. Each statute declares its character, regardless of whether it is a supermajority law or an ordinary law. However, according to the Romanian Constitutional Court, the same act may also contain ordinary and organic provisions.[203] The scope of Romanian organic law, especially in the institutional aspect, is outlined relatively broadly, but it correlates

[197] Djuvara (1995).

[198] Deleanu (2006), p. 220.

[199] Art. 74 (1) of the Constitution of Romania (December 8, 1991).

[200] Szentgáli-Tóth (2019), pp. 62–74.

[201] Gitiri and Szentgáli-Tóth (2021).

[202] In this regard, the Romanian approach follows exceptionally the Spanish logic instead of the French one.

[203] From the relevant Romanian practice please see: ruling of the Constitutional Court no. 88/2.06.1998, Official Gazette 207/3.06.1998; ruling of the Constitutional Court no. 442/10.06.10, Official Gazette 526/2015.07.15; ruling of the Constitutional Court no. 568/2015.09.15, Official Gazette 844/2015.11.12; ruling of the Constitutional Court of Romania, no. 622/2016.10.13, Official Gazette 60/20.01.2017.

with the less demanding form of a supermajority. Therefore, it impacts the whole legal system less significantly.

2.1.15 *Constitutional Law in Russia*

The dissolution of the Soviet Union was surrounded by significant political instability and rising tensions between various Russian groups of interest. Therefore, the extension of the Constitution had been considered during the drafting of the new constitutional framework. As a result, federal constitutional laws and federal laws have been distinguished in Russia.[204] The Constitution expressly provides that federal laws shall not contradict federal constitutional laws. Consequently, a clear hierarchy has been established between supermajority and ordinary laws.[205]

Regarding procedural rules, constitutional laws possess very similar requirements to constitutional amendments: while ordinary laws shall be passed by an absolute majority of both chambers or just approved implicitly by the second chamber,[206] federal constitutional laws shall be supported by a two-thirds majority in the House of Representatives (State Duma) and by a three-quarters majority in the Federation Council as the second chamber.[207] The president of the republic does not have such veto powers as in Azerbaijan or Kazakhstan: federal constitutional laws adopted by both chambers shall be signed and promulgated by the president within 14 days.

The scope of Russian federal constitutional laws is also dominated by the institutional fields: the work of the government,[208] the judiciary,[209] the Constitutional Court,[210] the commissioner of fundamental rights,[211] the national symbols,[212] national referenda,[213] and the composition of the Russian Federation, and the status and the territory of its member entities shall be covered by federal constitutional law.[214] Detailed rules on the state of emergency are also placed into federal

[204] Art. 76 (1) of the Constitution of Russian Federation (December 25, 1993).
[205] Art. 76 (3) of the Constitution of Russian Federation (December 25, 1993).
[206] Art. 105 (2) and (4) of the Constitution of Russian Federation (December 25, 1993).
[207] Art. 108 (2) of the Constitution of Russian Federation (December 25, 1993).
[208] Art. 114 (2) of the Constitution of Russian Federation (December 25, 1993).
[209] Art. 118 (3) of the Constitution of Russian Federation (December 25, 1993).
[210] Art. 128 (3) of the Constitution of Russian Federation (December 25, 1993).
[211] Art. 103 (1) point e) of the Constitution of Russian Federation (December 25, 1993).
[212] Art. 70 (1) of the Constitution of Russian Federation (December 25, 1993).
[213] Art. 84 point c) of the Constitution of Russian Federation (December 25, 1993).
[214] Art. 65 (2), 66 (5) and 137 of the Constitution of Russian Federation (December 25, 1993).

constitutional laws: the possible grounds for its declaration;[215] the extraordinary competences of the executive[216] and the exceptional restrictions of fundamental rights.[217]

2.1.16 Constitutional Law in Slovakia

Slovakia has created an interesting combination of the various sets of supermajority law known from other countries in the region. First, Slovak constitutional laws derive from the Constitution of Czechoslovakia, where constitutional laws existed with almost equal rank as the main text of the Constitution. Furthermore, the Austrian experience of constitutional reform, and Hungarian steps in this direction during the democratic transition may have affected the Slovak development.[218]

As a result of this combination, supermajority law has been implemented in Slovakia with strict procedural rules, but with a very narrow scope in comparison with other analyzed models. Simple majority means the backing of at least half of the parliamentarians present.[219] However, for the enactment or amendment of constitutional laws, three-fifths of all deputies should support the bill.[220] The Slovak Constitution further clarifies the legal rank of constitutional laws between the Constitution and ordinary laws: it is specified on the one hand, that ordinary laws shall not contradict constitutional laws.[221] On the other hand, constitutional laws shall be worded[222] and interpreted[223] in line with the Constitution. Although constitutional laws are subject to the same level of supermajority as the Constitution, this distinction creates an undoubted hierarchy for the sake of constitutional supremacy. To adopt a constitutional law for the accession of Slovakia to an international organization, not only the three-fifths parliamentary consent but also the holding of a referendum is required.[224]

The scope of constitutional laws is outlined in relatively narrow terms: the rules on referendums, the rules on the accession of Slovakia to an international organization;[225] the rules on a state of emergency,[226] and the borders of the Slovak

[215] Art. 88 of the Constitution of Russian Federation (December 25, 1993).

[216] Art. 56 (2) of the Constitution of Russian Federation (December 25, 1993).

[217] Art. 56 (1) of the Constitution of Russian Federation (December 25, 1993).

[218] Erdősová (2022), p. 158.

[219] Art. 84 (2) of the Constitution of Slovakia (September 3, 1992).

[220] Art. 84 (3) of the Constitution of Slovakia (September 3, 1992).

[221] Art. 125 point A) of the Constitution of Slovakia (September 3, 1992).

[222] Art. 152 (1) of the Constitution of Slovakia (September 3, 1992).

[223] Art. 152 (4) of the Constitution of Slovakia (September 3, 1992).

[224] Art. 93 (1) of the Constitution of Slovakia (September 3, 1992).

[225] Art. 7 and 86 point C) of the Constitution of Slovakia (September 3, 1992).

[226] Art. 102 point L) of the Constitution of Slovakia (September 3, 1992).

Republic[227] are covered by constitutional laws. Consequently, constitutional laws provide additional protection for some basic frameworks of the state. The institutional aspect and the protection of fundamental rights by supermajority have been downplayed. The National Council of Slovakia is the legislative body that could overrule the result of a referendum through a constitutional law, but if at least three years have not passed after the referendum, such a constitutional law should not be enacted validly.[228]

Similar to Slovakia, the Czech Republic has also inherited and adapted the concept of constitutional law from Czechoslovakia. However, in my view, Czech constitutional laws should not be classified as supermajority laws. These norms represent constitutional amendments rather than a special form of legislation adopted under the supermajority regime.[229]

2.1.17 Organic Law in Africa and Oceania

Organic laws in Africa were inspired by the decolonization process explaining why this concept is more common in Francophone rather than Anglophone countries. Organic laws in Africa do not qualify as models because they are mere adaptations of European versions modified to suit local circumstances. Newly formed African states after gaining independence were not cohesive states but rather ethnic enclaves created by colonial governments and forced to coexist. In Francophone countries, organic laws were adopted as a mechanism to promote internal stability, strengthen national cohesion, and avoid authoritarian tendencies.[230]

Organic laws in Africa are mostly variants of European legal frameworks from France, Spain, and Portugal. A cursory glance at the five groups of African states where organic laws have been adopted reveals that they were formerly colonized by the French and followed the French constitutional model such as the Maghreb, the first group.[231] The second group consists of West African states colonized by the French. The third group includes Francophone countries in East Africa (Djibouti), while the fourth group is in the Central African region, mainly influenced by both France and Belgium. Fifth, organic laws were implemented in Angola and Cape Verde as well, after the fall of the Salazar government in Portugal.

The African context of organic laws has undergone numerous changes arising from the genocide in Rwanda where an elevated majority system of three fifths of

227 Art. 3 (2) of the Constitution of Slovakia (September 3, 1992).

228 Art. 99 (1) of the Constitution of Slovakia (September 3, 1992).

229 Art. 9 of the Constitution of Czech Republic (December 16, 1992).

230 Gitiri and Szentgáli-Tóth (2021), p. 113.

231 Art. 145 of the Constitution of Algeria (November 1, 2020); Art. 67 of the Constitution of Mauritania (July 12, 1991); Art. 85 and 86 of the Constitution of Morocco (July 1, 2011).

the vote was required for the enactment of organic laws.[232] In addition, when the Arab Spring engulfed the Maghreb, Tunisia implemented certain changes to the characteristics of organic laws that brought them closer to Rwanda's position.[233] Several African constitutions stipulate that financial-related laws must be adopted on the basis of procedural rules close to organic law-making,[234] but some of these financial laws are themselves organic laws. Due to further French influence, the provision that organic laws concerning the second chamber can only be adopted by the two chambers with a completely identical text has also spread in Africa.[235]

The subject matters of organic laws follow the aforementioned two-fold model, namely the protection of institutional frameworks and fundamental rights and freedoms.[236] In Africa, the institutional function of organic law is given primary consideration as a mechanism that indirectly protects fundamental rights and freedoms.[237] Although the African concept of organic laws is heavily influenced by the French model, it has developed independent characteristics from the original concept. For example, its scope is narrower, focusing on the legislature[238] and the judiciary,[239] with the exception of Burundi, where other constitutional actors are also covered. Organic laws in Africa have also been extended to the regulation of electoral management bodies,[240] elections[241]and the conduct of referendums.[242] Although African organic laws generally do not directly protect fundamental rights and freedoms, in

[232] Art. 73 (1) of the Constitution of Rwanda (May 30, 1991).

[233] Art. 81 of the Constitution of Tunisia (January 26, 2014); Art. 75 of the Constitution of Tunisia (July 25, 2022).

[234] Art. 112 of the Constitution of Benin (December 02, 1990); Art. 151 of the Constitution of the Republic of Congo (October 25, 2015); Art. 88 (11) of the Constitution of Madagascar (November 14, 2010); Art. 75 of the Constitution of Tunisia (July 25, 2022).

[235] Art. 67 (4) of the Constitution of Mauritania (July 12, 1991); Art. 85 of the Constitution of Morocco (July 1, 2011).

[236] Fombad (2017), pp. 138–139.

[237] Gitiri and Szentgáli-Tóth (2021), p. 115.

[238] Art. 145 of the Constitution of Algeria (November 1, 2020); Art. 86 of the Constitution of Burkina Faso (June 2, 1991); Art. 148, 153, and 156 of the Constitution of Burundi (February 28, 2005); Art. 97 of the Constitution of Gabon (November 16, 2024); Art. 79 of the Constitution of Madagascar (November 14, 2010).

[239] Art. 145 of the Constitution of Algeria (November 1, 2020); Art. 236 of the Constitution of Burundi (February 28, 2005); Art. 126, 131, 134, 138 and 143 of the Constitution of Central African Republic (August 30, 2023); Art. 28 and 29 of the Constitution of Comoros (December 23, 2001); Art. 90 (2), 96 (2), 100 (2), and 104 of the Constitution of Equatorial Guinea (November 16, 1991); Art. 91 of the Constitution of Guinea (March 22, 2020); Art. 125, 136, and 141 of the Constitution of Niger (October 31, 2010); Art. 60 of the Constitution of Senegal (Januar 7, 2001).

[240] Art. 211 of the Constitution of Democratic Republic of Congo (February 18, 2006).

[241] Art. 79, 88 (3) and (10) of the Constitution of Madagascar (November 14, 2010); Art. 48 (1) of the Constitution of Mauritania (July 12, 1991); Art. 35 of the Constitution of Senegal (January 7, 2001).

[242] Art. 164 (g) of the Constitution of Angola (January 21, 2010); Art. 187 (1) c of the Constitution of Cape Verde (September 5, 1980); Art. 151 of the Constitution of the Republic of Congo (October 25, 2015).

the Maghreb this may also happen. In Morocco for example, the right to petition[243] or take industrial action[244] is also covered by organic laws.

While organic law as originally conceptualized in Europe was meant to build strong institutions, better protect fundamental rights and freedoms, combat possibilities of dictatorship, and ultimately lead to constitutional stability, in Africa, organic laws have had the opposite effect. In states that have adopted organic laws, such as Chad, these laws have extended the constitutional crisis, and existing constitutional regimes have not endured.[245] Numerous constitutional amendments and revisions ably demonstrate this in the Francophone countries of the continent.[246] The inherent instability and testimony show that organic laws have not been successful in Africa. This is further exacerbated by certain derivatives such as those practiced in Rwanda and Tunisia that require an elevated level of consent that goes beyond the two-thirds majority. They have been criticized for distorting parliamentary democracy.[247]

Geographically distinct from Africa, the Constitution of Papua New Guinea should also be mentioned, as it also operates with organic laws that require a two-thirds majority of all parliamentarians for the adoption of these statutes.[248]

2.1.18 *Organic Law in Latin America*

In Latin America, the diverse historical background has led to the implementation of organic laws. A full account of the national specificities would go beyond the scope of this volume, so only the importance of the French and Spanish examples is underlined.[249] Furthermore, the development of supermajority legislation is still ongoing. For instance, the draft constitution of Chile from 2022, which was rejected by a referendum, did not operate with the term "organic law" but only mentioned some legislative subject matters, that require the absolute majority consent of the Parliament.[250] The 2023 draft of the Chilean Constitution, also rejected by a referendum in December 2023, would have required a four-sevenths majority in both parliamentary chambers for the enactment of electoral laws, and an absolute majority in both chambers for the adoption of institutional laws on the functioning and organization of main constitutional actors.[251] Similar to the Chilean drafts, the

243 Art. 15 of the Constitution of Morocco (July 1, 2011).

244 Art. 29 of the Constitution of Morocco (July 1, 2011).

245 Art. 139 of the Constitution of Chad (December 29, 2023).

246 Gitiri and Szentgáli-Tóth (2021), p. 114.

247 Gitiri and Szentgáli-Tóth (2021), p. 114.

248 Art. 17 of the Constitution of Papua New Guinea (September 16, 1975).

249 Muñoz (2006), pp. 115–129.

250 Art. 271 of the proposed draft Constitution of Chile (September 4, 2022).

251 Art. 79 of the proposed draft Constitution of Chile (December 17, 2023).

Constitution of Colombia also allocates an absolute majority requirement for the enactment and amendment of certain acts. However, it does not establish a separate subcategory of laws.[252]

Regarding the procedural background, organic laws are usually distinguished from ordinary laws by an absolute majority requirement, which deems the less significance of this legal instrument in the Latin-American region.[253] Two exceptions can be provided: the Dominican Republic passes organic laws by a two-thirds majority;[254] while in Venezuela, two-thirds consent is also expected for this, and the Constitutional Chamber of the Supreme Tribunal shall review the constitutionality of any amended organic act before its promulgation.[255] Only the Constitution of Ecuador stipulates expressly the hierarchical supremacy of organic laws over ordinary laws,[256] the other relevant Latin-American constitutions leave this question open for interpretation.

The scope of organic laws is usually outlined by vague terms in Latin-American constitutions, which again demonstrate the less elaborate character of organic laws in the region. They may cover the dominance of the institutional aspect; however, organic law further concerns the direct safeguard of fundamental rights in the Dominican Republic,[257] Ecuador,[258] and Venezuela.[259] Nevertheless, protected fundamental rights are not enumerated expressly by these constitutions. Instead a general clause confers any role on organic law in the protection of fundamental rights, though it might be complemented by some additional exemplificative constitutional references. The legislation on regional structure and on the municipalities[260] is also sanctioned by more constitutions with organic laws.

References

Aladashvili I (2005) Guide to georgian legal research. GlobaLex www.nyulawglobal.org/globalex/Georgia.html (30 11 2020)

Ardant P, Mathieu B (2014) Droit constitutionnel et institutions politiques. 26ᵉ. LGDJ, Paris

Avril P, Gicquel J (2014) Droit parlementaire. Dalloz, Paris

[252] Art. 151 and 152 of the Constitution of Colombia (July 4, 1991).

[253] Art. 165 of the Constitution of Panama (October 11, 1972); Art. 106 of the Constitution of Peru (December 31, 1993).

[254] Art. 112 of the Constitution of the Dominican Republic (June 13, 2015).

[255] Art. 203 of the Constitution of Venezuela (December 20, 1999).

[256] Art. 133 and 425 of the Constitution of Ecuador (September 28, 2008).

[257] Art. 112 of the Constitution of Dominican Republic (June 13, 2015).

[258] Art. 133 (2) of the Constitution of Ecuador (September 28, 2008).

[259] Art. 203 of the Constitution of Venezuela (December 20, 1999).

[260] Art. 195 of the Constitution of Dominican Republic (June 13, 2015).
Art. 133 (3) of the Constitution of Ecuador (September 28, 2008).
Art. 16 and 169 of the Constitution of Venezuela (December 20, 1999).

Baric S (2016) The Transformative Role of the Constitutional Court of the Republic of Croatia: From the ex-Yu to the EU. Working Paper 6, Analitika – Center for Social Research Sarajevo. bib.irb.hr/datoteka/971606.constitutional_court_croatia.pdf (30 11 2020)
Bin R, Pitruzella G (2008) Diritto costituzionale. In: Giappichelli G (ed) Turin
Blacher P (2012) Le Parlement en France. LGDJ, Paris
Blacher P (2021) Droit constitutionell. 8e. Hachette Supérieur, Livre, Paris
Bonime-Blanc A (2010) Constitution making and democratization. The Spanish paradigm. In: Miller LE, Aucoin L (eds) Framing the state in times of transition: case studies in constitution making. Chapter 15. United States Institute for Peace, Washington, DC, pp 417–432
Braibant MG (1996) Normes de références du contrôle de constitutionnalité et respect de la hiérarchie en leur sein. Dalloz, Paris
Camby JP (1998) Quarante ans de lois organiques. Revue de droit publique 5–6:1686–1698
Carnat T (2005) Constitutional law. State University of Chisinau, Chisinau
Chabrier L, Haudrechy B (2020) Droit constitutionnel de la Ve republique. Ellipses Édition Marketing S A, Paris
Chofre Sirvent JF (1994) Significado y función de las leyes orgánicas. Tecnos, Madrid
Comella VF (2013) The framing of the Spanish constitution. In: Comella VF (ed) The constitution of Spain: a contextual analysis. Hart Publishing, Oxford
David R (1964) Les grands systemes de droit contemporains. Dalloz, Paris
Debré M (1959) La nouvelle Constitution. Revue française de science politique 9(1):7–29
Deleanu I (2006) Institutii si proceduri constitutionale. Constitutional institutions and procedures. C.H. Beck, Bucuresti
Djuvara N (1995) Între Orient şi Occident. Ţările române la începutul epocii moderne. Humanitas, Bucharest
Drašković ML (2015) Short guide through legislative and institutional protection of human rights in Montenegro. Centre for Civic Education, Podgorica
Erdősová A (2022) The constitutional development of Slovakia. In: Csink L, Trócsányi L (eds) Comparative constitutionalism in Central Europe: analysis on Certain Central and Eastern European Countries. Central European Academic Publishing, Miskolc–Budapest, pp 149–172
Fényes E (1843) Statistics of Hungary. n.k. Pest
Fombad CM (2017) Separation of powers in African constitutionalism. Stellenbosch handbook in African constitutional law. OUP, Oxford
Gárdos-Orosz F, Bán-Forgács N (2024) Introduction - the (non)resilience of the hungarian legal system: from populist constitutionalism to a permanent state of danger. In: Gárdos-Orosz F (ed) The resilience of the Hungarian legal system since 2010. A failed resilience? Springer Nature, Cham, Switzerland, pp 1–16
Giles F (1991) The locust years: the story of the Fourth French Republic, 1946-1958. Secker & Warburg, London
Gitiri J, Szentgáli-Tóth B (2021) The organic laws in francophone Africa and the judicial branch: a contextual analysis. Speculum Juris 35(1):106–117
Granger M-P (2011) Preamble(s) of the French constitution: content, status, application and amendment. Acta Iuridica Hungarica 52(1):1–18
Hajnóczy J (1791) Magyarország Országgyűléséről és annak szervezetéről szóló közjogi értekezés. In: Hajnóczy József közjogi-politikai munkái. Csizmadia Andor ed (1958) Akadémiai Kiadó, Budapest, pp 236–240
Hóman B, Szekfű G (1928) Magyar Történet. Királyi Magyar Egyetemi Nyomda, Budapest
II.1.Cristas A (2007) Portuguese Law, An Overview (Em Portuguese do Brasil) Lisboa, Almedina
Iliopoulos-Strangas J (2007) Cours supremes nationales et cours européennes: concurrence ou collaboration? In memoriam Louis Favoreu, Bruylant
Jakab A (2010) Az európai alkotmányjogi gondolkodás két szembenálló paradigmája: Ausztria és Németország. In: Chronowski N, Petrétei J (eds) Tanulmányok Ádám Antal professzor emeritusz 80. születésnapjára. Studia Iuridica Auctoritate Universitatis Pécs Publicata, vol 145. PTE ÁJK, Pécs, pp 127–148

Jakab A, Szilágyi E (2014) Sarkalatos törvények a magyar jogrendben. Új Magyar Közigazgatás 7(3):96–102

Kilényi G (ed) (1989) Emberi és állampolgári jogok. Alkotmányjogi Füzetek 2. ÉGSZI, Budapest

Könczöl M (2020) History and interpretation in the fundamental law of Hungary. Eur Pap 5(1):161–174

Lang I et al (2019) The constitution of Croatia in the perspective of European and global governance. In: Albi A, Bardutzky S (eds) National constitutions in European and global governance: democracy, rights, the rule of law. T.M.C. Asser Press, The Hague, pp 1139–1177

Luchaire F, Conac G (1987) La Constitution de la Ve République. Economica, Paris

Marczali H (1907) Az 1790/1-diki országgyűlés. MTA, Budapest

Mazza M (2013) The Hungarian fundamental law, the new cardinal laws and European concerns. Acta Juridica Hungarica 54(2):140–155

Mélin-Soucramanien F, Pactet P (2021) Droit constitutionnel. 40é Dalloz, Paris

Mezey B (2011) A Nemzeti Hitvallás jogtörténeti elemei. In: Kubovicsné Borbély A et al Az új Alaptörvényről elfogadás előtt: tanulmánykötet az Országgyűlés Alkotmányügyi, Igazságügyi és Ügyrendi Bizottsága által 2011. április 8-án azonos címmel megrendezett tudományos konferencián elhangzott előadások alapján. Országgyűlés Alkotmányügyi, Igazságügyi és Ügyrendi Bizottsága, Budapest, pp 35–47

Muñoz LF (2006) Leyes orgánico-constitucionales: insatisfactoria rigidización de la democracia, en Anuario de Derecho Constitucional Iberoamericano N° 12, Konrad Adenauer Stiftung

Noel J (2021) Le droit constitutionnel de la Ve Republique. Ellipses, Paris

Prakke L et al (2004) Constitutional law of 15 EU member states. 6e Kluwer

Roper SD (2008) From semi-presidentialism to parliamentarism: regime change and presidential power in Moldova. Europe-Asia Studies, Taylor & Francis Journals 60(1):113–126

Soltész I (2010) Az Országgyűlés Szervezete, Feladatai és Működése 1990-2010. Parlamenti Módszertani Iroda, Budapest

Széchenyi I (1864) Magyarország sarkalatos törvényei, s államjogi fejlődése 1848-ig. Eggenberger, Pest

Szentgáli-Tóth B (2014) Alkotmányos-e a minősített többség? Jogászvilág 26 Marc 2014. https://jogaszvilag.hu/szakma/alkotmanyos-e-a-minositett-tobbseg/

Szentgáli-Tóth B (2017) A minősített többségű törvényalkotás Magyarországon a rendszerváltástól napjainkig. In: Chronowski N et al (eds) A szabadságszerető ember Liber Amicorum István Kukorelli. Gondolat, Budapest, pp 770–779

Szentgáli-Tóth B (2019) Organic laws and the principle of democracy in France and Spain. Pro Futuro - a Jövő Nemzedékek Joga 9(4):62–74

Szentgáli-Tóth B (2020a) Supermajority laws as actors of the separation of powers. Hungarian J Legal Stud 61(2):210–228

Szentgáli-Tóth B (2020b) The regional migration of a constitutional idea: Supermajority laws as instruments for the protection of fundamental rights in Central Europe. In: Gábris T, Sombati J (eds) Central and Eastern Europe as a Double Periphery? Volume of Proceedings from the 11th CEE Forum Conference in Bratislava, Slovakia 25–26 April 2019. Peter Lang, Berne, pp 47–70

Szentgáli-Tóth B (2020c) Organic laws and the principle of democracy in France and Spain. In: Miras AP et al (eds) Setenta años de Constitución Italiana y cuarenta años de Constitución Española. Vol. 4. Retos en el siglo XXI. Centro de Estudios Políticos y Constitucionales, Madrid, pp 61–76

Szentgáli-Tóth B (2022) La diffusion de la loi qualifiée dans les régions d'Europe Centrale et de l'est. l'importation d'une idée constitutionnelle pendant la transition démocratique. Lettre de l'Est 29:3–18

Toldy F (1861) A Magyar Birodalom alaptörvényei. n.k.

Troper M (2008) Constitutional law. In: Berman GA, Etienne P (eds) Introduction to French law. Wolters Kluwer, Netherlands, pp 1–34

Troper M, Chagnollaud D (eds) (2012) Traite international de droit constitutionnel. Dalloz, Paris

Varju M et al (2016) Hungary: constitutional (r)evolution or regression? In: The role of national constitutions in European and global governance. T.M.C. Asser Press, Hága, Cambridge, pp 1–41
Verpeaux M, Bonnard M (2007) Le Conseil constitutionnel. The Constitutional Council. La documentation française, Paris
Wiederin E (2007) Grundlagen und Grundzüge staatlichen Verfassungsrecht: Österreich. In: von Bogdandy A et al (eds) Handbuch Ius Publicum Europaeum (IPE). C.F. Müller, Heidelberg, pp 389–449

Part II
The Potential Justifications of Supermajority Law

Chapter 3
Supermajority Law as the Extension of the Constitution

3.1 Theoretical Basis

In the following chapters, I briefly outline the main tools of interpretation and theories aimed at justifying the implementation of supermajority legislation. Academic scholarship distinguishes five justifications of supermajority laws linked to the three main distinctive characters of these constitutional instruments, which will be enumerated as follows:[1] first, the theory of extending the constitution; second, the safeguarding of a stable constitution will be highlighted. Then, various forms of supermajority laws will be scrutinized as political instruments as the third theory; as tools for the protection of fundamental rights related to supermajority law's scope in fourth place; and finally, supermajority law will be seen as a remarkable actor of separation of powers.

My purpose in conducting a comprehensive analysis of these theories is to emphasize the shortcomings of current concepts of supermajority law and to propose alternative solutions to address these issues effectively. In my opinion, the inclusion of supermajority law is justified in the constitutional system; however, it may be necessary to partially reconsider its legal rank and its procedural rules, while simultaneously narrowing the scope of supermajority law.

---

[1] Szentgáli-Tóth (2022).

B. A. Szentgáli-Tóth, *The Past, Present, and Future of Legislation with Supermajority*, Ius Gentium: Comparative Perspectives on Law and Justice 126,
https://doi.org/10.1007/978-3-031-99324-4_3

3.2 The Constitution as a Starting Point

The first theory is the extension of the constitution, which reflects on the uncertain legal rank of supermajority law highlighted by hypothesis 1. given at Sect. 1.3. This approach stems from the alleged quasi-constitutional character of supermajority laws, and despite the plausible dogmatic arguments supporting this framework; its practical implementation raises severe concerns.[2] The current vision on the hierarchy of legal sources bestows the constitution with a supreme character over the entire legal system. As one of its basic tenets it requires that all lower legal norms must be in harmony with its content.[3] However, the constitution has a limited scope; a constitutional document could only cover the most crucial rules.[4] The limited scope and specificity of constitutions have been discussed thoroughly in the scientific discourse.[5] One could easily assume that if each rule with greater significance will be transferred into the constitution, the constitution would be unlimitedly expandable. This does not happen, however, to norms deemed to be significant and are not incorporated into the constitution due to its limited scope. Thus, a near-constitutional protection should be provided to them. This raises the question of whether crucial rules on key institutions and fundamental rights should be enacted under the ordinary legislative procedure or be safeguarded by additional requirements, such as a supermajority.

The extension theory assumes that the constitution covers the most paramount issues, but it is not able to deal with the full regulation of these fields in detail. The proper scope of the constitution and supermajority laws constitutes an endless debate. The adequate answers to this dilemma depend on the regulatory structure of each field of supermajority legislation; on the constitutional framework of the particular state; on the political and legal culture; and on the mechanisms protecting the constitution. In Spain, the regulatory domain is reserved for organic laws,[6] while in Hungary the term "essential content" of fundamental rights provides orientation.[7] However, these only provide general frameworks, and their interpretation may open up the space for greater flexibility.

The extension theory relies primarily on the definition of the constitution and then proceeds to outline the limits of the constitution, while highlighting the quasi-constitutional character of supermajority laws.[8] The constitution is placed at the top of the legal system. As a consequence, it is always crucial to define a clear distinction between constitutional norms and norms with which lower-ranked legal instruments should comply.

---

[2] MacDonnell (2016), p. 522.

[3] Ahmed (2022), pp. 1370–1417.

[4] Dixon (2015), pp. 825–826.

[5] Elkins (2009), pp. 6–30.

[6] Field (2021), p. 551.

[7] 4/1993. (II. 12.) AB decision, ABH 1993, 48; JCC no. 236-2007.

[8] Eskridge and Ferejohn (2005), p. 198.

Several prestigious constitutional lawyers shared their thoughts on the definition of the constitution.[9] I only refer to the most well-known direction of this discourse, which is that the constitutional text is generally understood as a single document known as the constitution. However, an explicit declaration can give a legal norm constitutional status, or certain rules may be granted constitutional status through public consent. Supermajority laws can be given constitutional or quasi-constitutional status through explicit constitutional provisions, legal practice, or public consent.[10] What does the constitutional character mean? What should be understood under the term 'constitution'? These preliminary questions must be answered before elaborating on the interpretation of supermajority laws as an extension of the constitution.

The first concept of the ideal state, the oldest known description of a constitutional theory, was provided by Plato. He distinguished three main social layers among the inhabitants of the state: warriors, philosophers and merchants. Power should always be concentrated in the hands of the philosophers.[11] Some decades later, Aristotle examined the constitution of different city-states. He compared more than a hundred contemporary constitutional designs, thus becoming the first recognized scholar of comparative constitutional law.[12]

The first modern constitutions were passed at the end of the eighteenth century[13] as written documents summarizing the constitutional norms of a state. This stimulated a more sophisticated interpretation of the constitution: either as the legal document at the top of the legal system or as the collection of supreme rules that provide the political framework of the state at a given moment.[14] The fundamental norm character of constitutions was conceptualized by Hans Kelsen at the beginning of the twentieth century. He derived the whole legal system from the constitution and highlighted the constitutional conformity of the substance of all subordinate legal norms.[15]

The constitutional character of a norm depends on two factors. First, the subject matter of the particular norm. When any provision regulates the status, competence, or relationship of the key institutions of the state, these fall under the broader term of the constitution. Similarly, such norms are elements of the constitutional concept, outlining the legal relationship between the state and its citizens (such as rules on fundamental rights).[16] The other attribute establishes whether the particular norm stands at the top of the legal system, whether it should comply with any legal content with supreme effect. Certain, but not the exclusive criterion for this approach is

[9] As a recent overview from the various attempts of definition please see: Grimm (2016), pp. 5–25.

[10] Ahmed and Perry (2014), p. 514.

[11] Plato (2007).

[12] Ginsburg and Dixon (2011), p. 307.

[13] Blythe (2004).

[14] Grimm (2016), p. 12.

[15] Kelsen (1960).

[16] Künkler and Stein (2017), p. 238.

whether the norm is incorporated into a document defined as a constitution or whether it is regarded as a constitutional rule by the public.[17]

The huge diversity of constitutional definitions can be characterized by the idea that all political systems constructing a state should be seen as a constitution regardless of substantial requirements.[18] Therefore, totalitarian regimes and absolute monarchies can also rely on a constitutional framework according to this argument. Other scholars describe the constitutional character with certain substantive requirements: the protection of fundamental rights, the separation of powers, and the rule of law, legal certainty and further similar expectations.[19] Proponents of this approach essentially identify the constitution with the rule of law and speak of a constitution only when the fundamental values of the rule of law are respected.[20] This classification leads us to a further categorization: the distinction between the formal and substantive concepts of constitutionalism.[21] The concept of formal constitutionalism refers to a set of facade constitutional rules adopted lawfully but not respected in practice even by its framers, while the substantive constitution presupposes a constitutional text that prevails both in letter and spirit.

The distinction between codified and non-codified constitutions is historically well-established. The historical, non-codified constitution represents the outcome of long-term constitutional development and is composed of more constitutional documents and public conventions crystallized through centuries. By contrast, the codified constitution is embodied by a legal document enacted in a particular historical moment, passed under a procedure prescribed for constitution-making.[22] Each element of the codified constitution is found in explicitly written legal documents with normative force. On the contrary, non-codified constitutions always rely on non-written customary norms, and legal practice and public consent play a more impactful role in their elaboration. In reality, each constitutional regime represents a combination of these two frameworks. It is impossible to find any fully codified or fully uncodified constitution.[23] Uncodified elements might be found in codified constitutions. For instance, the president of a parliamentary republic is often authorized to submit bills to the parliament. However, such a step is quite unusual in a Westminster parliamentary structure. Moreover, after the legislative elections, the head of state gives a mandate to the leader of the stronger political force to establish a government, regardless of his/her political preferences.[24]

A further issue has emerged regarding the classification of constitutions: whether supermajority laws, as an extension of the constitution, can be considered part of the

[17] Chafetz and Pozen (2018).

[18] Bernholz (2017), pp. 51–62.

[19] Barber (2018), pp. 5–28.

[20] Ginsburg and Versteeg (2017), pp. 506–525.

[21] Schütze (2019), p. 40.

[22] Glenn (2006), pp. 421–440.

[23] Dorsen (2010), pp. 55–63.

[24] Ahmed et al. (2019), p. 798.

constitutional framework, or if they simply exist in close proximity to the constitution within the hierarchy of norms. To address this question, it is important to clearly distinguish between broader and narrower interpretations of the constitution.[25] The narrower contour of the constitution covers a legal document titled "constitution" that stipulates constitutional rules.[26] The narrower contour of the constitution covers a legal document titled "However, no country has constructed a system where all constitutional rules are incorporated into a sole document; at least certain external sources of the constitution always exist, and they serve as crucial tools of interpretation."[27] The narrower contour of the constitution covers a legal document titled as "However, no country has constructed a system where all constitutional rules are incorporated into a sole document; at least certain external sources of the From the countries operating with supermajority law, the French, the Austrian, and the Hungarian constitutional framework rely partly on uncodified contents, principles, and legal norms."[28] As already mentioned, the French Constitutional Council extended the scope of the constitution with certain repealed constitutional documents within the constitutional bloc. In Austria, the constitutional framework comprises a multi-level construction of legal norms, and the Austrian Constitutional Court clarified several details regarding the relationship of the norms with different ranks. Furthermore, during the adoption of the Fundamental Law in Hungary, a separate text was also drafted as "the transitory provisions of the Fundamental Law."[29] In principle, to secure the accountable constitutional transition, although the Constitutional Court of Hungary annulled this norm since its coverage overstepped its original function and overruled the original text of the Fundamental Law in several respects.[30] The drafters of the Fundamental Law intended to extend the constitutional framework further and considered supermajority laws as elements of the broader constitutional concept along with cardinal laws and the historical constitution of Hungary.[31] In practice, Hungarian cardinal laws have been far from being vested with quasi-constitutional force, but the presence of this approach demonstrates that the extension theory was still influential during the drafting of the Fundamental Law.

The term 'constitution' represents several different meanings; no broad consensus has been elaborated for its content. For the purpose of this book, I use a broad and substantial definition of constitution, consisting of each rule that fulfills the substantial requirements outlined earlier. This concerns fundamental rights or key institutions of the state, and it complies with the substantial standards of

[25] Albert (2015).

[26] Komesar (2017).

[27] Lyon (1988).

[28] Szentgáli-Tóth (2023), pp. 171–197.

[29] https://www.venice.coe.int/webforms/documents/default.aspx?pdffile=CDL-REF(2012)018-e

[30] 45/2012. (XII. 29.) AB decision, ABH 2012, 347.

[31] Ablonczy (2011), p. 210.

constitutionalism. One could not rely on the extension theory unless this extensive interpretation of the constitution is accepted.

3.3 Supermajority Laws as Quasi-Constitutional Norms: The Impact on the Hierarchy of Norms

As for starters, some points should be specified regarding the character of supermajority laws as legal sources and the alleged hierarchy between supermajority laws and the constitution. The exact rank of supermajority laws within the hierarchy of norms generates several theoretical and practical implications.[32] The clear hierarchy of legal norms forms an integral and indispensable element of the rule of law.[33] The different sources of law establish a clear hierarchical order; the lower-ranked norms should not substantially contradict the norms of supreme effect.

Constitutional systems prescribe three ways to determine the rank of supermajority laws as legal sources.[34] First, the constitution may explicitly stipulate the place of supermajority laws within the hierarchy of norms. Second, national constitutional courts interpret the relevant constitutional provisions. When a sufficiently precise constitutional orientation is missing, the body shall provide detailed orientations to address this issue. Third, legal scholars may establish theoretical frameworks for the legal status of supermajority laws, which can impact the legal practice. Several questions still remain open regarding the legal rank of supermajority laws, and numerous aspects should be taken into account to establ0ish a coherent set of interpretations.

The science of constitutional law provides alternative approaches to the role of supermajority laws as legal sources.[35] Supermajority laws undoubtedly fall somewhere between the constitution and ordinary laws; however, several problems still need to be clarified.[36] The most paramount issues are usually substantially reflected by the constitutional practice or the relevant legal regulation; legal scholars rarely focus deeply on supermajority laws. One should decide whether the quasi-constitutional or the statutory character of supermajority law shall enjoy priority, or these norms may constitute a completely separate level of legal sources between the two aforementioned categories. The practical consequences of the answer point to ordinary laws not containing any rule that contradicts a supermajority provision, and as will be demonstrated later, this broadens significantly the margin of movement of the constitutional court.[37] The role of supermajority laws as legal sources

---

[32] Troper and Chagnollaud (2012), p. 340.

[33] Pinelli (2016).

[34] le Divellec and de Villiers (2022), pp. 236–237.

[35] Drago (2020), pp. 351–354.

[36] Avril and Gicquel (2014), pp. 271–273; Tushnet (2013).

[37] Szentgáli-Tóth (2020), p. 222.

determines their function within a particular legal system. If supermajority laws do not exceed the constitutional framework in a broader sense, they should not conflict with the constitutional provisions. However, if supermajority laws have quasi-constitutional force, it would create significant uncertainty regarding which law takes precedence in the event of a contradiction between them. If supermajority laws are considered to have quasi-constitutional force, they are expected to override all other legal rules outside of the constitutional framework. Consequently, there should be no hierarchical order between supermajority laws and constitutional norms. Nevertheless, supermajority laws may be invoked during the constitutional review of lower-ranked norms due to their primacy.

The quasi-constitutional force of supermajority laws, represented by the widespread denomination of "constitutional law," may secure an elevated level of protection for certain fields of legislation. This confers additional prestige upon these legislative fields and hinders the passing of any amendment on them. From a political perspective, this tool of interpretation, especially in the two-thirds model, might serve as a safeguard for the opposition. The government would not be able to unilaterally amend the basic principles of the most important policies.[38] This argument carries more weight during a transitional period, when stakeholders deem it necessary to prevent the concentration of power while establishing the new order.

The aforementioned considerations clearly demonstrate that the quasi-constitutional status of supermajority laws, and the expansion of the constitution, have undeniable advantages, but also give rise to significant problems. At least eight concerns should be mentioned when extending the constitutional framework with supermajority laws.

- First, it matters whether all constitutional norms have been incorporated into a unitary document or if these rules are distributed among more legal sources. The unity and coherence of the constitution establish paramount principles of constitutional interpretation.[39] If supermajority law is incorporated into the constitutional framework, the limits of the constitution will be blurred, and the distinction between ordinary and supermajority laws remains uncertain. As a consequence, it is strongly contestable whether this extension of the constitution is in compliance with the theoretical bases of constitutional interpretation.[40] An example of this fragmented constitution is embodied by the Austrian constitutional model, which is not transparent and is continuously contested for these reasons.[41]
- The internal coherence of the constitution is the second consideration: it may not be absolutely necessary to gather constitutional norms into a single document to establish a workable constitutional concept. However, the internal logic of the constitutional framework must remain indispensably coherent, and the quasi-constitutional nature of supermajority laws jeopardizes this principle. Each part

[38] Tipler (2016), pp. 5–7.

[39] Tóth (2021), pp. 64–65.

[40] Jakab (2013), p. 1234.

[41] Klecatsky (1980), pp. 66–82; Eberhard and Konrath (2004–2005), p. 18, 20.

of the legal system is based on the constitution, constitutional provisions determine the significant range of lower-ranked norms, and the constitution specifies who has the right to enact legal norms, under what circumstances, and within which scope.[42] By contrast, supermajority laws constitute a special subcategory of laws regulating daily legal relationships among people, which are distinguished from ordinary laws but shall not lose their statutory character.

- The substantial side of constitutional coherence is an even more important consideration than the formal aspect of this principle. No constitution exists without contradictions, but the fragmentation of the constitution and the spread of quasi-constitutional norms significantly enhance the risks of substantial anomalies. If the scope of the constitution is not determined with sufficient precision, the constitutional review will face more severe difficulties. The relevant authorities should not decide at first instance whether a legal norm is constitutional. Instead, a preliminary question must be raised: which exact group of legal norms should be invoked during the constitutional review? Therefore, the extended framework of the constitution may have a tangible impact on the process of constitutional adjudication.[43]
- Third, it is possible for quasi-constitutional supermajority laws to possess equal legal force as the constitution. However, supermajority laws should not be included within the broad constitutional concept, since their quasi-constitutional character derives from the relevant constitutional provisions. A difference is still perceptible between the constitution and supermajority laws as the extensions of the constitution, since the legal rank and the regulatory scope of supermajority laws are always determined by the constitution.[44]
- The fourth question deals with whether awarding quasi-constitutional force to supermajority laws overextends the scope of constitutional regulation? The constitution designates a narrower set of rules on top of the legal system, serving as the basic point of reference for all other lower-ranked legal norms.[45] When supermajority laws form part of the constitution, they could support the stability of the constitutional document, while quasi-constitutional norms would be unreasonably expanded.
- Fifth, the rank of supermajority laws as legal sources may be specified by the constitution by explicitly mentioning this category among the enumerated list of legal sources. Some constitutions highlight supermajority laws as a special subcategory of law, while others establish a clear hierarchical order between the constitution, supermajority, and ordinary laws. However, these relatively clear constitutional directions are frequently debated by academics. For instance, András Jakab argues that the legal rank of supermajority laws might be dubious

[42] Gilligan (1993), p. 321.
[43] Tremblay (2003), p. 536.
[44] Verpeaux and Bonnard (2007), p. 101.
[45] Varga Zs (2010), pp. 21–25; Kilényi (1994), pp. 201–209.

despite the explicit constitutional rules on the issue.[46] Similar experience emerges from the relevant constitutional court case law: key rulings on supermajority laws are often heavily criticized by constitutional scholars.[47] Nevertheless, supermajority laws always have some constitutional characteristics as they are enacted or amended under stricter procedural regimes than ordinary laws, and they at least theoretically cover the most crucial fields of legislation. Nevertheless, supermajority laws must preserve their statutory character: their binding force comes from the constitution; their scope is provided by the constitution; they should be in compliance with the constitutional norms regarding their content, as the French Constitutional Council pointed out.[48]

- The relationship between supermajority laws and the constitution provides the sixth crucial point. A crucial precaution in the hierarchy of legal norms entails the proper distinction between the constitution and all other acts, below the constitution at the pyramid of legal sources. Supermajority laws with quasi-constitutional force significantly jeopardize the transparency of this distinction. Supermajority laws as quasi-constitutional norms could still retain some of their statutory characteristics; and the conflict is rooted in this dichotomy. A set of rules may be called "constitution", but this set of rules has equal legal rank as the most important acts, and not vested with supreme power over supermajority legislation. Consequently, ordinary laws need to comply with two—not just one—levels of laws enjoying supremacy. Hence, the Spanish-inspired concept of constitutional block is used in several countries where supermajority law exists.[49] The Spanish structure demonstrates the contradiction of statutory and constitutional characteristics well. Supermajority laws could function efficiently if the constitution clearly determines their place in the hierarchy of norms somewhere between the statutory and the constitutional level. This is not the case in any of the relevant constitutions; the statutory and constitutional side of supermajority laws are often juxtaposed. This may be proof that supermajority laws are somehow alien to the traditional setting of legal hierarchy, which operates with a constitution as a collection of the most crucial rules, a unitary category of laws below.[50]
- Seventh, the relationship between supermajority and ordinary laws represents an even more complex issue. According to the extension theory, constitutional laws will not just be laws adopted under a stricter procedural regime, but a separate category of legal norms with significant weight. Constitutional laws may have the same legal rank as the core text of the constitution, similar to Italy, and the constitutional court could invoke them during the constitutional review of ordinary laws. Since supermajority laws undoubtedly enjoy priority over ordinary

---

[46] Jakab and Cserne (2001).

[47] The most invigorating discourse demonstrates this from France, as an example please see: Hamon and Troper (2022), pp. 768–771.

[48] La décision du Conseil Constitutionnel, n°60-8 DC du 11 août 1960.

[49] JCC no. 142/1993.

[50] Jakab and Szilágyi (2014).

laws, a hierarchical relationship has clearly been established between the two categories, and ordinary laws should not substantially contradict supermajority laws vested with quasi-constitutional force.[51] In this case, supermajority laws fall much closer to the constitution in the procedural sense than to ordinary acts. Only the requirements for their adoption are slightly less demanding than the mechanisms established for constitution-making or amending processes.

- The eighth consideration carries a strong political character. What constitutes an important safeguard in the eyes of the opposition could mean a severe restriction for the governmental side.[52] If the scope of supermajority law is determined too broadly, supermajority and oppositional support would be necessary, even for minor amendments. As Rappaport noted, the government would be at least partly blocked, as supermajority and oppositional support would be indispensable for the revision of the most important laws.[53]

In conclusion, the extension theory operates with two distinct constitutional categories of laws. However, this model has never been properly deliberated, and the relationship between supermajority and ordinary laws is always based on a combination of the principle of competence and the principle of hierarchy. Consequently, even if a legal system implements the extension theory, supermajority laws should not be treated as norms equal to the constitution. This argument outlines that even if supermajority laws are more important than ordinary laws, they still remain statutes. However, one should not see the denomination of "act" as an exclusive factor to differentiate between statutes and the constitution. Several examples could be cited to demonstrate that certain constitutions were formally passed as regular acts, but their enactment or amendment are is subject to a supermajority, and their special status has not been questioned.[54] These examples support the idea that formal grounds should not be overgeneralized, and the exact configuration in a particular constitutional regime must be evaluated on a case-by-case basis.

3.4 Supermajority Laws as Constitutional Amendments

The extension theory operating with the quasi-constitutional force of supermajority laws should clearly be distinguished from the extension of the constitution with other written and unwritten norms. The extension with codified norms might be more transparent, as written constitutional norms may be easier to identify. The amendment of the constitution always requires a formal procedure, which serves the accountability of the system and legal certainty. By contrast, the unwritten

[51] 43/2012. (XII. 20.) AB decision, ABH 2012, 296.

[52] Ilonszki et al. (2021), p. 727.

[53] Rappaport (2014).

[54] For instance: Act. XX. of 1949 on the Constitution of Republic of Hungary, Art. 71 (1) and (2) (August 20, 1949).

constitutional amendments lack any established procedural framework, so the content of the constitution might be changed without a formal process.[55] This could be the source of misconduct but the constitution could also gain more flexibility.[56] The resilience and flexibility may be in conflict with each other in the field of constitutional law, but in my view, stability should enjoy priority at the final consideration. An uncodified constitution may be long-lasting with a strong constitutional culture, but without it, it would rather be a risk factor.[57] Furthermore, when a norm is adopted explicitly as a constitutional amendment, it is different from when a merely formally supermajority law, such as a constitutional law, has been modified. However, this will result in the amendment of the broader constitutional framework. In the former case, the constitutional amendment is deemed to be explicit; in the latter, it is deemed to be implicit.[58] This strong boundary should be highlighted between constitutional laws implementing constitutional amendments, and other constitutional laws specified by the constitution in Italy and elsewhere. If the amendment of supermajority laws means the modification of the constitution as well, this obviously presumes a formalized process with clearly established rules. However, this may not only result in the duplication of the constitutional framework, but also in the fragmentation of the higher norm at the top of the constitutional system.[59]

I have mapped out earlier how the coherence of the constitution creates an important theoretical tenet of constitutional law, but this does not mean that the constitution is necessarily unified in its appearance and as a legal document. In several constitutions, different requirements are set for the amendment of certain essential parts of the constitutional framework. In Bulgaria, a special body should be convened for the amendment of certain constitutional rules, while in Poland the key principles of the rule of law may only be changed via referendum.[60] The German Basic Law contains some unamendable provisions, which at least in principle, are not accessible to being amended.[61] Similarly, in France and Italy, the republican form of government shall not be subject to any amendment and is deemed to be eternal.[62] It seems that a well-known practice in the European legal culture encompasses a reasonable distinction between constitutional norms with regard to their form or their legal rank.[63] However, when this distinction is unreasonably complex,

[55] Albert (2017), p. 739.

[56] Dezső (1995), p. 231.

[57] McLean (2016), p. 120.

[58] Voigt (1999), p. 206.

[59] Venizelos (2020), p. 1010.

[60] Art. 157 and 158 of the Constitution of Bulgaria (July 12, 1991); Art. 235 (6) of the Constitution of Poland (April 2, 1997).

[61] Art. 79 (3) of the Federal Republic of Germany (May 8, 1949).

[62] Art. 89 of the Constitution of France (October 4, 1958); Art. 139 of the Constitution of Italy (December 22, 1947).

[63] Wischmeyer (2017), p. 1242.

the coherence of the constitution and fulfilling its function as a basic norm may be endangered.[64]

When multiple supermajority laws are bestowed with quasi-constitutional force, the distinction between the constitution and lower-ranked norms may be relativized, and the constitution could dwindle to the level of supermajority laws rather than vice versa. Despite the constitutional basis of quasi-constitutional supermajority laws, when the constitution confers upon several external norms the constitutional rank, it loses its central role among the many other quasi-constitutional rules. Should we interpret supermajority law as such a constitutional norm, which might be amended without the revision of the main constitutional document? In my view, this approach lacks convincing justification. Since supermajority laws detail the basic principles provided by the constitution, it is well-founded that they must be distinguished from the constitutional norms substantially, formally, and procedurally. Such an extension of the constitution would not be in conformity with constitutional functions, which require a narrow circle of constitutional norms at the top of the legal system.[65]

Moreover, if supermajority laws are considered quasi-constitutional norms, and the amendments of supermajority laws are seen as constitutional amendments, almost the entire legal system could be treated as constitutional norms. This would result in an overbroad margin of movement for the constitution-amending power, potentially undermining the balance between constitution-drafting and constitution-amending power.[66]

The domain of supermajority law undoubtedly encompasses crucial fields of legislation, which justifies their additional protection in comparison with ordinary laws. The most important laws cannot be selected without contention, and the exceptional significance of supermajority laws does not provide sufficient reason to recognize them as constitutional norms. While it may seem reasonable on formal grounds that supermajority laws constitute the more flexible part of the constitutional framework, this view should be rejected based on merit-based arguments.

A comparison between the two-thirds majority required for certain pieces of supermajority legislation and for constitution-making extends the assessment further. In the case of supermajority laws, the elevated majority requirement demands broad consent, and this sets considerably stricter conditions than the ordinary legislative process. By contrast, more challenging procedural rules may exist for constitutional amendments than the mere prescription of an elevated consent, as, for instance, a referendum may also be ordered.[67] This tension clearly shows that when the amendment of supermajority laws and the constitution are passed under

[64] Coan (2017), p. 850.

[65] Young (2008), p. 408.

[66] Roznai (2017).

[67] Dixon (2011).

identical or almost identical terms, the priority of the constitution on top of the legal system will be further undermined.[68]

Regarding the relationship between the constitution and supermajority laws, the Hungarian Constitutional Court argued that the procedural issue and the concerns related to the hierarchy of norms should be separated.[69] If supermajority laws are considered legal sources with equal footing to the constitution, substantial compliance with the constitution will not be expected from supermajority laws; appropriate contradictions may arise between the two levels. The procedural equivalence would mean that the requirements for supermajority legislation and for constitution-making would be similar to each other. Thus, the extension theory is in conflict either on procedural grounds with the approach that defines the constitution as a narrow, well-defined set of norms at the top of the legal system. A key characteristic of the constitution is that it stands at the top of the legal system. The binding force of lower-ranked legal norms always originates from the constitution. An extensive, fragmented, and opaque set of rules should not serve as the basis of the constitutional system.

3.5 The Limited Scope of the Constitution: Supermajority Laws as Instruments to Promote the Flexibility of the Constitution

During the assessment of the extension theory, the limited scope of the constitution must also be considered. An interesting issue of the science of constitutional law is how far the length of a constitution could be extended. Two different aspects can be distinguished between codified and uncodified constitutions in this respect. Quantitative methods should only be applied to the examination of codified constitutions, as the contours of an uncodified constitution are necessarily fluid and might be amended due to changing circumstances without any formal procedure.

The discipline of constitutional law has already reflected on the length of constitutional documents and the magnitude of difference between the longest and the shortest constitutional texts.[70] Any general conclusion cannot be drawn; nevertheless, the length of the constitution may vary within a well-definable interval.[71] These studies do not focus on the formal numbering of constitutional articles; this would be distortive and misleading. After the adoption of the constitution, new articles may be added to the text with special numbering; or a constitutional article seemingly under one number may cover more legal norms and regulatory matters.[72]

[68] McGinnis and Rappaport (1999), p. 393.

[69] 55/2010. (V. 5.) AB decision, ABH 2010, 366.

[70] Ginsburg (2010).

[71] Tushnet (2013).

[72] Landau (2011), pp. 611–614.

A deeper understanding of the issue is provided by the concept of specificity when considering the smallest units of text from a quantitative perspective. This involves determining the number of norms included in the constitutional text, which is determined by the number of sentences, words, or characters.[73] This quantitative approach estimates the link between the length and stability of constitutions. The longer, more detailed constitutions would likely be amended more frequently, while a constitution with restricted scope might be more long-lasting. These tendencies may also influence the requirements prescribed for the amendments of the constitution.[74] These analyses are based on formal and quantitative approaches. The goal was to estimate the potential length of the main constitutional text. It has not been examined whether the scope of the full constitutional framework is limited, how many documents the constitutional norms might be distributed amongst, and how far one can go in terms of the fragmentation of the constitutional framework, as happened in Austria.[75]

Therefore, two aspects of constitutional specificity should be distinguished: first, the extent of the formal, codified constitution, and second the complexity of the complete constitutional framework. From the perspective of supermajority legislation, this second, little-researched issue is worthy of further interest. Constitutional law is not able to identify the ideal complexity of a constitution, but one may outline helpful factors during the designation of a constitutional framework in the light of the particular circumstances.[76] The constitutional culture plays a crucial role in the background: when constitutional actors approach each other with mutual understanding and respect the margin of movement of other players, even a constitution with several codified or uncodified components might be feasible for the long run. The United Kingdom provides an excellent example of a long-lasting uncodified constitutional framework,[77] while Austria demonstrates the perspectives of a multilayered codified constitution.[78]

The countries with a less-established constitutional culture and democratic traditions tend to insist on a formal understanding of the constitution and constitutionalism.[79] A further aspect of the assessment considers the constitutional structure of the selected country: whether it is a unitary or a federal state; whether it has a parliamentary or a semi-presidential system. In light of the above, the quasi-constitutional nature of supermajority laws probably exceeds the reasonable scope of constitutional specificity, especially regarding the thirty to forty areas of legislation covered by supermajority laws in the relevant countries. If thirty to forty supermajority laws were given quasi-constitutional force, the original constitutional text would be

[73] Klein and Sajó (2012), pp. 419–436.

[74] Elkins et al. (2009).

[75] Albert (2023), p. 1629.

[76] Klein and Sajó (2012), pp. 419–436.

[77] Horsley (2022), p. 106.

[78] Wiederin (2023).

[79] Voermans (2023), p. 219.

expanded. However, when supermajority law is limited to four or five institutional matters, these might have equal legal status as the constitution without such consequences.

This idea leads to further undermining of the fundamental norm character of the constitution: whether the detailed rules on certain legislative matters can be adopted under the same procedure as what is required for constitutional amendments. It would comply more cohesively with the logic of the legal hierarchy if the constitution stipulated only some key provisions, and the details were provided by lower-ranked norms possibly subject to strict procedural requirements, but not equivalent to with the constitution-amending process. An additional tension is caused by the inherently different selection mechanisms of constitutional and supermajority legislative norms. The delimitation of the constitution is influenced by the function of the constitution being the point of reference for the whole legal system.[80] On the contrary, supermajority laws are never restricted to fundamental rights or to the key institutions of the state. Other fields of legislation may also be covered by this concept and are subject to political decisions. Thus owing to the inherently subjective filter of significance, the selection will always lack rational and objective grounds.[81] With the exception of Moldova, where the Parliament could pass organic laws on certain matters without explicit constitutional authorization,[82] the coverage of supermajority legislation is always stipulated by constitutional provisions.

If supermajority laws with quasi-constitutional force are seen as instruments to serve the flexibility of the constitution, this would give further perspectives to the extension theory. This connects to the function of supermajority law as a stabiliser, as will be demonstrated later, but this could only be feasible when supermajority laws are clearly separated from the main body of the constitution either procedurally and as sources of law. When supermajority laws are undoubtedly placed under the constitution within the hierarchy of norms, the detailed rules on constitutional matters should be covered by supermajority laws, and these will not extend further the main text of the constitution. This could serve the permanence of the constitutional framework, as only the most important reforms would be carried out via constitutional amendments. For less significant revisions, it may be sufficient to amend just supermajority laws. This still means a stricter procedure than ordinary legislation; however, this is far from the requirements of constitution-making or constitution-amending. With such a step, the safeguard element is maintained, but the functions of the constitutions are not undermined.

Keeping this in mind, if one looks back at the distinction between the broader and narrower sense of the constitutional framework, it may be argued that supermajority laws serve the stability of the narrower constitutional design. Considering the extension theory, the rules placed into supermajority laws with quasi-constitutional

---

[80] Widner and Contiades (2012), pp. 67–68.

[81] 4/1993. (II. 12.) AB decision, ABH 1993, 48.

[82] Roper (2008), p. 119.

force remain at the constitutional rank; the amendments of these provisions constitute just amendments of the broader constitutional framework.

3.6 Supermajority Laws with Quasi-Constitutional Force and the Constitutional Review

Constitutional review and the potential impact on the role of the constitutional court must also be analyzed during the conceptualization of the extension theory. Except in countries where the idea of unconstitutional constitutional amendments has been accepted,[83] the constitutional court may only review the compliance of lower-ranked norms with the constitution. The scope and weight of constitutional review depend on the particular constitutional framework. Constitutional courts focus exclusively on the conflicts between the constitution and lower-ranked norms. When the contradiction lies between two lower-ranked norms with a hierarchical order, other bodies might also be competent, such as the Supreme Court, or the power of deciding these matters might also be vested in constitutional courts.[84]

Two models of constitutional review are known in Europe and North America. One of them encompasses the constitutional court as a separate body, and its task revolves around the protection of the constitution.[85] This model has been implemented by most of the European countries. The other approach authorizes the supreme judicial body to exercise constitutional review, so the same body would hand down supreme judicial and constitutional rulings.[86] Here, the best-known example of this structure, the United States of America, should be highlighted. Meanwhile, the Scandinavian countries—Denmark, Estonia, Iceland, Norway, and Sweden—operate with similar solutions in Europe. Atypical structures are also worth contemplating in some European countries. In these countries, no constitutional review exists in its traditional understanding. These countries include the United Kingdom, the Netherlands, Switzerland, Greece, and Finland.[87]

Regardless of which model is implemented by a country, the margin of movement of the body entitled to exercise constitutional review (hereinafter referred to as the constitutional court) depends on the exact definition of the constitution. The implementation of supermajority law into the legal system establishes an additional competence for the constitutional court, as supermajority and ordinary laws are distinguished based on the relevant constitutional provisions. In case of uncertainties, the clarification would be the task of the constitutional court. The classification of supermajority laws as constitutional or statutory also describes an essential issue

[83] Stone (2018), p. 363.

[84] Lalisan (2020), pp. 4–13.

[85] Ginsburg and Versteeg (2014), p. 601.

[86] Mawcic (2018), pp. 5–32.

[87] Comella (2004), p. 461.

from this perspective. This would determine whether these norms could be invoked during the constitutional review of ordinary laws. In the case of the constitutional review of ordinary laws, the quasi-constitutional force or lack thereof may decide whether supermajority laws should be complied with by ordinary laws. If supermajority laws have a quasi-constitutional character, they would undoubtedly hold a higher position than ordinary laws in the hierarchy of legal sources. An ordinary law should not contradict a supermajority law. In other words, supermajority laws may be considered during the constitutional review of ordinary laws. On the other hand, if supermajority laws are not given a quasi-constitutional character, this could raise different issues. There is no strong hierarchy between supermajority and ordinary laws;[88] ordinary laws may be in conflict with supermajority laws, and the latter ordinary law may overrule the earlier supermajority law.

When greater importance is assigned to supermajority law in a constitutional system, the role of these norms will be stronger during the constitutional review, and this increases the margin of movement of the constitutional court, providing additional bases for constitutional interpretation. As a further consequence, the constitutional court will be involved more actively in the political discourse. This tendency may undermine the independence and professional integrity of the constitutional court, while the exact limits of the constitution will be contested permanently. Therefore, the constitutional court could not per se be left out from these debates.[89]

3.7 The Erosion of Constitutional Supremacy

Some further remarks should be added to the assessment of the extension theory. The first issue is the erosion of the constitutional role as a fundamental norm. I have already mentioned that the extension and fragmentation of the constitutional framework question the central role of the constitution. These are accompanied by several dilemmas of constitutional interpretation. How can we expect coherence from such a set of norms, which has not been enacted at a particular moment, but over a longer period of time? How should one expect cohesion from such a set of norms, which have elements with different legal status and rank? Are the methods of constitutional review applicable to solve such a conflict, when a substantial contradiction arises between certain constitutional provisions, and some sections of supermajority laws with quasi-constitutional rank?

The relationship between constitutional and statutory interpretation has been a contested issue in the field of constitutional law.[90] At least it seems certain that the two concepts differ considerably from each other.[91] If the existence of this difference

[88] Unless expressly provided for by the constitution, as is the case in Ecuador or Russia.

[89] Navarrete and Castillo-Ortiz (2020), p. 134.

[90] Stack (2004).

[91] Berger (2023).

is accepted, the methods of constitutional interpretation shall not be applicable without any adaptation to statutes or to supermajority laws, while vice versa, supermajority laws shall not be considered as parts of the constitution. Therefore, if we rely on the quasi-constitutional role of supermajority law, the interpretative framework of these norms will be unclear. Supermajority laws may be seen as parts of the constitution if the original intent during the drafting of the constitution was to complete the main text of the constitution with quasi-constitutional norms, and this should establish a coherent system of constitutional norms. In most cases, the weight of this expectation may not be overestimated, since supermajority laws have usually been implemented into the legal system during a political/constitutional transition as a reflection on specific circumstances. However, this would rarely result in a coherent constitutional framework. The status and scope of supermajority laws would be determined by political considerations.

The quasi-constitutional character of supermajority laws has been rumored in all constitutional systems where supermajority law has been implemented. The special and uncertain position of supermajority laws between the constitutional and statutory levels forms the background of this argument. Hierarchical elements are undoubtedly perceptible in the relationship of supermajority and ordinary laws, and in some cases, the quasi-constitutional character of supermajority laws also receives greater weight. However, the quasi-constitutional norms will undermine constitutional supremacy, relativize and question the borders of the constitution, and cause several theoretical and practical difficulties. In light of these concerns, in my view, even if one considers supermajority law as a well-founded legal concept, these norms should not be vested with quasi-constitutional character.

3.8 Known Examples of the Extension of the Constitution

The classic example of quasi-constitutional supermajority laws can be drawn from Hungary, with the introduction of constitutional laws in 1989.[92] During the same transitional moment, constitutional laws were also implemented in other post-communist countries such as Azerbaijan, Kazakhstan, Kyrgyzstan, Russia, Slovakia, and Tajikistan. The short lifespan of Hungarian constitutional laws justifies that the extension of the constitution hardly means an implementable concept in practice.[93]

The aforementioned Austrian sample serves as a similar model. Here, besides the text of the constitution, several acts also contain constitutional provisions, such as the data protection act.[94] During the subsequent decades, owing to political aspirations, the circle of these statutory provisions with quasi-constitutional force has

[92] Bruszt and Horváth (1990), p. 373.

[93] 66/1997. (XII. 29.) AB decision, ABH 1997, 397.

[94] Art. 1 of the Data Protection Act in Austria (Datenschutzgesetz), https://www.ris.bka.gv.at/GeltendeFassung.wxe?Abfrage=bundesnormen&Gesetzesnummer=10001597.

been continuously extended. A few provisions of certain acts have been supposed to be a constitutional norm, and they are clearly separated in the particular acts. This difference explains that despite a number of controversies, the codified but highly fragmented constitutional concept has been viable in Austria for the long run.

Italian constitutional laws have also been bestowed with quasi-constitutional force. These laws are subject to the same procedural mechanism as constitutional amendments. In case of norm conflict, these laws should prevail over formerly enacted constitutional provisions. In addition to the Austrian experience, Italy provides another model where supermajority laws with quasi-constitutional force have existed for decades.[95]

After having mentioned those models of extension directly involving supermajority legislation as quasi-constitutional norms, I turn to the assessment of other constitutional systems, where written or unwritten quasi-constitutional norms play a crucial role, or further elements with quasi-constitutional force complement the constitutional document. Consequently, such an interpretation results in the extension of the constitution; however, supermajority laws are not directly concerned. The exemplificative enumeration of such models could underline the distinction made at the beginning of Sect. 3.4.

Each constitutional system of the world is constructed by a combination of codified and uncodified norms; neither model prevails anywhere without reservations.[96] To support this argument, the historical constitutional concepts should be first mentioned, as their constitutional document is missing. The discipline of constitutional law usually classifies three current constitutional regimes as "historical" ones: Great Britain, Israel, and New Zealand.[97]

The English constitutional development provides the most popular example of historical constitutional entrenchment: some acts with greater significance have been vested with constitutional force during the consecutive centuries. The essential elements of the British Constitution are the following: the distinguished acts; the judicial precedent; the practice of the authorities; and the constitutional conventions.[98]

In Israel, after the declaration of independence of the newly-formed Jewish State in 1948, no consensus has been achieved regarding the drafting of a constitution. Instead, the Knesset passed four fundamental laws, which have served as the pillars of Israeli constitutional development. This solution was originally intended as a temporary framework, but it has survived for more than 75 years.[99]

The declaration of independence from British colonial power brought a series of constitutional revisions in New Zealand. The Pacific country extended its autonomy as a result of consecutive agreements; these were integrated into the legal system by

---

95 Cartabia and Lupo (2022), p. 42.

96 Goldsworthy (2018), pp. 109–110.

97 Robbers (2007), p. 791.

98 Blick and Blackburn (2012).

99 Orit (2007).

statutes with quasi-constitutional force.[100] The Canadian constitutional development shows several similarities with the model of New Zealand, so the North American country is also worthy of being mentioned at this point.[101]

The other constitutional regimes are usually seen as codified; however, this does not mean that the broader notion of the constitution would only cover a singular document. Besides Austria, it is also worth highlighting the French approach, where the aforementioned concept of constitutional block has been elaborated. The French constitutional practice and literature imply the preamble of the 1791 Constitution, the 1946 Constitution, the Declaration of Rights of Man and of the Citizen, the Environmental Charter (2004), and the acts on fundamental rights passed during the period of the Third Republic (right to association, right to assembly) within the broader constitutional concept.[102] According to the Constitutional Council, French organic laws fall outside of this framework of the constitutional block. More than a hundred years ago, the Third French Republic provided a great example of a multi-level constitution with the enactment of three organic laws with quasi-constitutional force.

Constitutional block also exists in Spain but with different content: this covers the collection of those norms, which may be invoked during the constitutional review of ordinary laws. The Spanish constitutional block can be interpreted as a technical set of norms rather than a coherent constitutional concept.[103]

The Swedish constitutional design also serves as a fascinating point of reference in this regard, grounded on four fundamental laws as four pillars.[104] In the last two centuries, four acts with quasi-constitutional force have been enacted (in 1809 on the succession of the throne; in 1949 on freedom of the press; in 1974 on governance; in 1991 on freedom of expression).[105]

In the Basic Law (Grundgesetz) of Germany, the reference to moral law in Article 2 (1) demonstrates that unwritten contents and principles shall be taken into account during the interpretation of the Federal constitution.[106]

Considering these models, one may argue that it is not alien to the European legal tradition to extend the main constitutional framework with either codified or uncodified quasi-constitutional norms. Three such examples might be mentioned, where supermajority laws have undoubtfully been covered by this concept: the Austrian and Italian constitutional frameworks for the longer term, while the constitutional laws in Hungary have only existed in this form for a few months. In conclusion, the presence of quasi-constitutional norms in the legal system generates more issues

---

[100] Soriley (2005) pp. 4–5; Rishworth (2016), p. 19.

[101] Mclachlin (2016).

[102] Emeri (1970), p. 608.

[103] Troper and Chagnollaud (2012), p. 346.

[104] Nergelius (2019), pp. 319–321.

[105] https://www.riksdagen.se/globalassets/03.-dokument-och-lagar/bestall-och-ladda-ner/other-languages/grundlagar-2023-engelsk-web.pdf.

[106] Basic Law (Grundgesetz) of the Federal Republic of Germany, Art. 2 (1) (May 8, 1949); Enders (2010).

than it solves. This uncertainty means a further distortive factor of constitutionalism, which may easily undermine its authority.

The extension theory as a method of argumentation might be essential, but it is hardly implementable in practice, as demonstrated by the complexity of the Austrian constitutional framework or the quick fall of Hungarian constitutional laws. Therefore, the other approach of supermajority law with a constitutional focus, which highlights its stabilizing function, has a greater long-term impact. Relying on the aforementioned considerations, I further analyze supermajority laws as acts somewhere between the constitution and ordinary laws, contributing to the stability of the constitutional framework.

References

Ablonczy B (2011) Az Alkotmány nyomában. Beszélgetések Szájer Józseffel és Gulyás Gergellyel. Elektromédia Kft, Kerepes

Ahmed A (2022) A theory of constitutional norms. Mich Law Rev 120(7):1370–1417

Ahmed F, Perry A (2014) The quasi-entrenchment of constitutional statutes. Cambridge Law J 73(3):514–535

Ahmed F et al (2019) Judging constitutional conventions. Int J Const Law 17(3):787–806

Albert R (2015) How Unwritten "Constitutional Norms Change Written Constitutions". (July 9, 2015), Dublin ULJ 38:387, Boston College Law, School Legal Studies Research Paper No. 364, Available at SSRN: https://ssrn.com/abstract=2628460

Albert R (2017) Quasi-constitutional amendments. Buffalo Law Rev 65(4):739–770

Albert R (2023) Multi-textual constitutions. Virginia Law Rev 109(8):1629–1898

Avril P, Gicquel J (2014) Droit parlamentaire. Dalloz, Paris

Barber N (2018) The principles of constitutionalism. OUP, Oxford

Berger E (2023) Constitutional conceits in statutory interpretation. Adm Law Rev 75(3):479–564

Bernholz P (2017) The constitution of totalitarianism. In: Totalitarianism, terrorism and supreme values. Studies in public choice. Springer

Blick A, Blackburn R (2012) Mapping the path to codifying - or not codifying - the UK's constitution Centre for political and constitutional studies. King's College, London Parliament UK 2

Blythe MJ (2004) The ideal government and the mixed constitution in the middle ages. PUP, Princeton

Bruszt L, Horváth GK (1990) 1989: the negotiated revolution in Hungary. East Europe: where from, where to? Summer 57(2):365–387

Cartabia M, Lupo N (2022) The constitution of Italy: a contextual analysis. Bloomsbury Publishing

Chafetz J, Pozen DE (2018) How constitutional norms break down. UCLA Law Rev 65:1430–1459

Coan A (2017) The foundations of constitutional theory. Wisconsin Law Rev 16–24:833–882

Comella VF (2004) The European model of constitutional review of legislation: Toward decentralization? Int J Const Law 2(3):461–491

Dezső M (1995) Az alkotmány népszavazással történő elfogadása. In: Takács I (ed) Az alkotmányozás jogi kérdései. ELTE Eötvös, Budapest, pp 231–235

Dixon R (2011) Constitutional amendment rules: a comparative perspective. In: Ginsburg T, Dixon R (eds) Comparative constitutional law. Elgar Edwar, Cheltenham, pp 96–112

Dixon R (2015) Constitutional drafting and distrust. Int J Const Law 13(4):819–846

Dorsen N (2010) (eds) Comparative constitutionalism: cases and materials. 4e American Casebook Series, St. Paul, Thomson/West

Drago G (2020) Contentieux constitutionnel francais, 5[é] Presses Universitaires de France, Paris

Eberhard H, Konrath C (2004–2005) Der Österreich-Konvent. JAP/Juristische Ausbildung & Praxisvorbereitung
Elkins Z et al (2009) Identifying risks to constitutional life. In: Elkins Z et al (eds) The endurance of national constitutions. CUP, Cambridge, pp 6–30
Emeri C (1970) Le bloc de la constitutionnalité. RDP, Paris
Enders C (2010) A right to have rights - the german constitutional concept of human dignity. NUJS Law Rev 3(3):253–264
Eskridge W, Ferejohn J (2005) Quasi-constitutional law: the rise of super-statutes. In: Devins N et al (eds) Congress and the constitution. Duke University Press, New York, pp 198–219
Field BN (2021) Spain: single-party majority and minority governments. In: Bergman T et al (eds) Coalition governance in Western Europe, comparative politics. Oxford Academic, Oxford, pp 544–573
Gilligan TW (1993) Information and the allocation of legislative authority. J Inst Theor Econ 149(1):321–341
Ginsburg T (2010) Constitutional Specificity, Unwritten Understandings and Constitutional Agreement. University of Chicago Public Law &Legal Theory Working Paper 330
Ginsburg T, Dixon R (2011) Comparative constitutional law: introduction. University of Chicago Public Law & Legal Theory Working Paper 362
Ginsburg T, Versteeg M (2014) Why do countries adopt constitutional review? J Law Econ Org 30(3):587–622
Ginsburg T, Versteeg M (2017) Constitutional correlates of the rule of law. In: Adams M et al (eds) Constitutionalism and the rule of law: bridging idealism and realism. CUP, Cambridge, pp 506–525
Glenn P (2006) Comparative legal families and comparative legal traditions. In: Reimann M, Zimmermann R (eds) The Oxford handbook of comparative law. OUP, Oxford, pp 421–440
Goldsworthy J (2018) The implicit and the implied in a written constitution. In: Elkins Z, Stone A (eds) The invisible constitution in comparative perspective. CUP, Cambridge, pp 109–145
Grimm D (2016) Constitutionalism: past, present, and future. OUP, Oxford
Hamon F, Troper M (2022) Droit constitutionnel. 42ᵉ LGDJ, Lextenso, Paris
Horsley T (2022) Constitutional functions and institutional responsibility: a functional analysis of the UK constitution. Legal Stud 42(1):99–119
Ilonszki G et al (2021) Can opposition parties be responsible? Parliam Aff 74(3):722–740
Jakab A (2013) Judicial reasoning in constitutional courts: a European perspective. German Law J 14(8):1215–1275
Jakab A, Cserne P (2001) A kétharmados törvények helye a magyar jogforrási hierarchiában. Fundamentum 5(2):40–49
Jakab A, Szilágyi E (2014) Sarkalatos törvények a magyar jogrendben. Új Magyar Közigazgatás 7(3):96–102
Kelsen H (1960) Reine Rechtslehre 2. Franz Deuticke, Wien
Kilényi G (1994) Az alkotmányozás és a "kétharmados" törvények. Jogtudományi Közlöny 49(5):201–209
Klecatsky RH (1980) Bundes-Verfassungsgesetz und Bundesverfassungsrecht. In: Schambeck H (ed) Das österreichische Bundes-Verfassungsgesetz und seine Entwicklung. Duncker & Humbolt, Berlin, pp 66–82
Klein C, Sajó A (2012) Constitution-making: process and substance. In: Rosenfeld M, Sajó A (eds) The Oxford handbook of comparative constitutional law. UPR, Oxford, pp 419–436
Komesar NK (2017) Constitutions as basic structure. (December 30, 2017). Univ. of Wisconsin Legal Studies Research Paper, 1435
Künkler M, Stein T (2017) Fundamental rights as constitutional principles: on the current state of interpreting fundamental rights (1990). In: Künkler M, Stein T (eds) Constitutional and political theory: selected writings. OUP, Oxford, pp 235–265
Lalisan S (2020) Classifying systems of constitutional review: a context-specific analysis. Indiana J Const Design 5(1):4–13

Landau D (2011) The importance of constitution-making. Denver Univ Law Rev 89:611–633

le Divellec A, de Villiers M (2022) Dictionnaire du droit constitutionnel. 13é Dalloz, Paris

Lyon N (1988) An essay on constitutional interpretation. Carswell, Toronto

MacDonnell V (2016) A theory of quasi-constitutional legislation. Osgoode Hall Law J 53(2):508–539

Mawcic AM (ed) (2018) Constitutional review systems around the world. Vandeplas Publishing

McGinnis JO, Rappaport MB (1999) Supermajority rules as a constitutional solution. William & Mary Law Rev 40(2):365–470

McLachlin B (2016) Introduction. In: Dodek A The Canadian constitution. Dundurn Press

McLean J (2016) The unwritten political constitution and its enemies. Int J Const Law 14(1):119–136

Navarrete RM, Castillo-Ortiz P (2020) Constitutional courts and citizens' perceptions of judicial systems in Europe. Comp Eur Polit 18(2):128–150

Nergelius J (2019) The constitution of Sweden and European influences: the changing balance between democratic and judicial power. (Springer, 2019). In: Albi A, Bardutzky S (eds) National constitutions in European and global governance: democracy, rights. The rule of law, Haag. T.M.C. Asser Press, pp 315–358

Orit R (2007) Forming a collective identity: the debate over the proposed constitution 1948–1950. J Israeli Hist 26(2):251–271

Pinelli C (2016) Theories concerning the hierarchy of norms. Max Planck Encyclopedia of Comparative Oxford Constitutional Law [MPECCoL]

Plato (2007) The Republic. Translated by Desmond Lee, the introduction was written by Melissa Lane. Penguin Books LTD

Rappaport MB (2014) More on Supermajority Rules: May's Theorem' Library of Law and Liberty. (22 January 2014) http://www.libertylawsite.org/2014/01/22/more-on-supermajorityrules-mays-theorem/

Rishworth P (2016) Writing things unwritten: common law in New Zealand's constitution. Int J Const Law 14(1):137–155

Robbers G (2007) (ed) Encyclopedia of World Constitutions II. nk. New York

Roper SD (2008) From Semi-Presidentialism to Parliamentarism: regime change and presidential power in Moldova. Europe-Asia Stud Taylor & Francis J 60(1):113–126

Roznai Y (2017) Towards a theory of constitutional unamendability: on the nature and scope of the constitutional amendment powers. Jus Politicum 18

Schütze R (2019) Constitutionalism(s). In: Masterman R, Schütze R (eds) The Cambridge companion to comparative constitutional law. Cambridge companions to law. CUP, Cambridge, pp 40–67. https://doi.org/10.1017/9781316716731.003

Soriley JMc (2005) The New Zealand constitution. Parliamentary Library: Wellington, New Zealand

Stack KM (2004) The divergence of constitutional and statutory interpretation. Colorado Law Rev 75:1–52

Stone A (2018) Unconstitutional constitutional amendments: between contradiction and necessity. Int Const Law J 12(3):357–368

Szentgáli-Tóth B (2020) Supermajority laws as actors of the separation of powers. Hungarian J Legal Stud 61(2):210–228

Szentgáli-Tóth B (2022) Organic/Cardinal Laws. In: Grote R et al (eds) Max Planck Encyclopedia of comparative constitutional law. (MPECCoL). OUP, Oxford, p Paper e302

Szentgáli-Tóth B (2023) The Legal transplant during the democratic transition: the regional migration of a constitutional idea: The spread of supermajority law in the central and East-European regions. Studia Prawnicze 227(1):171–197

Tipler K (2016) Review. Counting the many: the origins and limits of supermajority rule. Contemp Polit Theory 15(1):5–7

Tóth ZJ (2021) (ed) Constitutional interpretation. Analysis on Certain Central European countries studies of the Central European Professors' Network. Central-European Academic Publishing, Budapest/Miskolc

Tremblay LB (2003) General legitimacy of judicial review and the fundamental basis of constitutional law. Oxford J Legal Stud 23(4):525–562

Troper M, Chagnollaud D (eds) (2012) Traite international de droit constitutionnel. Dalloz, Paris

Tushnet M (2013) Constitution-making: An Introduction. TLR 91(7). www.texaslrev.com/wp-content/uploads/2015/08/Tushnet.pdf

Varga Zs A (2010) Some thoughts on the new constitution of hungary. Iustum Aequum Salutare 6(4):23–28

Venizelos E (2020) From the relativization of the constitution to the augmented constitution. ERPE 32(3):973–1017

Verpeaux M, Bonnard M (2007) Le Conseil constitutionnel. The Constitutional Council. La documentation française, Paris

Voermans W (2023) Concepts, shapes and types of constitutions. In: The story of constitutions: discovering the we in us. Comparative constitutional law and policy. CUP, Cambridge, pp 201–236

Voigt S (1999) Implicit constitutional change-changing the meaning of the constitution without changing the text of the document. EJLE 7(3):197–224

Widner J, Contiades X (2012) Constitution-writing processes. In: Tushnet M et al (eds) Routledge handbook of constitutional law. Routledge Taylor & Francis Group, London and New York, pp 57–69

Wiederin E (2023) The evolution and gestalt of the Austrian constitution. In: Bogdandy A von et al (eds) The Max Planck handbooks in European Public law: Volume II: constitutional foundations. Oxford Academic, pp 1–54

Wischmeyer T (2017) Unconstitutional constitutional amendments. Int J Const Law 15(4):1242–1247

Young EA (2008) The constitutive and entrenchment functions of constitutions: a research Agenda. Univ Pa J Const Law 10(2):399–411

Chapter 4
Supermajority Law as an Instrument for Promoting the Stability of the Constitution

4.1 Various Instruments for Promoting the Stability of the Constitution

Apart from interpreting supermajority laws as the extended arms of the constitution, this legal instrument with special rank in the hierarchy of norms also constitutes a mechanism that potentially serves the stability of the constitution.[1] Supermajority legislation would protect the Constitution, as most reform attempts would focus on supermajority laws rather than the Constitution itself. The interpretation of supermajority law as a stabilizer should be understood in the context of these instruments, which aim to enhance the durability of the constitutional framework.[2] Several researchers have focused on the endurance of constitutions; the average lifespan of a national constitution is around seventeen years.[3]

As the most important and impactful factor, the resilience of the constitutional should be mentioned.[4] Remarkably, there is less chance of modifying a more rigid constitutional framework. The endurance of a constitution depends on several factors, primarily the constitutional safeguards applied to maintain a permanent constitutional framework. Additionally, the internal structure, culture, and attitudes of political life, social/economic circumstances, geographical surroundings, and external relations of the particular country also play a crucial role.[5] Within this concept, supermajority legislation may carry significant weight. Several constitutional

[1] Avril and Gicquel (2014), p. 270.

[2] McGinnis and Rappaport (1999), pp. 365–370.

[3] Ginsburg (2010).

[4] Dixon (2011), pp. 96–112.

[5] Ginsburg (2011), pp. 112–129.

B. A. Szentgáli-Tóth, *The Past, Present, and Future of Legislation with Supermajority*, Ius Gentium: Comparative Perspectives on Law and Justice 126,
https://doi.org/10.1007/978-3-031-99324-4_4

functions and risks might be conferred upon supermajority laws instead of the constitution.

More dimensions may be distinguished for describing constitutional stability.[6] The frequency of constitutional revisions might be used as a possible indicator: the adoption of a new constitution and the abrogation of a former one, or an extensive modification of the existing constitutional framework.[7] However, in several cases, a minor constitutional change may be achieved without the establishment of a new constitutional framework, so the frequency of constitutional amendments may also be important data. The average time lasting between two constitutional amendments or the average number of enacted constitutional amendments during a year may be determined.[8]

In addition to this, the literature has not elaborated on a concise definition of constitutional amendment: the constitution could be amended not only by modifying the explicit wording of the text itself. The constitutional framework may be changed with the overruling of former constitutional practices, or with the continuous development of unwritten constitutional conventions.[9] The number of such implicit constitutional amendments may not be easily calculable since several of them do not have any perceptible format in the legal system.[10] However, it is beyond doubt that when considering the endurance of constitutions, the amendment of these uncodified norms and principles should also be taken into account.[11]

The level of constitutional rigidity is a key aspect of describing a constitutional framework. When considering the stability of the constitution, we focus on the characteristics that elevate it above lower-ranked norms within the legal system. It is important to examine the special safeguards in place to protect the Constitution, as well as the political and societal attitudes towards it. The Constitution can serve as the primary source of a legal system and should be the point of reference for all lower-ranked norms, as long as it is respected by society. However, constitutional provisions are considered permanent and accountable, and amendments should only be initiated in rare cases with strong justification.[12]

The frequent amendment of the constitutional framework undermines its authority in the eyes of society since the constitution would be the instrument and victim of daily political battles. In the long run, only those constitutions could retain their reputation which could remain distant from political debates and function as a framework rather than an instrument.[13]

[6] Dixon (2011).

[7] Law (2022), pp. 89–90.

[8] Ginsburg and Melton (2015), pp. 686–687.

[9] Voigt (1999), p. 198.

[10] Ginsburg and Melton (2015), p. 695.

[11] Albert (2015), pp. 657–658.

[12] Raz (2009).

[13] Scheppele (2017), p. 49.

The stability of the constitution depends on several other factors; however, it also has a considerable impact on a wide range of surrounding social relationships. The permanence of the constitution may contribute to the development of political culture and the establishment of accountable social and economic policies. The regular revision or amendment of the constitution, usually explained by social, political, economic, or moral crises, appears as explicit signs of deeper social transformations.[14]

So one should not see the endurance of the Constitution as merely a technical issue. The deeper understanding of constitutional stability also contributes to the contextualization of numerous social tendencies. For this reason, it is extremely important to look for mechanisms to stabilize the constitution and to assess how supermajority legislation could serve in reducing the constitutional amendment rate.

4.2 Supermajority Laws and the Resilience of the Constitution

The stability of the constitution is primarily determined by the rules for amending it, although these rules alone are not enough to measure the resilience of the constitutional framework. It is important to distinguish between the power to create a constitution and the power to amend it. The entity responsible for creating the constitution (constituent power) may have the authority to establish a new constitutional framework without considering the existing constitutional norms. On the other hand, the power to amend the constitution (constituted power) is always limited in scope. It can only modify specific elements of the constitutional framework, but cannot revise the entire constitutional design.[15] As the most common requirement for constitutional amendments, constitutions often operate with an elevated level of prescribed majority. Simple parliamentary backing is not sufficient to amend the constitutional rules.[16] A two-thirds majority appears as the most common precondition for constitutional reforms, but especially in bicameral systems, another form of supermajority is also widespread: instead of a simple majority, a three-fifth proportion of votes is are needed for constitutional amendments.[17] Moreover, in France, most amendments to the constitution shall be confirmed by a referendum.[18] Such solutions are also known, where certain chapters of the constitution may be amended by the parliament, while for the modification of certain key provisions, a special constitution-drafter assembly should be convened.[19]

---

[14] Blake et al. (2021), pp. 1–9.

[15] O'Donoghue (2014), pp. 56–57.

[16] Sajó (1995), pp. 54–55.

[17] Pardo-Álvarez (2023).

[18] Art. 89 of the Constitution of France (October 4, 1958).

[19] Art. 158 of the Constitution of Bulgaria (July 31, 1991).

As this will be demonstrated later, the constitution-making function of a supermajority has a clear impact on the status of supermajority laws; therefore, certain examples should be mentioned for this requirement. In Denmark, due to the strict demands to amend the Constitution, during the last 175 years, no smaller constitutional amendment has been enacted. Instead, constitutional revisions have been adopted, the last time being in 1953.[20] Numerous constitutions provide a stricter form of multiple supermajorities vis-á-vis the proportion of votes prescribed for supermajority laws. In more countries, the parliament shall declare its dissolution after the ratification of the constitutional amendment, and the new parliament set after the elections decides again on the matter,[21] such as in Belgium[22]and Luxembourg.[23]

Popular participation in the constitution-making process constitutes a separate issue.[24] In several countries, a referendum is required for the amendment of the constitution, or at least for the amendment of certain constitutional clauses.[25] Referendum is commonly referred to as a central element of the Swiss constitutional framework.[26] Poland should also hold a referendum on the amendments concerning the sovereignty of the state and the rule of law.[27]

A further stabilizing instrument is providing the competence of substantial constitutional review for the constitutional court over constitutional amendments. It makes a meaningful difference between constitutional systems, whether the constitutional court is entitled to exercise substantial constitutional review over constitutional amendments.[28] Most countries reject at least the substantial constitutional review of these norms. In this case, the constituent power enjoys in principle complete freedom in terms of content; however, in reality, international legal obligations and constitutional culture impose meaningful restrictions on the constitution drafter's margin of movement. The constitutional culture varies from country to country, so where it is less established the frequency and content of constitutional amendments are less predictable. Some scholars have argued recently that international tribunals, global public opinion, and NGOs exercise informal control over the constitution, so the constitution shall not be seen anymore as such a set of norms that should not comply with superior legal norms.[29]

By contrast, the formal requirements of constitutional amendments are provided by the constitution. Only such content could be incorporated into the constitution,

[20] Christensen (2020); Art. 88 of the Constitution of Denmark (June 5, 1848).

[21] Albert (2014).

[22] Art. 195 of the Constitution of Belgium (February 7, 1831).

[23] Art. 114 of the Constitution of Luxembourg (October 17, 1868).

[24] Elster (1998).

[25] Elster (1998), p. 98.

[26] Serdült (2014), pp. 87–88.

[27] Art. 235 (6) of the Constitution of Poland (April 2, 1997).

[28] Roznai (2013a), p. 557; Roznai (2013b), pp. 657–660; BVerfGE 1, 14 (1951).

[29] Sadurski (2009), p. 38.

which is adopted under this procedural regime. Compliance with these formal requirements constitutes a precondition of a valid constitutional amendment. Therefore, the constitutional court is usually authorized to review the prevalence of these safeguards.

The stability of the constitution is heavily influenced by the circle of initiators who are vested with the power to submit any constitutional amendment to the competent body for approval.[30] As a widely accepted option, the same actors might be authorized to initiate constitutional amendments and statutes. This concept assumes that the constitution stands on top of the legal system just like a law with supreme effect over all other legal norms.[31] In several countries, only a narrow circle of constitutional actors is entitled to submit constitution-amending bills.[32] For instance, the president of the republic, the speaker of the parliament, the prime minister, the leaders of the parliamentary groups, and the ombudspersons can be such initiators. Moreover, the broader public may also be involved in the initiation process. In principle, even each citizen could have this right. However, this popularized approach would lead to the permanent contestation of the constitutional framework.[33]

One should bear in mind that the circle of initiators should be considered in the broader context of the entire constitutional framework as a determining factor of constitutional rigidity. To provide an example, even though each deputy could submit a constitutional amendment bill, if the amendment needs to be supported by three consecutive parliaments, the constitutional framework would be stable or, in other words, rigid.[34] In contrast, if the circle of initiators is narrowly defined, and the submitted bill can be incorporated into the constitution with just a two-thirds majority parliamentary vote, the stability of the constitution is not adequately safeguarded. Consequently, from the perspective of stability, the procedural requirements set for constitutional amendments are considered to be more important than the exact circle of initiators.

The alleged hierarchy within the constitution may also concern its stability.[35] The idea of hierarchical order may appear when the amendment of certain constitutional provisions is subject to stricter safeguards than the general constitutional amendment procedure. According to this line of argumentation, one should not describe the constitutional framework as a homogeneous unity; the most crucial constitutional norms may enjoy additional protection.[36] This solution highlights the primary role of the constitutional rules, especially the fundamental constitutional principles; therefore, this approach should not correlate with the quasi-constitutional status of supermajority laws. Nevertheless, the hierarchy within the constitution serves the

[30] Reitz (2003), p. 437.

[31] Amar and Tushnet (2009), pp. 3–4.

[32] Ginsburg (2012), pp. 71–72.

[33] Report 469/2008 of the Venice Commission on constitutional amendments, sections 30–33.

[34] Tsebelis (2022), p. 294.

[35] Gárdos-Orosz (2017), p. 610.

[36] Al-Dulaimi et al. (2018), p. 54.

stability of the constitution at least in principle. The bases of the constitutional framework such as the form of the state or the fundamental economic structure shall not be amended unless very strict conditions are met.

Unamendable constitutional provisions may also raise several questions at this point. For instance: can any constitutional norm be classified as eternally unamendable?[37] The eternity clauses should remain indefinitely in the constitution with unamended content, which clearly goes beyond the aforementioned limited endurance of constitutions. All of those attempts which target the abrogation or the amendment of eternal clauses might be in conflict with the constitution since they lead to a contradiction with a constitutional provision. This contradiction may be tackled with the proper distinction of the constitution-making and constitution-amending power: eternity clauses are adopted by the constitution-drafter with the intent of limiting the margin of movement of the constitution-amending power.

With the enactment of unamendable provisions, the weight of supermajority laws would diminish in the legal system, since these norms will be more distant from the supreme constitutional provisions on the very top of the legal system. If certain constitutional articles shall not be touched, certain reform attempts will probably target supermajority laws instead of the Constitution.

4.3 Supermajority Laws in Relation to Other Tools That Serve the Stability of the Constitution

In the foregoing, the aforementioned stabilizer instruments will be enumerated again; moreover, their relationship with supermajority laws will be examined in depth.

Supermajority laws have several similarities with the constitutional amendments enacted with supermajority mentioned amongst the stabilizer instruments, but significant differences should be underlined between the two circles of issues as I have mentioned and I will demonstrate also later. In the case of passing or amending the constitution with a supermajority, the constitution-making, the constitution-amending, and the supermajority legislative power constitute three different actors in substance. These are essentially the same from a merely formal perspective; just the three tasks to be fulfilled differ considerably.

It has been analyzed in depth that the parallel existence of constitution-making, constitution-amending, and supermajority legislator two-thirds majority raises several concerns regarding the permanence of the constitutional framework. The elevated level of the prescribed majority shall be interpreted as a technical or substantial requirement. In my view, which is in harmony with the approach of the French Constitutional Council, as well as the Spanish and Hungarian constitutional courts, the proper interpretation in all three cases considers supermajority as a substantial

[37] Albert and Oder (2018), p. 5.

requirement, which embodies not only a certain quantity of votes but also the broad consent behind this wide support.[38] However, a supermajority may be seen as the unjustified distortion of the logic of parliamentarians from the perspective of supermajority laws[39] but may also be considered as a not sufficiently strict concept from the side of constitution-making, which is not able to protect the constitution from undue political attacks.[40]

Despite the formal equivalence, constitution-making, constitution-amending and supermajority legislative power should be clearly distinguished since these three serve inherently different goals.[41] In the case of constitution drafting, the aim is to elaborate a set of rules for the long term, which should be a point of reference for a series of consecutive generations. However, the circumstances are constantly changing, and constitutional amendment might be a legitimate reflection on the latest challenges, so if surrounded by sufficient prudence, a constitutional amendment should be a reasonable option. By contrast, in general terms, supermajority laws are more important than ordinary ones but may still cover daily social relations among people. In light of these different characteristics, legislative and constitution-amending supermajorities constitute two merely different issues, and their parallel existence may establish a factor of uncertainty in the constitutional system.

Referendum as a constitutional instrument opens up further perspectives, which are strongly linked to supermajority legislation. A referendum is a double-edged weapon that potentially serves to protect the constitution, but it may also create an additional risk factor. The organization of a referendum is a more time- and cost-demanding process compared to a parliamentary debate and vote, and it leads to less predictable outcomes. These factors reduce the likelihood of frequent referenda. Meanwhile, direct democracy often favors more radical views, which can be incorporated into the constitution through plebiscites. Additionally, the outcome of a referendum with millions of participants is always less predictable than the decision-making process of a few hundred politicians.[42]

Nevertheless, these statements should be sophisticated in light of the local social circumstances and political culture. For instance, a Swiss referendum may not be comparable to a constitution-making referendum in other countries, since such events do not represent the exception in Switzerland, but rather form part of the ordinary political agenda. If the constitution can only be amended through a referendum, supermajority law would be the highest legal source, which would be enacted solely by the legislative body without involving direct democracy. This would increase the role of supermajority laws in the legal system but also highlight the distinction between the constitution and supermajority laws. Decisions made

[38] A supermajority prescribed by the Constitution for the amendment of certain supermajority laws constitutes not only a formal precondition of legislation but also a substantial safeguard ensuring the broad consent of parliamentarians [1/1999. (II. 24.) AB decision, ABH 1999, 25.].

[39] Buchanan and Tullock (1999).

[40] Pasquino (2015), p. 85.

[41] Rappaport (2014).

[42] Qvortrup and Trueblood (2023), p. 204.

through direct democracy always carry stronger legitimacy than norms adopted by the parliament,[43] so the constitution would be more clearly distinguished from lower-ranked legal norms, and its fundamental norm character would be strengthened.

The other consequence of a binding constitutional referendum might be the greater significance of supermajority laws as a factor of flexibility. The referendum requirement implements a significant limitation on constitutional reform attempts, since the amendment of the constitution would be possible only via an uncertain and long-lasting process. So the constitution contains relatively rigid clauses, and the unwritten norms and principles as well as supermajority laws are easier accessible for revisions. In light of the above, in the case of constitutional referenda, supermajority laws may contribute to the stability of the constitutional framework at least on the theoretical level. But no such practical sample could be provided, which would enlighten this construction under real conditions.

It follows that the scope of supermajority law would also carry more weight once a constitutional referendum has been implemented, as supermajority law would still be the most powerful tool in the hands of the parliament. The coverage of supermajority law would likely be reduced under these circumstances, as the amendment of ordinary laws would be left as the primary responsibility of the pro-governmental parliamentary majority. In this context, supermajority laws would be reviewed with a wider political consensus, while constitutional amendments could be passed through referenda.

The restricted scope of constitutional amendment initiators may also have an impact on the status of supermajority laws. The right to initiate should be kept for a narrow circle of constitutional actors to protect the Constitution from regular influence of political pressure. However, this right should be allocated carefully, as the possibility of initiation should not be monopolized by the governmental side or the political sphere.[44] Nevertheless, despite these concerns, substantial and well-founded ideas should be integrated into the constitutional framework; therefore, a too restrictive approach also excludes numerous channels from this discourse. This configuration strengthens again the role of supermajority law as such a legal instrument, which falls outside the constitution, so it might be amended relatively easily with broad political consent. In the case of a narrow circle of initiators, supermajority laws might be the main vehicles for modernizing the legal system. These norms might serve flexibility rather than stability owing to the broader margin of maneuver left for their amendments.

By contrast, if the circle of constitutional amendment initiators is broader, each citizen may submit such proposals, while supermajority laws would be further removed from direct democracy. Despite their special character, supermajority laws are still laws in the end. Therefore, their enactment and amendment may be initiated by the actors who are entitled to submit legislative bills. Direct popular participation

[43] Bogdanor (1994), pp. 47–61.

[44] Klein and Sajó (2012), p. 419.

has limited influence on supermajority laws, and a referendum may only be held if the usually strict requirements are met. However, the constitution, as the foundation of the entire legal system, also takes into account various extra-legal considerations. Societal, political, and other interests may also be represented by this set of norms. Consequently, if the circle of initiators were expanded, the distinction between the constitution and supermajority laws might be lessened, and the quasi-constitutional nature of supermajority laws might be emphasized. Therefore, the exact circle of constitutional amendment initiators has a great influence on the rank of supermajority laws in the constitutional system; the level of this impact depends on how this circle is determined.

It has already been conceptualized that the eternity clauses may undermine the coherence of the constitutional framework.[45] Nevertheless, one may argue that in most of the known cases, unamendable provisions provide only some general principles or framework rules, just the form of state or the sovereignty as well as the territorial integrity of the country appear in these clauses. The unamendable character of such framework rules has less impact on the status of supermajority laws at most insofar, that supermajority laws are not subordinate to a unitary set of constitutional norms on the top of the hierarchy of norms. If not the whole constitution means the supreme law of the legal system, but just its well-defined part, supermajority laws will be found only at the third level, since the constitutional norms, and amongst these, especially the unamendable provisions as a separate category will have supremacy over them.

After assessing the relationship between the unamendable provisions and supermajority laws, one may find that there is no link between these two stabilizer instruments, except for the aforementioned indirect contact. The scope of unamendable provisions is narrower compared to other stabilizer instruments and only covers certain well-defined basic principles. Due to the limited coverage of eternity clauses, the connection between these provisions and supermajority laws should not be strong.

When the constitutional court is entitled to review the merits of constitutional amendments, while supermajority laws are also found in the legal system, this may entail noteworthy consequences. If the constitutional court also reviews the merits of constitutional amendments, an important difference might disappear between supermajority laws and the Constitution. Supermajority laws—even if they are over ordinary laws within the hierarchy of norms shall comply with the constitutional articles either on substantial or formal grounds. By contrast, as far as constitutional provisions are concerned, the review lacks clear standards[46] on which ground one may argue that certain constitutional articles shall prevail over the others.[47] Herbert

[45] Suteu (2021), p. 3.

[46] Romeo (2020), p. 918.

[47] Roznai (2013a), p. 562.

Küpper, a German-Hungarian scholar, argued that such hierarchy could be established only by the explicit terms of the constitution.[48]

When the constitutional court cannot exercise substantial review over constitutional amendments, it highlights the distinguished role of the Constitution. The absence of this substantial review presents an important distinction between the constitution and supermajority laws, as supermajority laws can be examined for their compliance with constitutional standards. In contrast, if there is a potential for substantial review of constitutional amendments, it brings the constitutional court closer to the political arena, and rulings from the court are likely to face significant opposition. In legal systems that accept the substantial review of constitutional amendments, such as Austria and the Czech Republic, this is the case.[49] The broader implementation of supermajority laws might be advantageous in this regard, since most relevant constitutional rulings would focus on supermajority laws instead of constitutional amendments.

The rank of supermajority laws within the hierarchy of norms may also influence the level of constitutional rigidity on at least two grounds: the relationship between supermajority laws and the constitution on the one hand, and the scope of supermajority regulation on the other hand. Supermajority laws that are closer to the constitution mostly undermine the distinguished role of the constitution, as detailed earlier. The constitutional- or quasi-constitutional character of supermajority law is rarely raised, as in Italy; or in Hungary during 1989–1990, supermajority laws usually resemble ordinary ones. The status of supermajority laws as legal sources is usually contested, even if supermajority law is not deemed to serve the permanence of the constitutional framework.

Moldova provides an excellent example where the professional discourse has been very limited on the dogmatic background of supermajority laws. Nevertheless, the relationship between the Constitution, supermajority, and ordinary laws remains a highly debated issue. The Constitutional Court has not satisfactorily reflected on these challenges. The hierarchical and competence[50] principles provide adequate theoretical concepts to describe supermajority laws as legal sources; however, the exact content of these principles has not been crystallized neither in Moldova nor elsewhere.

Moreover, the exact scope of supermajority legislative requirements opens up further factors of uncertainty: to what extent should a supermajority legislative matter be regulated under a stricter procedural regime?[51] Since the rank of supermajority law as a legal source and the coverage of legislative supermajority cannot be precisely determined, these always pose matters of huge concern in the legal system. As a consequence, the relevant constitutional case law and practice regarding the status of supermajority laws are highly controversial; the legal scholarship

[48] Küpper (2013), pp. 7–8; Küpper (2022), p. 20.

[49] Garoupa et al. (2021), p. 229.

[50] Sirat (1960), pp. 153–160.

[51] n° 84-177 DC du 30 aout 1984; 4/1993. (II. 12.) AB decision, ABH 1993, 48.

dealing with this issue also shows a deeply divided character. Therefore, the presence of supermajority laws within the hierarchy of norms undermines constitutional stability.

The impact of supermajority laws on constitutional stability also depends on the applied procedural model of supermajority legislation.[52] In an absolute majority system, the role of supermajority laws in protecting the constitution would be less significant under the less demanding form of a supermajority. However, it also establishes a legitimate approach that supermajority laws would not distort the logic of parliamentarism to the same extent as the two-thirds majority requirement. The softer, absolute majority model of supermajority legislation has less impact on the endurance of the constitution, meaning it imposes a less demanding restriction on the power to amend the constitution compared to a two-thirds majority.[53]

Supermajority laws adopted with a two-thirds majority enjoy significantly stronger protection than ordinary laws, so supermajority laws will be closer to the constitutional level. The usual mechanisms of parliamentary work would be changed; the two-thirds requirement entails fundamental novelties in the constitutional and political sphere. The enactment and amendment of supermajority laws will be more difficult; consequently, the gap will be narrower between the constitutional and the supermajority legislative procedure. These factors increase constitutional uncertainties caused by supermajority laws enacted with a two-thirds majority.

In Francophone countries and also in Venezuela, a mandatory a priori constitutional review should be conducted before each supermajority law comes into effect. If this is done, the hierarchy between the constitution and supermajority laws would be beyond doubt. The quasi-constitutional role of supermajority laws should not be raised. Their effectiveness depends on their compliance with the constitution, so these norms function as special statutes with some doubt. Consequently, a mandatory a priori constitutional review has less impact on constitutional stability. Its significance only appears in cases where a motion may also be submitted to the constitutional court, as will be demonstrated later in Portugal.

4.4 Supermajority Laws as Instruments for Ensuring the Stability of the Constitution Within Specific National Legal Systems

After providing the theoretical foundations, it is necessary to examine the national contexts of supermajority laws where supermajority laws are seen as a means of safeguarding the constitution.[54] In France, organic laws are subject to an absolute majority requirement, so the distinction between the two types of statutes is not as

[52] Elkins et al. (2009), p. 6.

[53] Vermeule (2007), p. 654.

[54] Kunenko (2022), p. 65.

clear-cut as in countries that follow the two-thirds model. However, due to the bicameral structure, the second chamber holds more influence in the supermajority legislative process compared to the ordinary mechanism. Therefore, the organic nature of these laws serves as a significant limitation on their amendment.[55]

In France, and in the Francophone countries following the French example, as well as in Venezuela, a mandatory a priori constitutional review might also be introduced. The impact of this concept would be significant on constitutional stability if a motion should or may be submitted to the constitutional court during this review process. When organic laws are sent to the constitutional court without any explicit motion referring to the constitutionally contestable provisions, as is the case in France, the constitutional review would lack direction. Due to the excessive workload on these bodies, a careful assessment of paramount issues should not be expected. Consequently, the robustness of the constitutional review would be at least questionable. Moreover, the French Constitutional Council usually follows a pragmatic approach and interprets constitutional provisions in a restrictive manner.[56] This pragmatic approach has lost its dominance since the elaboration of the constitutional block; nevertheless, recent French constitutional rulings still provide cursory reasoning and rigid interpretation.[57]

The effect of mandatory a priori review had been further relativized by the lack of a posterior review in France until 2008. Therefore, a priori review was the main path to raise constitutional concerns involving organic laws, and this situation highlighted the necessity of precise motions. Consequently, a priori review was not one among more instruments for safeguarding the Constitution; it was the main path for the Constitutional Council to protect the Constitution, and its role remains dominant so far.

A major constitutional reform was enacted in the summer of 2008, which introduced preliminary rulings on constitutionality (QPC).[58] According to the new rules, any party in a legal controversy could initiate the constitutional review of the applicable law before the ordinary court. If the ordinary court finds the request well-founded, it forwards it to the Conseil d'État (State Council) or to the Cour de Cassation (Court of Cassation). If these high judicial bodies also support the request, it will be heard by the Constitutional Council.[59] The Constitutional Council will decide on the constitutionality of the particular norm based on the constitutional block.

One may see from this that the French constitutional design has developed remarkably during the last few decades, and this has also affected the role of organic laws in promoting the stability of this framework. However, one may conclude that mandatory a priori review could best serve the stability of the constitutional

[55] Debbasch (2021), pp. 136–137.

[56] Jouanjan (2020), p. 259.

[57] Rogoff (2011), p. 263.

[58] Balladur (2007), p. 209.

[59] Guillaume (2010).

framework if a detailed motion is attached to the particular law, and if the mandatory a priori review is supplemented by the widely accessible option of a posterior review as a corrective mechanism. In contrast to France, a priori review is subject to motion in Portugal; however, in that country, prior constitutional scrutiny is only an opportunity reserved for the initiation of the main constitutional actors and has not been rendered as a mandatory requirement of the organic legislative process.

In Spain, the transitory role of organic law was more influential.[60] This may be explained by the political and ethnic diversity, which I have already mentioned earlier. For retaining Spain's territorial integrity, all instruments were considered for the promotion of inclusivity and the stability of the constitutional framework. This led the framers of the French sample to the implementation of organic law.[61] Nevertheless, Spanish organic laws are less complex from a procedural point of view than their French counterparts. Only an absolute majority of parliamentary votes is required in the first chamber. I have argued that the absolute majority is less capable of promoting constitutional rigidity. This is definitely true in Spain, where an absolute majority is expected only in the lower house of Congress. So in Spain, the stable governmental majority has almost unlimited power to modify organic laws. The additional protection is less tangible than in France, except from the statutes of the autonomous communities.[62] On the contrary, Spanish case law focuses on the same issues as the rulings of the French Constitutional Council. Therefore, one may conclude that despite the significant French inspiration of the Spanish model, Spanish organic laws are less influential as a concept within the constitutional framework than their French counterparts.

The Romanian solution combines elements from French and Spanish organic laws when it comes to the stabilizer function of this concept. The primary motivation there is to promote constitutional stability. The introduction of organic laws was part of a post-revolutionary consolidation package. In terms of the structure of the state, the supermajority serves not only social cohesion but also the moderation of political competition between the stronger parties. The Romanian model notably follows the French one regarding procedural rules, so the role of organic laws as stabilizers should be limited, despite the required absolute majority in both chambers of the legislation. In line with this tendency, fundamental rights do not fall under the scope of organic law in Romania, which further delimits the impact of supermajority.[63]

In Hungary, the stability of the constitution relies on the long-standing traditions among theories for the justification of cardinal laws. The Hungarian public law literature elaborated on this centuries ago, stating that through cardinal law, certain

[60] Conversi (2002).

[61] Conversi (2002), p. 230.

[62] Roca (1997), p. 142.

[63] Decision of the Constitutional Court of Romania, no 442/10.06.2015, Official Gazette no 526/15.07.2015.

elements of the constitutional framework can be reconsidered while maintaining the coherence and unity of the entire constitutional framework.[64]

After 1989, the transitory role of supermajority laws was highlighted: this special category of laws played a significant role in securing the transition with peaceful means. The safeguard approach was over-generalized in Hungary; this resulted in the establishment of the short-lived category of constitutional laws. During the two decades following the democratic transition, two-thirds laws served obviously the permanence of the constitutional framework, but the regular presence of a two-thirds parliamentary majority gave the special state of play for all political actors.

When the government gained the ability to amend the Constitution with a two-thirds majority unilaterally,[65] supermajority law was used as a tool to strengthen governmental policies rather than safeguarding the Constitution. It hampered constitutional development instead of protecting the Constitution from undue intentions. One may experience here in practice the aforementioned phenomena, that stability or rigidity does not constitute objective values. We could just assume that the proper balance should be targeted. The Hungarian Constitutional Court also stressed the importance of the stabilizer function during the elaboration of the concept of Hungarian supermajority laws.[66]

During the drafting of the Fundamental Law, the vision of supermajority laws as safeguards was deemed to be the most influential.[67] This was further strengthened by the series of inherently new policies incorporated by the two-thirds parliamentary majority into cardinal laws with the intent of retaining them for the long run.

From each national example, one may feel the central role of stability concerns during the implementation of supermajority laws. Besides this, the supermajority law has been a contested legal instrument wherever it has been introduced: apart from the alleged safeguard function as one side of the coin, the presence of supermajority laws from the other side always entails discussion on their legitimacy due to their conflict with the basic logic of parliamentarism.[68]

Supermajority laws may have a further channel to influence constitutional permanence if their political impact is taken into account. If supermajority laws are adopted with broad consent, with the participation of more political stakeholders, the interest of all participating political actors will be mirrored by the commonly established values, the constitution, and supermajority laws. In such cases less controversy may arise between the government and the opposition regarding the very substance of the constitutional and political framework. The fault lines are marked by some key social and economic issues. The opposition does not primarily aim at reconsidering the constitutional framework but capturing the power with

[64] Hajnóczy (1791), pp. 236–240.

[65] Between 1994 and 1998 and from the parliamentary elections in 2010 so far, except for a short period between 2015 and 2018.

[66] 26/1992. (IV. 30.) AB decision, ABH 1992, 135.; 66/1997. (XII. 29.) AB decision, ABH 1997, 397.

[67] Ablonczy (2011), p. 105.

[68] Neil (2024), p. 396.

constitutional means. The political discourse tends to be less sharp, and the debates on matters of public interest remain within a moderate space.[69]

When political debates revolve around the constitutional framework, particularly in populist regimes, the opposition often obstructs parliamentary sessions and tries to alter the government and the constitutional framework through alternative means. As constitutional amendments typically have stringent requirements, the opposition can only achieve its objectives by violating the constitution. The government accuses the opposition of lacking constructive engagement, while the opposition criticizes the absence of meaningful negotiations and perceives authoritarian tendencies.[70]

I have already mentioned that supermajority laws have a special status under the two-thirds parliamentary majority requirement, but such a situation should be analyzed further. When a stable two-thirds parliamentary majority supports the government, the government does not forcibly cooperate or at least negotiate with the opposition parties. In these situations, two aspects of constitutional stability should be highlighted. On the one hand, the pro-government parliamentary supermajority should be reluctant to amend its own laws, while the opposition with less than one-third of the parliamentarians has a limited chance of obtaining a two-thirds parliamentary majority within the foreseeable future. In other words, the priorities of a two-thirds parliamentary majority could prevail in the long term regardless of the outcome of forthcoming elections. On the other hand, a constitution adopted exclusively by a sole political formation with a two-thirds majority obviously generates strong hostile feelings from those who were left out of the constitution-making process or who decided to leave it. As I have mentioned before, these sentiments could potentially turn into ambitions to further constitutional revisions, in other words, to undermine the endurance of the constitution.

The aforementioned thoughts may be valid only for supermajority laws adopted with a two-thirds majority. If an absolute majority is prescribed to enact supermajority laws, the government would not need as broad parliamentary support as in the two-thirds model, while the opposition would have a greater chance in the future to achieve the absolute parliamentary majority. Consequently, the absolute majority requirement may eliminate some destabilizing factors that may arise once supermajority laws are adopted under the two-thirds regime.

[69] Kishishita and Yamagishi (2022), p. 153.

[70] Szente (2023), p. 131.

4.5 The Role of Supermajority Laws During Transitional Periods

The brief enumeration of the main national models relies multiple times upon the transitory role of supermajority law; I will focus on this aspect in the foregoing. During these moments, the established frameworks of social life are always questioned, while the main directions of the changes include several factors of uncertainty.[71] The complexity of formulating a new political order and setting up a new governance structure precludes accurate predictions. These uncertainties are elevated when the transition involves replacing a dictatorship with a democracy: there is a great deal of fear surrounding the potential return of the previous authoritarian regime, whether perceived or realistic, which greatly influences political behavior. Furthermore, the unclear intentions of the new political forces and their polarized views further complicate the situation[72] Looking for stabilizer legal instruments reflecting on these unpredictable circumstances explains the introduction of supermajority law either in Spain, Portugal, Hungary, or also in a number of Central and Eastern European countries. By contrast, in France, the less drastic political changes in 1958 vis-à-vis the already mentioned democratic transitions entailed also the demand of developing constitutional stability as a key consideration.

Supermajority reinforces the need for broad consent during political transitions, as consolidation is expected to come from inclusive political dialogue. The participants adopt only a few framework rules to outline the main constitutional contours. The most contested issues are addressed through compromises, resulting in the enactment of laws requiring a supermajority, or they are simply neglected and left unresolved.

In certain cases, supermajority laws might be important factors in constitutional stability, but their role varies significantly depending on the particular circumstances. Consequently, supermajority laws should only play a secondary role in promoting constitutional rigidity. Therefore, the argument of constitutional stability has limited weight in justifying supermajority laws, as these norms may not significantly contribute to the increase of constitutional endurance.[73] It should be highlighted again that the discourse on constitutional stability does not focus on absolute values; just the proper balance is sought between flexibility and rigidity. Beyond doubt, supermajority law may have a stabilizing function in certain respects (for instance: constitutional review and constitutional referenda), however, it relies just on secondary importance, and the concept of supermajority law as a safeguard of constitutional stability could not provide convincing arguments for the justification of this legal instrument. One may also raise the question of whether the alleged advantages of the promotion of constitutional stability could counterbalance the disadvantages (for instance: the distortion of parliamentarism).

---

[71] Grover (2024), p. 83.

[72] Elster (2012), pp. 7–9; 21–37.

[73] Goss (2018), p. 178.

The science of constitutional law has elaborated two different, but closely linked arguments for the justification of supermajority laws. Both lines of argumentation, in my view, reject the overbroad scope of supermajority legislation. Supermajority laws, whether seen as extensions of the constitution or as stabilizing factors, could best fulfill their functions with a reasonably restricted regulatory domain. All in all, the concept of stabilizing instruments sounds more plausible and aligns closer to the constitutional reality in my opinion. However, the prolongement theory may also be influential, especially during transitory periods. Supermajority law could best serve a stable constitutional framework with a narrow scope. Extensive supermajority legislation would inevitably generate forced cooperation between different political stakeholders for regulating all of these fields, leading to lengthy negotiations and severely limiting the margin of movement of the government.[74]

To continue the enumeration of main justificative arguments, the next chapter will explore the political implications caused by the supermajority law.

References

Ablonczy B (2011) Az Alkotmány nyomában. Beszélgetések Szájer Józseffel és Gulyás Gergellyel. Elektromédia Kft, Kerepes

Albert R (2014) The structure of constitutional amendment rules. Wake Forest Law Rev 49:913–975

Albert R (2015) Amending constitutional amendment rules. IJCL 13(3):655–685

Albert R, Oder BE (2018) The forms of unamendability. In: Albert R, Oder B (eds) An unamendable constitution? Unamendability in constitutional democracies. Ius Gentium: comparative perspectives on law and justice, vol 68. Springer, Cham, pp 1–26

Al-Dulaimi AO et al (2018) Are all constitutional rules created equal? Substantive hierarchy in constitutions in theory and practice. J Malays Comp Law 45(1):47–72

Amar VD, Tushnet M (ed) (2009) Global perspectives on constitutional law. OUP, New York

Avril P, Gicquel J (2014) Droit parlamentaire. Dalloz, Paris

Balladur E (2007) Une Ve Republique plus démocratique - Comite de reflexion et de proposition sur la modernisation et le reequilibrage des institutions de la Ve Republique. La documentation francaise, Vie Publique

Blake WD et al (2021) Social capital, institutional rules, and constitutional amendment rates. UMBC Faculty Collection. American Political Science Review, pp 1–9

Bogdanor V (1994) Western Europe. In: Butler D, Ranney A (eds) Referendums around the World: the growing use of direct democracy. Macmillan, London, pp 47–61

Buchanan JM, Tullock G (1999) The calculus consent. Logical Foundations of Constitutional Democracy. Liberty Fund

Conversi D (2002) The smooth transition. Natl Ident 4(3):223–244

Debbasch R (2021) Droit constitutionnel. 13[e] Lexis Nexis, Paris

Dixon R (2011) Constitutional amendment rules: a comparative perspective. In: Ginsburg T, Dixon R (eds) Comparative constitutional law. Elgar Edwar, Cheltenham, pp 96–112

Elkins Z et al (2009) Identifying risks to constitutional life. In: Elkins Z et al (eds) The endurance of national constitutions. CUP, Cambridge, pp 6–30

Elster J (1998) Deliberation and constitution making. In: Elster J (ed) Deliberative democracy. Cambridge studies in the theory of democracy. CUP, pp 97–122

[74] Klingsberg (1993), pp. 44–48.

Elster J (2012) Constitution-making and violence. J Leg Anal 4(1):7–39
Gárdos-Orosz F (2017) The stability of constitutions and their role in promoting intergenerational justice. Croat Comp Public Adm 17(4):593–610
Garoupa N et al (2021) Procedural and substantial amendment rules: an empirical exploration. German Law J 22(2):216–237
Ginsburg T (2011) The endurance of national constitutions. In: Ginsburg T, Dixon R (eds) Comparative constitutional law. Elgar Edwar, Cheltenham, pp 112–129
Ginsburg T (2012) Comparative constitutional design. CUP, New York
Ginsburg T, Melton J (2015) Does the constitutional amendment rule matter at all? Amendment cultures and the challenges of measuring amendment difficulty. IJCL 13(3):686–713
Ginsburg T et al (2010) The endurance of national constitutions. John M. Olin Program in Law and Economics Working Paper, No. 511
Goss C (2018) Interim constitutions and the invisible constitution. In: Dixon R, Stone A (eds) The invisible constitution in comparative perspective. Comparative Constitutional Law and Policy, CUP, pp 167–192
Grover L (2024) Out of the shadows: illuminating the distinctiveness and exceptional use of interim constitutions. IJCL 22(1):83–110
Guillaume M (2010) La question prioritaire de constitutionnalité. Justice et cassation, revue annuelle des avocats au Conseil d'État et à la Cour de cassation, www.conseil-constitutionnel.fr/conseil-constitutionnel/root/bank_mm/QPC/qpc_mguillaume_19fev2010.pdf
Hajnóczy J (1791) Magyarország Országgyűléséről és annak szervezetéről szóló közjogi értekezés. In: Hajnóczy József közjogi-politikai munkái. Csizmadia Andor ed (1958) Akadémiai Kiadó, Budapest, pp 236–240
Jouanjan O (2020) Constitutional justice in France. In: von Bogdandy A et al (eds) The Max Planck Handbooks in European Public Law: Volume III: Constitutional Adjudication: Institutions. Oxford, pp 223–278
Kishishita D, Yamagishi A (2022) Do supermajority rules really deter extremism? The role of electoral competition. J Theor Polit 34(1):145–172
Klein C, Sajó A (2012) Constitution-making: process and substance. In: Rosenfeld M, Sajó A (eds) The Oxford handbook of comparative constitutional law. UPR, Oxford, pp 419–436
Klingsberg E (1993) Safeguarding the transition. East Eur Const Rev 2(2): 44–48
Kunenko IS (2022) The concept and significance of constitutional and organic laws in legal science and legislation of different countries. J Int Leg Commun 4(1):65–74
Küpper H (2013) Az alkotmánymódosítás és az alkotmánybírósági kontroll - megoldás az örökkévalósági klauzula? Közjogi Szemle 6(4):1–17
Küpper H (2022) The politics of the past and their effect on the new constitutions. In: Ismatov A et al (eds) Dynamics of contemporary constitutionalism in Eurasia: local legacies and global trends. Berliner Wissenschafts-Verlag, Berlin, pp 15–28
Law DS (ed) (2022) Constitutional drafting and revision. In: Constitutionalism in context. Comparative Constitutional Law and Policy, CUP, pp 87–182
McGinnis JO, Rappaport MB (1999) Supermajority rules as a constitutional solution. William Mary Law Rev 40(2):365–470
Neil S (2024) The collective costs of strict supermajority requirements. In: The collective-action constitution, theoretical perspectives in law. Oxford Academic, New York, pp 395–446
O'Donoghue A (2014) Who benefits? Constituent and constituted power. In: Constitutionalism in global constitutionalisation. CUP, pp 54–86
Pardo-Álvarez D (2023) The sovereign minority: the supermajority rule for constitutional amendments. Revista de Investigações Constitucionais 10(3):1–28
Pasquino P (2015) Flexible and rigid constitutions: a post-Kelsenian typology of constitutional systems. In: López-Guerra C, Maskivker J (eds) Rationality, democracy, and justice: the legacy of Jon Elster. CUP, pp 85–96
Qvortrup M, Trueblood L (2023) The case for supermajority requirements in referendums. IJCL 21(1):187–204

Rappaport MB (2014) More on supermajority rules: May's Theorem' Library of Law and Liberty. (22 January 2014) http://www.libertylawsite.org/2014/01/22/more-on-supermajorityrules-mays-theorem/
Raz J (2009) On the authority and interpretation of constitutions: some preliminaries. Between authority and interpretation: on the theory of law and practical reason. OUP, Oxford
Reitz JC (2003) Standing to raise constitutional issues. Am J Comp Law 50(Special issue):437–461
Roca FJG (1997) La 'decostruzione' della Legge del Parlamento. In: Rolla G, Ceccherini E (eds) Profili di Diritto Parlamentare in Italia e in Spagna. Giappichelli, Torino, pp 127–180
Rogoff MA (2011) French constitutional law: cases and materials. Carolina Academic Press, Carolina
Romeo G (2020) The conceptualization of constitutional supremacy: global discourse and legal tradition. German Law J 21(5):904–923
Roznai Y (2013a) The theory and practice of 'supra-constitutional' limits on constitutional amendments. Int Comp Law Q 62(3):557–597
Roznai Y (2013b) Unconstitutional constitutional amendments – the migration and success of a constitutional idea. AJCL 61(3):657–719
Sadurski W (2009) Twenty years after the transition: constitutional review in Central and Eastern Europe. Syd Law School Res Pap 9(69):1–38
Sajó A (1995) Az önkorlátozó hatalom. KJK-MTA Állam- és Jogtudományi Intézet, Budapest
Scheppele KL (2017) The social lives of constitutions. In: Blokker P, Thornhill C (eds) Sociological constitutionalism. CUP, Cambridge, pp 35–66
Serdült U (2014) Referendums in Switzerland. In: Qvortrup M (ed) Referendums around the world. Palgrave Macmillan, London, pp 65–121
Sirat C (1960) La loi organique et la constitution de 1958. Dalloz, Paris
Suteu S (2021) Introduction: the rise of eternity clauses in democratic constitutionalism. Eternity clauses in democratic constitutionalism. Oxford comparative constitutionalism, Oxford
Szente Z (2023) The myth of populist constitutionalism in Hungary and Poland: populist or authoritarian constitutionalism? IJCL 21(1):127–155
Tsebelis G (2022) Constitutional rigidity matters: a veto players approach. Br J Polit Sci 52(1):280–299
Vermeule A (2007) Absolute majority rules. Br J Polit Sci 37(4):643–658
Voigt S (1999) Implicit constitutional change-changing the meaning of the constitution without changing the text of the document. EJLE 7(3):197–224

Chapter 5
Supermajority Laws as Instruments to Construct Political Compromise

5.1 The Impact of Supermajority Laws on Political Dialogue

Moving away from the legal rank of supermajority law, its third potential approach focuses on the procedural rules attached to this concept, and represents an inherently political one. Various forms of supermajority law entail distorted political discourse, therefore, the identification and the reconsideration of procedural short-comings could tackle the challenges raised in this chapter (Figs. 5.1 and 5.2).

The political interpretation also demonstrates well that the various justifications of supermajority laws are based on multiple, sometimes controversial assumptions. The political aspect of the analysis revolves around the following key terms: the distorted logic of parliamentarism, the link with the electoral system, the two-thirds governmental majority, and the protection of minorities. In the following, I briefly conceptualize how these terms coincide with the description of supermajority laws as primarily political tools.

Supermajority law as an instrument of consensus-building may play multiple, potentially coincident roles. According to one of these two narratives, supermajority only sets a technical requirement which prescribes a higher level of necessary consent for the enactment of some crucial laws. If one shares this view in its entirety, most theses of the current volume would be irrelevant. The constitutional and political functions, which are assessed here, would not be conferred upon supermajority laws. Although the fact that the doctrine of technical rule has not been officially implemented anywhere, it undeniably impacts the discourse on supermajority laws either in the constitutional case law or in the academic scholarship. Such argumentation creates an important point of reference for all attempts to undermine the significance of supermajority laws.

B. A. Szentgáli-Tóth, *The Past, Present, and Future of Legislation with Supermajority*, Ius Gentium: Comparative Perspectives on Law and Justice 126, https://doi.org/10.1007/978-3-031-99324-4_5

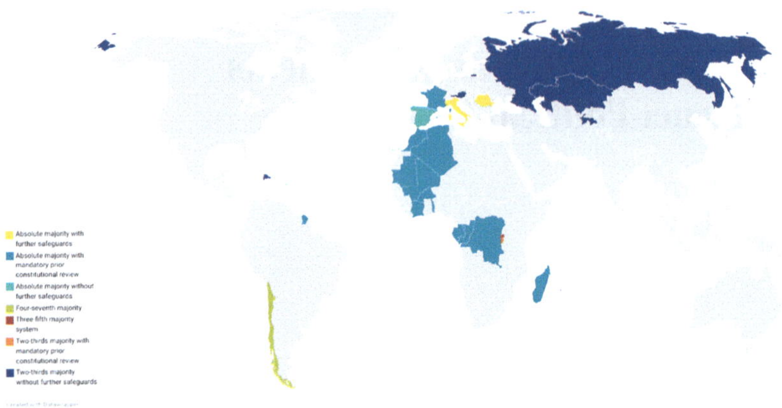

Fig. 5.1 Various models of supermajority laws in bicameral systems. Source: desk research of the author

However, national constitutional courts usually do not share this interpretation and consider supermajority as a substantial constitutional requirement.[1] Consequently, its ignorance would lead to a severe constitutional violation.[2] If supermajority law was seen as a purely technical concept, the non-compliance with this demand would lead to the invalidity of the law simply on procedural grounds. However, instead of this, such constitutional issues are usually tackled as substantial ones in the relevant case law.

By contrast, the description of supermajority as a substantial constitutional requirement is supported by several arguments; the political impact of this legal instrument should be also examined in the light of this classification. "The supermajority legislation explicitly rendered by the constitution means a substantial constitutional limitation on even the reasonable endeavors of the ordinary majority."[3] This explains that in all legal systems the broad consent requirement is supposed to influence the main lines of the political discourse.[4] As a political target, supermajority law also promotes inclusivity. With its quantitative character it may involve as many stakeholders in the decision-making process as possible. Each country operates with a political spectrum divided into economic, regional, cultural and religious factions; political formations distinguish themselves on the ground of these fault lines. Supermajority laws provide a valuable opportunity in this context to represent diverse interests during the decision-making processes.

From this perspective, supermajority law may open up new horizons for a country: this may support the inclusive, tolerant and flexible political discourse.[5]

[1] For instance: N° 87-234, DC du 7 janvier 1988, Rec. p. 2.

[2] For instance: CC, 25 mars 2014, 2014-386 QPC.

[3] 1/1999. (II. 24.) AB decision, ABH 1999, 25.

[4] Tipler (2016), pp. 5–7.

[5] Schwartzberg (2013), p. 36.

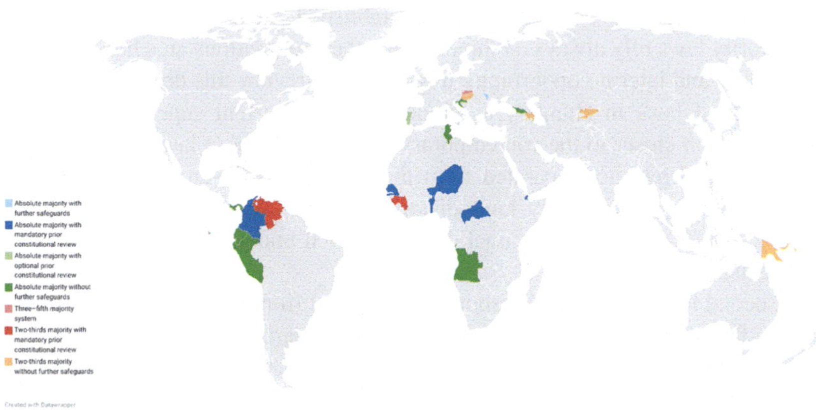

Fig. 5.2 Various models of supermajority laws in unicameral systems. Source: desk research of the author

However, this theoretical model assumes that the political actors might be forced by legal instruments to greater mutual tolerance. By contrast, one may argue that real inclusion might be promoted only for the internal motivation of the political and social stakeholders; legal means would have a limited influence on their behaviour. Consequently, it would depend on the exact circumstances, whether, despite their primarily quantitative character, supermajority laws are able to build constructive compromises in the political practice. Consent itself is always just a noteworthy, but exclusively quantitative indicator. However, the meaningful involvement of the opposition is not guaranteed: an act adopted by the strong parliamentary majority and accompanied by the clear exclusion of all other political groups would be deemed to be constitutional, at least from a formal sense, in spite of the limited inclusivity of the drafting process.

At least two levels of inclusivity should be distinguished at this point. On the one hand, the impact of supermajority law may be perceptible for the whole society at least in principle. The sociological assessment of supermajority law may clarify the attitudes of a particular political community towards this legal instrument. Are supermajority laws and their legal implications well-known for the whole society? Does this legal concept produce impact on the daily public discourse?[6] Despite the lack of any statistical measurement or relevant survey-based research, as one may experience, the complex and contested concept of supermajority law falls really far from the social discourse, this issue raises only the interest of a narrow group of legal experts.

We have seen, and will investigate further also, that most characteristics of supermajority laws differ significantly from the ordinary political and constitutional process, so this special category causes difficulties even for legal scholars and politicians. The lack of clear doctrinal framework also introduces an obstacle for

[6] Rappaport (2014).

supermajority laws to be socially well-established.[7] The implementations of supermajority laws rely always on direct political considerations attached to a transitory period, and later no opportunity might arise to review this decision. The historical cardinal laws in Hungary as predecessors of current supermajority laws might have been closer to the contemporary people since these laws embodied the constitution, and had not separated from the constitution, even procedurally. By contrast, current supermajority laws distort the logic of parliamentarism which entail a series of sharp constitutional debates, which undermine the reputation of these norms.[8]

The second level of inclusivity should be assessed from the view of the political actors. A frequently expressed critical appraisal of parliamentarism, that policy-making would be dominated by the parliamentary majority which would exclude the opposition from the decision-making process. The presence of supermajority laws reconsiders this situation, since a series of parliamentary decisions would forcibly need oppositional support unless the government would have two-thirds parliamentary backing. However, inclusivity in the political sense can to be easily misconceptualized. Certain political actors can use their position to blackmail their rivalries, so instead of looking for compromises, the conflicts would be deepened. One may again argue that the willingness to political consensus cannot be successfully forced via legal means. Supermajority law as a consensus-building tool constitutes always a final resort when other instruments fail to invigorate the dialogue between the opposing parties. The Spanish and the Hungarian development also support the validity of this statement.[9] Since supermajority law functions practically as a replacement of well-founded cooperation, its implementation into the legal system is always contested.

The political stage of the law-making process takes place within the internal fora of the governmental administration, or at most the pro-governmental parliamentary majority: the decisions are taken in the sittings of parliamentary groups, or in the formal and informal meetings of government officials. Only in matters of paramount importance public consultation or prior consultation with the opposition are held. The parliamentary stage of legislation constitutes mostly a formal step, and the opposition could rarely achieve the conceptual reconsideration of a governmental bill.[10]

Supermajority laws also modify the preparation of a bill. Instead of the internal governmental discussion, the opposition is advised to be involved before the parliamentary submission, since the parliamentary failure of a negotiated bill could be a serious issue for the government. The opposition may be called for dialogue even by the overly strong governmental majority, but these platforms usually discuss marginal aspects, focusing just on some less important details of the matters

[7] Binder (2007), pp. 152–154.
[8] Bradley and Pinelli (2012), p. 657.
[9] Pozsár-Szentmiklósy (2017), p. 288.
[10] König (2023), p. 594.

concerned.[11] The political stage of law-making demands a more careful approach for supermajority legislation, when apart from coordinating the coherent governmental approach, the views of external stakeholders should be also seriously taken into account. This feature of supermajority law offers considerable potential: in an ideal case, owing to the more prudent preparation, better tailored legal norms might be enacted. But these allegations do not always prevail in practice. By contrast, the fault lines might deepen and the law-making process might be blocked. For instance, several examples could be mentioned from Hungary between 1990 and 2010 when the lack of parliamentary supermajority backing caused the rejection of a bill.[12] To set a concrete example, the regulation on the remuneration of parliamentarians has not been amended for years due to the missing political consensus on the matter, despite the fact that all stakeholders opposed the existing framework.[13] This once more illustrates that supermajority law could easily function as a distorting actor rather than a safeguard; we are dealing with an easily manipulated concept.

The relationship between supermajority laws and political culture should be also assessed here, which has been already highlighted earlier. In an ideal case, the broader consent requirement means a compelling factor for the political stakeholders to foster constructive dialogue with each other to elaborate feasible compromises. This attitude could not be promoted with purely legal instruments in political life; mutual respect and tolerance are indispensable from the participants of the political debates. These precautions spread increasingly in those countries, where deeply rooted democratic and constitutional traditions have been entrenched, so the established culture of political dialogue is based with greater probability on constructive and mutual acknowledgements. But supermajority laws are implemented even in these countries as reflections on particular historical circumstances, so their long-term contribution to the political dialogue could solely rely on the joint willingness of various influential political stakeholders.[14]

Without an elaborated political culture in the background, supermajority law would be an instrument of allocating power rather than a safeguard. Supermajority would mean for the opposition the sole means to directly influence the decision-making process and this position can be used for the blocking of the government. The opposition might be politically motivated to hamper even the reasonable initiatives of the government, since the failure of the law-making process would be attributed by the public opinion to the government rather than to the opposition. So the opposition may gain political benefit by misconceptualizing supermajority[15] as we have seen in the case of the Hungarian act on parliamentary remunerations. The same mechanisms may be perceptible in the opposite direction when the governmental side uses supermajority to establish an exclusive political arena while

[11] Béteille (2012), p. 42.

[12] Szentgáli-Tóth (2020), p. 214.

[13] Szente (2021).

[14] Seleny (1999), p. 486.

[15] Ilonszki et al. (2021).

denying to the opposition the chance of implementing any reform, which does happen in Hungary since 2010.[16]

One may conclude from the above that supermajority law only has limited impact on the political culture, if any at all. Only in the case of deeply rooted political willingness can it institutionalize the set of unwritten norms already elaborated by a particular political community.

5.2 Supermajority Laws from the Perspective of Different Political Actors

The political stakeholders with different background might construct diverse views from supermajority laws; their attitude often depends on their position in the political arena.[17] For the government with a simple parliamentary majority, a supermajority is seen as an obstacle, which means a limit on the governmental margin of maneuver. The government cannot realize its intentions in the most important issues without oppositional support, so instead of conducting the ordinary legislative process, long-lasting and uncertain negotiations are initiated. As a consequence, supermajority laws heavily affect the governmental margin of movement, and even the governability of the country may be undermined.[18] It causes severe difficulties for the current government if public policy matters are also covered by supermajority laws. By contrast, the institutional matters form the basis of the constitutional framework, so the opposition legitimately expects to be involved in the enactment of these regulations, which provide the main rules on the political competition for all stakeholders. However, the government should be able to legislate the pension system, tax system, education, public health system, public administration, as well as some other sectors within the constitutional limits, as part of the governmental competence to establish the framework of social relationships.[19] If some of these matters fall within the scope of supermajority law, the government supported by simple majority would only be able to lead the country within the restrictions imposed by supermajority laws. From the point of view of the government supported by a simple parliamentary majority, supermajority laws outline the borders of the governmental margin of maneuver.

If a two-thirds parliamentary majority stands behind the government, this changes the situation remarkably. Such a government is not restricted anymore by the supermajority requirement and supermajority laws may be amended in practice under similar mechanisms as ordinary laws. In this situation, supermajority law means a unique opportunity for the government rather than an obstacle:

[16] Mazza (2013).

[17] McGinnis and Rappaport (1995).

[18] Vermuele (2014).

[19] Johnson (2006); Lee (2018), p. 419.

supermajority legislative matters may be regulated unilaterally without oppositional participation. The marginalized position of the opposition increases the value of supermajority: a weak political actor doesn't have a realistic chance to obtain two-thirds parliamentary majority in the foreseeable future to reconsider certain supermajority laws.

Therefore, a weaker government is keen on narrowing the scope of supermajority law, while pro-governmental parliamentary supermajority may have opposite ambitions, because in case of broader domain under supermajority, more governmental policies might be retained for the long term.[20]

In the case of two-thirds parliamentary majority, the political stage of legislation varies also remarkably from the previously outlined model. The governmental side can hold the substantial debates in its internal platforms; the main issues have been already decided when parliamentary debates take place. So the pro-governmental supermajority has an overly strong position which entails huge tensions around the oppositional actors pushed into the background. This always leads to the strengthening of political polarization, so the distorting effect of supermajority remains considerable.[21] For the prevention of such situations, the moving or substantive supermajority rule may mean a proper solution, which is also a contested concept. The so-called substantive supermajority would not provide a specific proportion of votes for the fulfillment of these criteria. Instead, the consent of various political stakeholders is required for the enactment or amendment of supermajority laws.[22]

Without broad governmental dominance, the strong opposition can benefit considerably from a supermajority. Such parties can often have a decisive role owing to the requirement of elevated parliamentary backing. Since the survival of the government depends also on the support of the strong opposition in supermajority matters, the views of these parties may take effect through political compromises even in certain crucial fields. Consequently, the strong opposition may benefit from the broad scope of supermajority law under the same term as the pro-governmental parliamentary supermajority. Therefore, a supermajority requirement also favours the stronger stakeholders' vis-à-vis the weaker political actors.[23] Smaller political groups may have less benefit from the implementation of supermajority regardless of their current governmental or oppositional position. So one may argue that the supermajority law could serve the interests of political parties with greater influence, relying on a well-established circle of voters.

For a smaller oppositional party, supermajority law provides mostly disadvantages, but these political actors rarely gain a decisive role. Broad consent is usually

[20] Szentgáli-Tóth (2015).

[21] Mahajan et al. (2023), p. 974.

[22] Pozsár-Szentmiklósy (2017).

[23] This tendency is probable but not necessary. If the government obtained almost two-thirds parliamentary support, the agreement of a smaller oppositional party could secure the required level of majority. These additional votes might be gained on a case-by-case basis from different stakeholders including parliamentarians outside parliamentary factions like happened in Hungary between 2015 and 2018.

grounded in the attitude of larger parties, so supermajority legislative procedure would probably not better represent the interest of smaller political factions. The oppositional involvement in political decision-making has a greater chance, but usually it is not the smaller parties who benefit from these additional opportunities.[24] By contrast, the political system might be centralized, as the presence of supermajority law would inspire political stakeholders to establish larger political groups better exploiting the potential benefits. Since a fragmented parliamentary environment reduces the frequency of broader consent, stronger parties appear in most of the legal systems operating with supermajority.[25] This structure of the political landscape undermines further the viability of smaller political parties.

This tendency seemingly contradicts the function of inclusivity, which has been assessed earlier. But in reality, these two concepts supplement each other. Since under the supermajority law regime, more supporting votes are necessary for legislation, several interests need to be harmonized to establish the required compromises. In the meantime, supermajority law inspires various politicians to explore the perspectives of long-term cooperation to be able to regulate crucial fields of social life with supermajority laws. So in constitutional systems operating with supermajority law, the political structure comprised fewer but stronger political parties.[26]

5.3 Social Attitudes Towards Supermajority Laws

A systematic survey-based research of this subject is still to be conducted. However one may assume that for those citizens who do not regularly follow legal and political discourse, the term supermajority law does not say anything. Most of the people are not aware of the fact that statutes do not constitute a unitary category and a stricter form of legislative process also exists.[27] Even for those who are informed about this distinction, the constitutional, political and further implications of these laws are not known, and only a narrow circle of constitutional experts focus more deeply on these issues. In the future, a separate volume might be devoted to the social attitudes towards supermajority law in different countries; as a methodological disclaimer, during such a research project, the reflections of constitutional lawyers, political actors and the civil society should be clearly separated.

Despite the fact that these laws concern the daily life of each citizen, the different procedural regime for the enactment of supermajority laws enjoys very limited attention in the long run. It may open up further perspectives for supermajority law if consensus-building was extended towards the direct participation of the society through the more intense implementation of democratic innovations. Such a

[24] Uhr (2009).

[25] Montero and Gunther (2002), p. 29.

[26] Szentgáli-Tóth (2019), p. 66.

[27] Canen et al. (2023), p. 1093.

concept could also get closer supermajority law to the broader society, so the ideal model of supermajority law may contain this element.[28] Innovative channels for social participation during the supermajority legislative process might be created, such as plebiscites, consultations, participatory budgets, or direct consultative fora.[29]

5.4 Supermajority Laws and the Electoral System

The political impact of supermajority legislation depends also on the exact form of the electoral system. This determines the circumstances under which absolute or two-thirds parliamentary majority might be achieved.[30]

A mixed electoral system is applied in most European countries where the elements of the majoritarian and the proportional concepts are combined. Mixed electoral systems may have several exact forms; these show a huge diversity around the world. In some mixed regimes, most of the mandates are allocated on proportional grounds; however, some countries operate with a dominant majoritarian component.[31] The relationship between mixed electoral systems and supermajority law are determined by the proper balance of these two elements (the proportional and majoritarian). Proportionality always increases diversity in the parliament, so one political formation would have less chance to be vested with absolute, or two-thirds majority. By contrast, the majoritarian model favors the stronger parties, so the political system is divided into two or maximum three key political factions. In this framework, two-thirds as the larger form of parliamentary supermajority might be a feasible target, as less than 50 percent of the votes cast could be sufficient for this.[32] However, such an electoral success should amount to an exceptional victory in a pluralistic society, since in a free and fair electoral system, such emphatic results are extraordinary. Nevertheless, supermajority electoral victories have been experienced among others in Austria, Hungary, and Romania, while two-thirds parliamentary majority is almost impossible in Spain due to the huge level of diversity and the fragmented structure of the political arena.

In my view, either the supermajority law or the electoral system should be seen in their entirety, and neither of them should enjoy priority vis-à-vis each other: their conceptualization is strongly interdependent. One may raise a further question: does the presence of several supermajority laws in the legal system justify such constitutional considerations? Should the proportional element have greater weight in the electoral regulatory framework to counterbalance the impact of the supermajority

[28] Czapanskiy and Manjoo (2008).

[29] Kovács Szitkay et al. (2024), pp. 215–216.

[30] Gallagher (1991).

[31] Norris (1997), p. 305.

[32] Kurunczi (2022), p. 423.

requirement?[33] In a purely majoritarian system, the stronger party can obtain a larger proportion of the mandates than in a mixed proportional framework: only the votes cast on the winner of the constituency result in the distribution of mandates and all other votes disappear. Thus, the majoritarian electoral system favours the stronger parties and helps in achieving a parliamentary supermajority.[34]

The parallel existence of a majoritarian, or mostly majoritarian electoral system and supermajority requirement constitutes a significant risk factor, hence two-thirds governmental parliamentary majority might be a regular state of play. Since the electoral regime prefers powerful stakeholders, supermajority law does not protect the interests of parliamentary minorities but stabilizes the positions of the current government.[35] This explains that in the majoritarian systems, especially in most of the Anglo-Saxon countries, supermajority laws are neglected. The reason is that the combination of a mostly majoritarian electoral system and supermajority legislation would significantly distort the political competition. Such a solution would eliminate smaller factions from the most important decisions on the one hand, but would promote parliamentary effectiveness on the other hand.

In case of a proportional electoral framework, supermajority laws may raise different concerns. The distribution of the mandates better mirrors the number of the votes cast on different parties which increases the fragmentation of the parliamentary composition.[36] On the one hand, this fosters inclusivity; however, on the other hand, it undermines parliamentary effectiveness as smaller parties would need more rounds of negotiation to find proper compromises.[37] In a proportional framework, two-thirds parliamentary majority for a sole political stakeholder is considered as extraordinary especially, for the long term. Under these circumstances, the consent-builder function of supermajority should be highlighted with all of its advantages and disadvantages. The elevated majority requirement forces the different stakeholders to cooperate. However, this willingness would be motivated externally, by supermajority as a constitutional mean. The government could easily lose control over the legislative process while the opposition or certain oppositional actors might have decisive word in certain questions. We can refer back to that hypothetical situation when a political formation wins the elections, but it gains only severely restricted possibilities to implement its intentions.

---

[33] Pozsár-Szentmiklósy (2017), p. 284.

[34] Baldini and Pappalardo (2009), p. 52.

[35] Goldfinger (2007), pp. 615–617.

[36] Bochsler et al. (2024).

[37] Lijphart (1994).

5.5 Supermajority Laws and the Logic of Parliamentarism

The link between supermajority laws and the electoral system highlights the discrepancy between the supermajority requirement and the inherent logic of parliamentarism.[38] In the ideal Westminster model of parliamentarism, the government and the parliament are strongly interdependent; the governmental proposals are passed relatively easily if the government enjoys the stable confidence of the pro-governmental parliamentarians. On the one hand, the parliamentary opposition exercises the control over the government by highlighting continuously the alleged mistakes of the governmental policies.[39] On the other hand, the margin of manoeuvre of the government is narrowed by the need of good electoral records: neither government could undertake unpopular measures without risking an emphatic electoral defeat.

Supermajority laws heavily influence the functioning of this theoretical model.[40] The will of the government and the legislative power will be different in several cases, especially when two-thirds parliamentary majority is needed for legislation. In this case, it would be almost impossible to identify who should bear the responsibility for certain decisions.[41] In the framework of parliamentarism, a clear governmental majority stands behind the acts of the parliament, but in case of supermajority law, oppositional votes are also necessary for passing a supermajority law, which affects the allocation of the responsibility for instance for the failure in the forthcoming elections. The electorate holds the parliamentary majority liable, but the special character of supermajority law would not be distinguished for most of the people owing to the aforementioned attitudes towards this legal instrument. So the opposition might block certain governmental measures without being politically responsible for this step.

A further characteristic of parliamentarism is that the competing parties have a relatively broad margin of movement when governing the country while they have a real chance in the oppositional status to shift the government and to gain power. In case of constructing parliamentary supermajority behind a certain political actor, the supermajority requirement may be a proper tool to eliminate this dynamic element which could facilitate the concentration of the political power in the long run. However, this dynamic element itself should obviously not be described as an absolute value as it also generates disadvantageous consequences: for instance, governments do not have the opportunity to elaborate and implement long term policies.[42]

The supporters of supermajority often highlight the role of this legal instrument in the protection of minorities as a political tool. The potential role of supermajority for the protection of minority interest should not be underestimated; however, the

[38] Basset (1965), p. 23.

[39] Stone (2014), p. 19.

[40] Stone (2014), p. 23.

[41] Ilonszki (2021), p. 736.

[42] Ogami (2024).

weight of this function should be revisited in the light of the aforementioned disadvantages. The protection of parliamentary minorities and the safeguard of inclusivity should be important considerations during democratic transitions when the intentions of the different stakeholders were not clear and authoritarian practices of the previous regime had been recently experienced.[43] In my view, once the pluralistic framework has crystallized, the situation should be assessed differently. In spite of its mistakes, the democratic framework provides numerous safeguards for outlining fundamental rights and freedoms feasibly, and effective remedies should be also available for individuals if any of the fundamental rights has been supposedly violated.

The opposition can contest the governmental decisions through several available international fora. Moreover, the opposition also has broad parliamentary competences.[44] For instance, the mechanisms of parliamentary inquiries[45] as well as obstruction stand at its disposal.[46] However, the political manoeuvres should not only take place in the parliamentary debates, but public demonstrations may be also organized to put additional pressure on the government.[47] Besides this, the opposition may also rely on remedial mechanisms: judicial or constitutional court proceedings might be initiated,[48] or the action of the authorities competent for the protection of fundamental rights might be requested. In addition to this, beyond the borders of a country, several international actors, courts and international organizations monitor the respect of democracy and the rule of law in each state.[49] Nevertheless, for measuring efficiency as a remedy, the practice of the relevant national stakeholders (courts, constitutional courts, ombudspersons) should be also assessed,[50] while several concerns might be formulated regarding the enforceability of international monitoring mechanisms.[51] In several cases, one may not access effective remedies through these means. Bearing in mind all of these aspects, the function of supermajority fostering minority protection remains undoubtedly compelling under the current circumstances, but it may have less weight in consolidated democracies than during democratic transitions.

Moreover, the role of supermajority in the protection of minorities should not be overestimated as also mentioned earlier during the analysis of the two-thirds parliamentary majority scenario. So the alleged advantages in the field of minority protection have limited effect, while the potential distortion of parliamentarism might constitute meaningful risk. The easy misconceptualization of supermajority law

[43] Elster (2012), pp. 21–23.

[44] König (2023), p. 595.

[45] Szabó (2024), pp. 64–67.

[46] Arlettaz et al. (2012), p. 211.

[47] Wouters and Walgrave (2017).

[48] Rivera Leon (2024), p. 8.

[49] Collins (2008), p. 166.

[50] Piątek (2019), p. 165.

[51] Dickson (2022), pp. 16–19.

could lead to a more polarized political landscape; therefore, even the reasonable amendment of certain supermajority laws would be postponed for the long term.

Supermajority may show up differently in unicameral and bicameral parliaments. In unicameral systems, the two-thirds majority model appears more frequently, while in bicameral structures, sometimes only absolute majority is required in the first chamber. The second chamber adds an additional check to the legislative process: one of its functions is that supermajority laws should be adopted under stricter, and more inclusive mechanisms, and after more careful considerations than ordinary laws.[52] This role of the second chamber closely aligns with certain justificatory arguments supporting supermajority. Therefore, the coexistence of the supermajority requirement and the second chamber may result in the duplication of these elements.

In France and Spain, where legislative bodies consist of two chambers, we do not experience the two-thirds majority requirement. Bicameralism and two-third majority requirement correlate only in Central-Asia where this coexistence represents a rigid component. If both two-thirds majority and the second chamber were implemented, this would mean a severe distortion of the legislative process which would safeguard this kind of law-making at the same level like the enactment of a constitution. It has been demonstrated that in most of the countries, even the amendment of the constitution is not safeguarded with such high standards than the combination of supermajority and bicameralism. The presence of the second chamber explains why bicameral countries tend to introduce less demanding forms of supermajority. Supermajority has less constitutional weight in the absolute majority model. In these constitutional frameworks, absolute majority complements the simple parliamentary majority model with less implication and the allegedly missing safeguards might be replaced by other mechanisms like the second chamber or the mandatory a priory constitutional review.

The presence of supermajority law and the second chamber correlate with mutual impact on each other. This interdependence demonstrates well that supermajority laws may not be interpreted properly unless the whole legal system is taken into account as a broader context.[53] As a consequence, despite the paramount importance of laying down the general principles as points of reference, the reasonability and the assumed ideal model of supermajority law should be subject to thorough country-specific assessments. This volume attempts to determine the factors which may be considered during the analyses of various national solutions.

It has already been mentioned several times that supermajority law erodes the traditional system of parliamentary responsibility. The government should be responsible for the parliament, which means in practice that it should inform from its measures the parliament dominated by the pro-governmental parliamentary majority. Formal confidence ensures the loyalty between the parliamentary majority and the government until legislation with supermajority reconsiders this seemingly

[52] Lee (2016).

[53] le Divellec and de Villiers (2022), pp. 236–237.

simplified vision. Supermajority laws undermine the traditional interpretation of parliamentarism based on the consent of a simple parliamentary majority and launch a framework of responsibility with limited transparency.

Going further, if the constitutional court reviews the constitutionality of supermajority laws before their entry into force, this may influence the political role of this set of norms.[54] This requirement may eliminate at least in principle unconstitutional contents from the circle of supermajority laws. If we consider the additional significance of supermajority laws vis-á-vis ordinary laws, this advantage should not be underestimated. However, mandatory a priory review strengthens the political character of the constitutional court since the enactment of a supermajority law with greater significance is always a divisive political issue. The constitutional court would interfere with daily political debates and decide the constitutionality of current political endeavours. This statement ought to be relativized by the fact that supermajority laws should not solely mirror the ambitions of the government, so the constitutional court should not only position itself with the governmental priorities on a permanent basis. However, the annulment of a law supported by several political forces can immediately put the body in the crossfire of noteworthy political attacks from various directions. A further argument contests the doctrine of mandatory a priory review on the ground that supermajority law should not safeguard the substantial constitutionality or the endurance of supermajority laws, but to provide additional legitimacy for these norms.

Supermajority law is often referred to as an important political instrument in the case law of several constitutional courts. Most of the constitutional courts highlight the role of supermajority law in consensus-building and underline the importance of the elevated level of required majority. The constitutional case law has never treated supermajority law as an exclusively constitutional category and the political character of this legal instrument has always been acknowledged.[55] The constitutional practice highlights all of the aforementioned political aspects, and among those special weight is conferred upon inclusivity. The constitutional courts take into account that supermajority laws may be able to involve broader political and societal groups in the political discourse. The consent requirement constitutes neither a technical rule nor targets to promote compromises between the parliamentarians. Instead of these, supermajority might aim to establish broader social consent behind legislation which may increase the legitimacy of each decision.[56]

---

[54] Troper (2006).

[55] Ardant and Mathieu (2014), pp. 344–345.

[56] As an example please see: 1/1999. (II. 24.) AB decision, ABH 1999, 25.

5.6 Supermajority Laws and Vote of No Confidence

A parliamentary government cannot survive without stable confidence. The government can remain in place and lead the country if it can maintain confidence between the pro-governmental parliamentary majority and the government.[57] If the parliament expresses its disagreement with the politics of the government, the government should be removed. In general terms, the majority of parliamentarians should support the government. Without this, the confidence is deemed to be removed.

The vote of no confidence may be initiated by the prime minister or by a certain number of parliamentarians.[58] Some constitutions, like the Fundamental Law of Hungary stipulates that apart from holding a separate vote of no confidence, the vote on a governmental bill might also be are coupled with a vote of no confidence. In this case, the majority required for the enactment of the particular bill is necessary for the confirmation of parliamentary confidence.[59] This means that if a vote of no confidence is requested jointly with the enactment of a supermajority bill, two-thirds majority should be reached for retaining the confidence in the government. In case of this regulatory surrounding, requesting a vote of no confidence for the enactment of a supermajority law is almost equivalent with political self-assassination unless the prime minister has an extremely strong parliamentary position.

In other countries, like in France and the Francophone states, the approach of this matter differs considerably: confidence is conferred upon the simple parliamentary majority and is not linked to the issue of supermajority legislation; therefore, a vote of no confidence cannot be requested jointly with the enactment of supermajority laws.[60]

5.7 Supermajority Laws and Minority Governments

A minority government entails an extraordinary configuration in constitutional systems operating with supermajority laws. The minority government lacks the permanent confidence of the parliamentary majority, so continuous oppositional support is indispensable to pass its bills.[61] A minority government does not necessarily cooperate with potential oppositional partners; the required additional votes may be obtained from different parties on a case-by-case basis. For a minority government, the primary task is not to achieve supermajority, but to secure the simple parliamentary support depending on the daily political state of play. In these circumstances, enacting or amending supermajority legislation is supposed to be an almost hopeless

[57] Tuttnauer and Hazan (2024), p. 852.

[58] Lento and Hazan (2021), p. 502.

[59] Art. 21 (4) of the Fundamental Law of Hungary (April 25, 2011).

[60] Camby (1998), p. 1690.

[61] Hazell and Paun (2009).

undertaking: even the agreement of one oppositional group would not be sufficient; the consent should be extended considerably to enact the particular supermajority bill. For this reason, in constitutional systems operating with supermajority law, minority government amounts to a rare, if not extraordinary, phenomena.

Since majoritarian electoral regimes favour minority governments vis-á-vis proportional frameworks,[62] a minority government appears on a regular basis in the common law legal systems. In these frameworks, the political orientation of the government and the parliamentary majority may diverge easily from each other. Several minority governments have been set up either in Canada and Australia. However, we should not draw the conclusion from this that, at least for shorter transitory periods, minority governance would not be feasible without a stable parliamentary majority in countries where supermajority laws exist. For instance, in Hungary, between May 2008 and June 2010 the socialist party established a minority government which was supported by the liberals as external partners. This government was able to maintain its operation for two years despite the massive presence of supermajority laws.[63] Nevertheless, it stands beyond doubt that the implementation of supermajority law diminishes significantly the probability of forming minority governments.

5.8 The Political Character of Various Supermajority Law Concepts in Different National Legal Systems

The historical role of supermajority laws has already been briefly analysed; this should now be revisited in the light of the political instrument doctrine. The comparison results in interesting similarities between all relevant models: the implementation of supermajority law was primarily motivated by political considerations. This explains why the logic of this legal instrument does not comply with the already existing structure of the hierarchy of legal sources.

In France, de Gaulle and his colleagues drafted the Constitution of the Fifth Republic after such a period when the government could not rely on effective instruments vis-à-vis the parliament, governments were faced with permanent crises and the average lifespan of governments did not exceed a year.[64] Due to these issues, each main reform attempt has been rejected. As a consequence, armed and peaceful independence movements were invigorated in the French colonies. Therefore, strong countermeasures and an accountable political environment were required. For these reasons, De Gaulle and his closest collaborators have not focused on the dogmatic aspects of supermajority law; organic laws were exclusively treated as a special subcategory of laws. Under the banner of the "rationalization of

[62] Thürk and Krauss (2023), p. 119.

[63] Petrétei and Tilk (2009).

[64] Debré (1959), p. 7.

parliamentarism," additional instruments were meant to provide the government with more possibilities to influence the legislative process.[65]

It has been already argued that the absolute majority formation of supermajority does not guarantee such wide opportunities to the opposition as two-thirds majority. Nevertheless, even the softer form of elevated consent means a limitation on the legislative power of the parliamentary majority. The mandatory a priory constitutional review of the Constitutional Council represents an even more crucial precondition since no organic law could enter into force without the Constitutional Council ruling on its constitutionality. The introduction of organic law in France is not comprehensible without the consideration of the political context. The concept of organic law has been raised primarily by politicians and the legal and historical aspects played only a secondary role.[66] The cohesion of the political and legal elements may be comparable with the Hungarian democratic transition as I will demonstrate.

As Spain could not rely on any direct tradition connected to supermajority laws, the political approach was also influential during the implementation of organic laws. Contrary to France, the Spanish framers did not intend to reconsider the democratic framework and its self-protection ability but the elaboration of constitutionalism based on the rule of law. However, this was a difficult task in a country where the former democratic endeavours had failed tragically after a few years. Besides this, uncertainty constituted a key consideration. Even contemporary political actors could not estimate the weight and the intents of each other. In retrospect, the democratic transition might be seen as a linear process. However, the participating actors to date could not foresee even the attitudes of the new king, Juan Carlos II (whether he aimed to continue the authoritarian tendencies or to establish a pluralist political arena based on free discussion on matters of public interest). In these circumstances, around three years were necessary after the death of Francisco Franco to crystallize the democratic framework. The aforementioned fragmentation of Spanish political life also contributed to the complexity of the democratic entrenchment.

Similarly to France and Hungary, supermajority law was also implemented in Spain simultaneously with the introduction of constitutional review, however establishing the latter was explained mainly with legal, while the former with political arguments.[67] The stakeholders of the negotiations did not focus on the protection or the prolongation of the constitution or the protection of fundamental rights. Investigations were limited to the impact of the new arrangement on the political configuration and the legislative process. Due to extreme prudence and risk aversion, Spanish supermajority laws cover a broad range of institutional matters and fundamental rights; this was later narrowed by the Constitutional Tribunal with the restrictive interpretation of the organic legislative domain.[68]

---

[65] Formery (2020), pp. 101–103.

[66] Sales (2022), pp. 240–245; 275–280; 366–369.

[67] Conversi (2002), p. 230.

[68] SJCC 76/1983, of 5 August, LC 2; 160/1987, of 27 October LC 2.

We have seen that both historical arguments and foreign examples were influential in Hungary during the democratic transition.[69] However, it should not be left out from the analysis that supermajority laws in Hungary were always adapted to the current political needs not only during the implementation, but also during the last three and a half decades. They served political rather than legal purposes.[70] Constitutional laws during 1989–1990 supported the direct management of the democratic transition and restricted the margin of movement of all constitutional actors with special regard to the government. Contrary to Spain, instead of the Constitutional Court, the political parties made the final step to correct the overly cautious approach for the sake of safeguarding the long-term governability of the country. Moreover, political considerations also justified two decades later that, despite legal criticism,[71] supermajority laws did not only remain in the Hungarian legal system during the enactment of the Fundamental Law, but their scope was further extended.

Hungarian supermajority laws have a unique line of development, during these three decades. At least three significantly different models of this legal instrument have been introduced into the Hungarian legal system. Such flexible and opportunistically[72] adopted frameworks are not known in other countries. In France and Spain, supermajority laws served the feasibility of a transitory period, and after consolidation this mechanism was vested with additional functions. By contrast, the Hungarian political elite always classified supermajority law as an instrument to strengthen or weaken the power of current competing actors and the attitude towards the elevated level of majority was determined by political ambitions.

During the enactment of the Fundamental Law of Hungary, the historical cardinal laws were mentioned which opened up a further possible interpretative dimension of supermajority laws. I have analysed earlier in depth the relationship between historical cardinal laws and the current ones. Underlining this point of reference cannot be understood without considering the political role of supermajority laws. The reinstatement of the historical terminology was an attempt to get supermajority laws closer to broader layers of society and to provide additional legitimacy for the two-thirds majority requirement.

As a final remark under this chapter, the political doctrine approach of supermajority laws should not mean a value-based argumentation. Legal arguments should not have primacy over political considerations. However, it should be taken into account that the alleged political advantages always serve the targets of a tighter interest group with greater political involvement, while the distorting effects in the legal system are tangible for each citizen even if the consequences might not be associated with supermajority law in the public discourse. The advantages of supermajority law for an incumbent governmental party or for a strong oppositional

[69] For more details please see: Tóth (2016).

[70] For more details please see: Kukorelli (2016).

[71] From these please see: Jakab and Szilágyi (2014).

[72] For more please see: Kukorelli (1994).

stakeholder should not be underestimated, but they only represent one part of the overarching picture. On the basis of the political instrument doctrine, I conclude that an elevated level of majority requirement has undeniable advantages, but these can be easily outweighed by the unwanted consequences.

References

Ardant P, Mathieu B (2014) Droit constitutionnel et institutions politiques. 26e. LGDJ, Paris

Arlettaz J et al (2012) Pouvoirs et démocratie en France. Pouvoir et démocratie en France. Broché, CRDP, Montpellier

Baldini G, Pappalardo A (2009) Majoritarian systems. In: Elections, electoral systems and volatile voters. Palgrave Macmillan, London, pp 38–59

Basset RG (1965) The essentials of parliamentary democracy, 2nd edn. Barnes & Noble

Béteille A (2012) Government and opposition, democracy and its institutions. Oxford Academic, Delhi

Binder SA (2007) Supermajority constraints as majority choice. Rev Polit 69(1):152–154

Bochsler D et al (2024) How proportional are electoral systems? A universal measure of electoral rules. Electoral Studies, https://api.semanticscholar.org/CorpusID:266072008}

Bradley AW, Pinelli C (2012) Parliamentarism. In: Rosefeld M, Sajó A (eds) The Oxford handbook of comparative constitutional law. OUP, Oxford, pp 650–770

Camby JP (1998) Quarante ans de lois organiques. Revue de droit publique 5–6:1686–1698

Canen N et al (2023) Social interactions and legislative activity. J Eur Econ Assoc 21(3):1072–1118

Collins TM (2008) The significance of different approaches to human rights monitoring: a case study of child rights. IJHR 12(2):159–187

Conversi D (2002) The smooth transition. Natl Ident 4(3):223–244

Czapanskiy KS, Manjoo R (2008) The right of public participation in the law-making process and the role of legislature in the promotion of this right. Duke J Comp Int Law 19(1). scholarship.law.duke.edu/cgi/viewcontent.cgi?article=1060&context=djcil

Debré M (1959) La nouvelle Constitution. Revue française de science politique 9(1):7–29

Dickson B (2022) International human rights monitoring mechanisms. Edward Elgar

Elster J (2012) Constitution-making and violence. J Leg Anal 4(1):7–39

Formery S-L (2020) La Constitution commentée. Article par article. 23e Hachette Livre, Vanves cedex

Gallagher M (1991) Proportionality, disproportionality and electoral systems. Elect Stud 10(1):33–51

Goldfinger J (2007) The logic of democracy: reconciling equality, deliberation, and minority protection; and deliberation, social choice, and absolutist democracy. Perspect Polit 5(3):615–617

Hazell R, Paun A (eds) (2009) Making minority government work: Hung parliaments and the challenges for Westminster and Whitehall. Institute vor Government

Ilonszki G et al (2021) Can opposition parties be responsible? Parliam Aff 74(3):722–740

Jakab A, Szilágyi E (2014) Sarkalatos törvények a magyar jogrendben. Új Magyar Közigazgatás 7(3):96–102

Johnson N (2006) A "super" bad idea: requiring a two-thirds legislative supermajority to raise taxes protects special interest tax breaks and gives budget veto power to a small minority of legislators. Center on Budget and Policy Priorities

König T et al (2023) Government dominance and the role of opposition in parliamentary democracies. EJPR 62(2):594–611

Kovács Szitkay E et al (2024) Democratic innovations in an illiberal landscape: three ideas from Hungary. In: Fiket I et al (eds) Participatory democratic innovations in Southeast Europe. Routledge, London and New York, pp 214–230

Kukorelli I (1994) Az alkotmányozás néhány koncepcionális kérdése. Magyar Közigazgatás 44(8):449–456

Kukorelli I (2016) Az MDF és az SZDSZ megállapodása utáni alkotmány-módosítás és következményei. In: Kukorelli I, Tóth K (eds) A rendszerváltozás államszervezeti kompromisszumai. Antológia, Lakitelek, pp 5–185

Kurunczi G (2022) Electoral systems. In: Comparative constitutionalism in Central Europe: analysis on certain Central and Eastern European countries. Central European Academic Publishing, Miskolc; Budapest, pp 423–440

le Divellec A, de Villiers M (2022) Dictionnaire du droit constitutionnel. 13[e] Dalloz, Paris

Lee D (2016) Supermajority rule and bicameral bargaining. Public Choice 169(1/2):53–75

Lee S (2018) Do states circumvent constitutional supermajority voting requirements to raise taxes? State Polit Policy Q 18(4):417–440

Lento T, Hazan RY (2021) The vote of no confidence: towards a framework for analysis. West Eur Polit 45(3):502–527

Lijphart A (1994) Electoral systems and party systems: a study of twenty-seven democracies, 1945–1990. OUP, Oxford

Mahajan A et al (2023) Interfaces with other disciplines supermajority politics: equilibrium range, policy diversity, utilitarian welfare, and political compromise. EJOR 307(2):963–974

Mazza M (2013) The Hungarian fundamental law, the new cardinal laws and European concerns. Acta Juridica Hungarica 54(2):140–155

McGinnis JO, Rappaport MB (1995) The constitutionality of legislative supermajority requirements: a defense. Yale Law J 105(2):483–511

Montero RJ, Gunther R (2002) Introduction: reviewing and reassessing parties. In: Gunther R et al (eds) Political parties: old concepts and new challenges, comparative politics. Oxford, pp 1–36

Norris P (1997) Choosing electoral systems: proportional, majoritarian and mixed systems. IPSR 18(3):297–312

Ogami M (2024) The conditionality of political short-termism: a review of empirical and experimental studies. Polit Gov 12. https://www.cogitatiopress.com/politicsandgovernance/article/view/7764/3760

Petrétei J, Tilk P (2009) A kisebbségi kormányzás sajátosságairól. In: Sándor P, Vass L (eds) Magyarország Politikai Évkönyve 2008-ról. Demokrácia Kutatások Magyar Központja Közhasznú Alapítvány, Budapest, pp 456–472

Piątek W (2019) The right to an effective remedy in European law: significance, content and interaction. China-EU Law J 6:163–174

Pozsár-Szentmiklósy Z (2017) Supermajority in parliamentary systems – a concept of substantive legislative supermajority: lessons from Hungary. Hung J Leg Stud 58(3):281–290

Rappaport MB (2014) More on supermajority rules: May's Theorem' Library of Law and Liberty. (22 January 2014) http://www.libertylawsite.org/2014/01/22/more-on-supermajorityrules-mays-theorem/

Rivera Leon MA (2024) Supermajorities in constitutional courts. Routledge, New York

Sales É (2022) Le droit constitutionnel de la Ve Republique. 2e Ellipses, Paris

Schwartzberg M (2013) Prelude: acclamation and aggregation in the ancient world - the origin of supermajority rules. Counting the many: the origins and limits of supermajority rule. CUP, Cambridge

Seleny A (1999) Old political rationalities and new democracies: compromise and confrontation in Hungary and Poland. World Polit 51(4):484–519

Stone B (2014) Opposition in parliamentary democracies: a framework for comparison. Australas Parliam Rev 29(1):19–31

Szabó Zs (2024) Parliamentary inquiries as minority rights: are legal transplants possible? Theory Pract Legis 12(1):55–72

Szente Z (2021) Parliamentary law and practice in Hungary in populist times. Int J Parliam Stud 1(1):127–145

Szentgáli-Tóth B (2015) Some points against legislating with two-thirds majority. https://www.lawyr.it/index.php/articles/reflections/543-some-points-against-legislating-with-two-thirds-majority

Szentgáli-Tóth B (2019) Organic laws and the principle of democracy in France and Spain. Pro Futuro - a Jövő Nemzedékek Joga 9(4):62–74

Szentgáli-Tóth B (2020) Supermajority laws as actors of the separation of powers. Hung J Leg Stud 61(2):210–228

Thürk M, Krauss S (2023) The formalisation of minority governments. West Eur Polit 47(1):113–141

Tipler K (2016) Review. Counting the many: the origins and limits of supermajority rule. Contemp Polit Theory 15(1):5–7

Tóth K (2016) A kétharmados törvények. In: Kukorelli I, Tóth K (eds) A rendszerváltozás államszervezeti kompromisszumai. Antológia, Lakitelek, pp 187–253

Troper M (2006) La V Republique et la separation des pouvoirs. Droits 43(1):33–44

Tuttnauer O, Hazan RY (2024) Government–opposition relations and the vote of no-confidence. Polit Stud 72(3):845–866

Uhr J (2009) Parliamentary oppositional leadership. In: Kane J et al (eds) Dispersed democratic leadership: origins, dynamics, and implications. Oxford, pp 59–82

Vermuele A (2014) The filibuster does not protect minority interests. And other reasons to reject supermajority requirements. The New Republic, January 15, 2014. https://newrepublic.com/article/116172/against-filibusters-super-majorities-melissa-schwartzberg-reviewed. Accessed 21 Oct 2017

Wouters R, Walgrave S (2017) Demonstrating power: how protest persuades political representatives. Am Sociol Rev 82(2):361–383

Chapter 6
Supermajority Laws as a Means of Protecting Fundamental Rights

Turning to the topical coverage of supermajority law, in this chapter, I attempt to shed light on the potential impact of requiring a supermajority to enact certain laws protecting fundamental rights, as well as the assumed risks and advantages of neglecting this concept in this field. First, a deeper understanding should be provided of the concept of fundamental rights and the main institutions and mechanisms established to safeguard them. Therefore, before examining the role of supermajority legislation in this regard, a cursory glance will be taken at the theoretical and institutional background of fundamental rights.

6.1 Development, Concept and Logic of Fundamental Rights

Long historical development led to the crystallization of fundamental rights during the Enlightenment period, specifically at the end of the eighteenth century.[1] In addition to fundamental rights, one can also refer to individual rights, collective rights, civil rights, constitutional rights, or human rights. However, fundamental rights typically encompass the rights that define the relationship between the individual and the state, and can be enforced vis-á-vis the state under certain circumstances.[2] As a main rule, individuals or other private stakeholders (legal entities, NGOs) benefit from fundamental rights; however, in certain countries, the fundamental rights of state authorities and the government have also been rumored and even, sporadically, acknowledged by the judicial case law. Besides this, fundamental rights usually impose duties on public authorities. However, the consideration of fundamental

[1] Ferrone (2017), p. 130.

[2] Vašek (2023), p. 341.

B. A. Szentgáli-Tóth, *The Past, Present, and Future of Legislation with Supermajority*, Ius Gentium: Comparative Perspectives on Law and Justice 126,
https://doi.org/10.1007/978-3-031-99324-4_6

rights with horizontal effect among private stakeholders,[3] or in exceptional cases, the potential violation of the public authority's fundamental rights by a private stakeholder, have also been conceptualized.[4]

A further distinction differentiates between fundamental rights and freedoms. The prevalence of fundamental rights requires not only abstention from interference on behalf of the state but also positive steps to ensure a credible and foreseeable environment where each individual could exercise fundamental rights without facing undue limitations. By contrast, as regards fundamental freedoms, state authorities have to remove all potential barriers unjustifiable in a democratic society from the exercise of these freedoms, while the level of exploiting these freedoms depends exclusively on the citizens themselves.[5]

Despite the significant similarities, no generally accepted list of fundamental rights has been elaborated. Each constitution contains different catalogues of fundamental rights. The interdependent dogmatic backgrounds merge the different visions of fundamental rights relevant in the context of legal relationships between the state and its citizens.

The development of fundamental rights has not been terminated by laying down the theoretical foundations during the Enlightenment period. By contrast, to set a clear example of further improvements, three generations of fundamental rights have gradually taken shape.[6] The first generation is linked to participation in public life, the second to economic, social, and cultural rights, and the third to collective rights.[7]

The logic of fundamental rights has been created to protect the freedom of the individual and to ensure the necessary conditions for this. As a consequence, most fundamental rights may be subject to reasonable limitations in a democratic society, as fundamental rights may often conflict with each other.[8] Moreover, each constitution sets out broad objectives which the states must seek to promote. Constitutions also often provide for the possibility of limiting fundamental rights necessary for the promotion of objectives set out in the constitution. Controversies regarding limitations on fundamental rights always arise when determining whether a specific measure or regulation adheres to the constitutional requirements of fundamental rights restrictions. In the case of certain fundamental rights, such as the right to life, restrictions are unequivocally prohibited.[9] Similarly, the rights to be free from torture or inhuman treatment, as well as the right to human dignity, cannot be restricted.[10] However, frequent state interferences do impact a majority of fundamental rights.

---

[3] Rödl (2013), p. 1021.

[4] Joyner and Roscini (2015), pp. 471–474.

[5] de Cecco (2014), pp. 383–385.

[6] Vasak (1977).

[7] Domaradzki et al. (2019), pp. 423–443.

[8] Barak (2012), pp. 131–174.

[9] Bedau (1968), pp. 550–572.

[10] Nederman and Pasnau (2009).

The role of supermajority voting in the protection of fundamental rights might be approached only through the most important relevant mechanisms established for this purpose; therefore, in the following, I will briefly review the current main instruments and trends serving the protection of fundamental rights before analyzing the potential impact of supermajority in this field.

6.2 The Protection of Fundamental Rights: Latest Tendencies

Most current constitutional systems operate with a wide range of instruments for the protection of fundamental rights within all branches of state administration, but these do not always provide effective guarantees. The exact competences, the level of independence and the practice of each body must all be taken into account in order to assess the adequacy of any mechanism protecting fundamental rights.[11]

Turning to the specific instruments, first of all the general fundamental rights limitation clauses in the national constitutions should be highlighted.[12] Apart from this, the legitimate conduct of public authorities and the judicial case law[13] provide the two primary guarantees of fundamental rights protection. In criminal cases, the involvement of fundamental rights shall not be explained,[14] while in civil cases the question of the horizontal scope of fundamental rights arises, i.e. the extent to which this approach can be applied in disputes between parties in a horizontal relationship.[15] Meanwhile, in administrative court proceedings, applicants seek redress against the allegedly unlawful activities of public authorities.[16]

Ordinary courts contribute to the protection of fundamental rights through various instruments. When interpreting the law, the court ideally takes into account fundamental rights and gives judgments protecting those for whom it considers a violation has been proven. In addition to their adjudicative activity, courts may also, upon request or following their own decision, refer a case to the Constitutional/Supreme Court if the applicable law is deemed to be contrary to the constitution.[17] The Constitutional/Supreme Court usually has exclusive competence to carry out such a review in the final instance, and it has the power to nullify any unconstitutional law. Throughout constitutional court proceedings, the ordinary court would

[11] Zysset and Çalı (2023), p. 164.

[12] Grimm (2015), pp. 16–17.

[13] Gardbaum (2008), pp. 749–753.

[14] Clapham (2016), pp. 11–15.

[15] Gardbaum (2003), pp. 387–398.

[16] Corder (2020), pp. 493–506.

[17] Jayawickrama (2017), pp. 70–101.

suspend the hearing of the particular case; during this period, no substantive procedural steps may be taken.[18]

The judge may also seek redress outside of the country to clarify certain aspects of fundamental rights protection: in the case of a question of interpreting applicable international treaties subject to judicial enforcement, the matter might be referred to the relevant international court. Regional international courts have developed various approaches protecting human rights.[19] However, a recent slow emergence of arguments operating with human rights considerations might be experienced.[20]

In the context of ordinary courts, their activity in the defense of fundamental rights correlates primarily with their level of independence.[21] The ordinary court confronts fundamental rights violations in individual cases and aims to remedy them, although in certain countries, a constitutional complaint directly against the applicable law also gives the court leeway to initiate abstract constitutional review.

The constitutional/supreme court, as the highest and only body with national competence to exercise constitutional review, may take action against individual infringements of rights or seek to remove legislation from the legal system that threatens a systemic violation of fundamental rights by general terms. The weight of both individual and collective fundamental right violations depends on the exact constitutional framework that we investigate.

The Constitutional Court has several instruments at its disposal to protect fundamental rights. If applicable, abstract ex-post review empowers the constitutional court to annul legislation that has already entered into force. Usually a short list of selected constitutional and political actors may turn with such claims to the constitutional court.[22]

Preliminary scrutiny requires a constitutional review of legislation before it enters into force. By contrast, a constitutional complaint provides a remedy for those who have suffered a fundamental right violation in an individual case.[23] In addition, the Constitutional Court can provide abstract interpretation of certain constitutional provisions or declare a constitutional violation by omission.[24] The Constitutional Court exercises continuous control over the administration and the legislature, thus acting as a strong deterrent against breaches of fundamental rights and can intervene effectively if such breaches do occur.[25]

The ombudsperson-type of legal protection stems from Sweden, and instead of protecting fundamental rights in a directly enforceable way, ombudspersons

---

[18] Sinani (2024), pp. 156–173.

[19] Carozza and Shelton (2013), pp. 29–32.

[20] Fariss (2018), pp. 239–271.

[21] Keith (2002), pp. 194–200.

[22] Sadurski (2001), pp. 315–334.

[23] Chakim (2019), pp. 96–133.

[24] For a comparative analysis of the role of constitutional courts in protecting fundamental rights, see: Brewer-Carias (2011), pp. 5–25.

[25] Rauchegger (2020), pp. 258–278.

monitor the whole administration in the broadest sense on an ongoing basis to identify and make public violations of individual rights.[26] Ombudspersons shall investigate cases of fundamental rights abuses that come to their attention and, as a result, take appropriate action for the protection of fundamental rights. The ombudsperson shall not be vested with the authority to take binding and legally enforceable decisions but to make recommendations, make a matter public, or initiate judicial or administrative proceedings.[27] Publicity constitutes the greatest weapon of the ombudsperson: in practice, despite the lack of legal embeddedness, the addressees usually show willingness to respect the recommendations of the ombudsperson in order to avoid unpleasant scandals reported widely by the media.[28] As a further means of legal protection, the ombudsperson may turn to the Constitutional Court with any request for constitutional review.

In principle, the ombudsperson is empowered to act in cases of any violation of fundamental rights, but in practice, the ombudsperson's activities usually concentrate on certain well-defined areas: ombudspersons usually pay particular, but not exclusive attention to the protection of children, people with disabilities, women, and future generations.[29]

The implementation of the ombudsperson model signals the development of democratic institutions, as it introduces a permanent check on the activities of the public administration from a fundamental rights perspective. The ombudsperson may, at any time, upon request or ex officio, monitor the application of the law by a wide range of administrative bodies.[30]

6.3 The Role of Civil Society and the Reinforced International Legal Protection of Fundamental Rights

A constitutional democracy aims to establish a vibrant civil society as a precaution: the state does not impose unreasonable restrictions on citizens' self-organization, people are allowed and encouraged to foster their own initiatives to achieve their legitimate goals.[31] On the contrary, dictatorships and authoritarian regimes always target them by additional difficulties making unpredictable and uncontrollable social initiatives impossible. The civil sector is gaining increasing importance in the protection of fundamental rights, and the emphasis is slowly but gradually shifting from the internal mechanisms of the state towards social self-organization. NGOs channel citizens' views and help to express and make visible and audible the united

---

[26] Creutzfeldt (2020), pp. 380–393.

[27] Reif (2004), pp. 9–10.

[28] Sripati (2005), pp. 1137–1142.

[29] Reif (2004), pp. 223–226.

[30] Creutzfeldt (2020), p. 384.

[31] Edelenbos et al. (2018), pp. 52–66.

will of like-minded citizens. Social organizations often raise their voices when governmental decisions are deemed to violate the principle of the rule of law or directly attack certain fundamental rights. Such social pressure often achieves a change in the government's intentions. Hence, the importance of these actors in the constitutional arrangements of the twenty-first century.[32] In such cases, the government usually accuses the critical voices of civil society of latent political ambitions undermining national sovereignty.[33] NGOs often provide legal protection, even free of charge, to victims of rights violations, enabling them to exercise rights of redress that they would not be able to exercise on their own. Legal representation places a very heavy financial burden on the claimant, who would be unlikely to succeed without sufficient legal expertise. Moreover, where applicable, mandatory legal representation sets a requirement of exhausting certain remedies (for instance, constitutional complaints, appeal proceedings before higher courts).[34]

An even more recent phenomenon in civil participation has been the establishment of supranational NGO networks dealing also with the protection of fundamental rights.[35] These networks could coordinate the endeavors of numerous stakeholders with similar purposes to promote common goals through cross border joint efforts.

International civil society advocacy opens up new horizons to launch a more effective form of social pressure than ever before. However, from the perspective of national sovereignty, this phenomenon allows external actors to interfere with the national discourse on fundamental rights rather than promoting the self-organization of citizens.[36]

Cross-border civil society cooperation brings to the forefront the international legal protection of fundamental rights and the importance of international legal cooperation in this field. Apart from the aforementioned internal mechanisms, respecting fundamental rights is closely monitored by stakeholders completely independent of state authorities.[37] Political manoeuvres, especially those managed by populist or authoritarian leaders, may be able to dismantle, partly or completely, autonomous bodies within the country, which may also influence the fundamental rights standards applicable in the particular country. However, governments cannot obtain dominant positions in international organizations, including supranational NGO networks. The only possibility is to expel such entities from the country, which is seen nowadays as a highly radical and far-reaching measure on behalf of any state, generating considerable international resonance.[38]

International cooperation for the protection of fundamental rights is formulated in geographical terms on several levels. The United Nations and a few other

[32] Donnelly (2011), pp. 496–508.

[33] Marcinkutė (2011), pp. 52–77.

[34] Váradi (2022), pp. 372–385.

[35] Boli and Thomas (1997), pp. 171–190.

[36] Munoz (2012), pp. 75–88.

[37] Woodiwiss (2006), pp. 30–58.

[38] Dijkstra and Debre (2022).

international organizations around the world promote respect for fundamental rightsfrom a global perspective.[39] In addition to global cooperation, we must take into account regional rights protection regimes, which generally have more extensive instruments and certainly a deeper insight into national legal systems than global actors. Such mechanisms exist on almost every continent in the world, including Africa, the Americas, Asia and the Arab world.[40] At a regional level, in Europe, the Council of Europe has played the most important role in the field of rights protection, and this international organization has always declared the protection of fundamental rights to be its main objective.[41] The European Union has traditionally focused on economic issues, and concerns regarding fundamental rights have only emerged during the recent decades in all fields of European integration.[42]

International cooperation could not have achieved major breakthroughs in the field of human rights protection had state authorities not been involved in these mechanisms. As a consequence, most international organizations cannot apply binding sanctions against sovereign states;[43] however, these organizations monitor processes, conduct investigations, make recommendations and possibly initiate actions.[44] Monitoring itself constitutes a significant deterrent effect, but the most effective mechanisms are those accompanied by legally binding and enforceable decisions. However, such direct intervention would enjoy a controversial reception, since such activities of international organizations are often considered as an external intervention into the internal affairs of a sovereign state.[45]

International judicial mechanisms may enable enforceable judgments for the protection of fundamental rights. This is represented in Europe by the European Court of Human Rights and, more recently, by the Court of Justice of the European Union. The ECtHR has a more extensive relevant case law and relies on incomparably broader experience in the field of fundamental right protection. Therefore, this will be briefly discussed in the following. Anyone who considers that a right enshrined in the ECHR has been violated by one of the contracting Parties may turn to the ECtHR if the requirements of admissibility have also been fulfilled. The ECtHR does not have the power to amend the legislation of a contracting State or to explicitly order the national authorities to take a particular action. Therefore, the ECtHR can award damages in its judgments. Moreover, the publicity of ECtHR's decisions and the envisaged damages are generally sufficient to ensure that the contracting parties comply with the ECtHR's case-law.[46]

---

[39] Shaw (2008), pp. 265–272.

[40] Donnelly (2003), pp. 135–140; Shaw (2008), pp. 350–353.

[41] European Convention for the Protection of Human Rights and Fundamental Freedoms (ECHR).

[42] Charter of Fundamental Rights of the European Union (2000/C 364/01).

[43] Oppong and Niro (2014), pp. 344–371.

[44] Bódig (2020), pp. 64–88.

[45] Follesdal (2021), pp. 118–138.

[46] Harris et al. (2014), pp. 7–24.

The ECtHR has developed extensive case law on all fundamental rights protected by the ECHR over the subsequent decades. This case law serves as a point of reference, and the enforceability of fundamental rights before an international court against a State should be of utmost importance for an effective protective mechanism. The frequency of court proceedings and the number of judgments against a national government are important indicators of human rights protection. Frequent awarding of damages may cause serious loss of prestige to a country and, in the long term, the resulting financial burden can also be equivalent to considerable financial resources in the case of consistent violations. Although international judicial mechanisms for the protection of fundamental rights face significant difficulties,[47] international courts can be seen as viable tools of legal protection with considerable perspectives[48] outside of Europe as well.[49]

In the following, the most important relevant international treaties protecting human rights will be enumerated. After the two world wars, the United Nations adopted the Universal Declaration of Human Rights, which has been the cornerstone of human rights thinking worldwide to this day.[50] Following this development, a number of other conventions have been concluded, focusing on the protection of the interests of certain particularly vulnerable groups. These include the Convention on the Rights of the Child,[51] the Convention on the Rights of Women,[52] and international standards for people with disabilities.[53] The three generations of fundamental rights have been protected by the International Covenant on Civil and Political Rights[54] and the International Covenant on Economic and Social Rights.[55]

Such supranational political and economic organizations as the European Union also play an emerging role in the protection of human rights. The European Union was not primarily established for the protection of fundamental rights; instead, the member states mainly aimed at coordinating their economic policies. However, the fundamental rights approach gradually gained ground in EU policies and later in the institutional framework. As a result, EU bodies constantly monitor the rule of law, democracy and respect for fundamental rights in the Member States. Moreover, the

---

[47] Financial obstacles for the claimants to reach the court; the rapidly evolving caseload; the limited background of the court regarding the local conditions and social circumstances. For more details, see: Keller et al. (2010), pp. 1025–1048.

[48] Flogaitis et al. (2013), pp. 6–32.

[49] Pasqualucci (2003), pp. 1–26.

[50] https://www.un.org/en/about-us/universal-declaration-of-human-rights.

[51] https://www.ohchr.org/en/instruments-mechanisms/instruments/convention-rights-child.

[52] https://www.ohchr.org/en/instruments-mechanisms/instruments/convention-elimination-all-forms-discrimination-against-women.

[53] https://www.ohchr.org/en/instruments-mechanisms/instruments/convention-rights-persons-disabilities.

[54] https://www.ohchr.org/en/instruments-mechanisms/instruments/international-covenant-civil-and-political-rights.

[55] https://www.ohchr.org/en/instruments-mechanisms/instruments/international-covenant-economic-social-and-cultural-rights.

due respect and protection of human rights have become part of the Copenhagen criteria.[56]

The founding treaties also include valuable references to human rights; these were completed by the enactment of the Charter of Fundamental Rights. The establishment of the position of European Ombudsperson also provides a further tool to monitor the activities of EU bodies from a fundamental rights perspective. In the case law of the Court of Justice of the European Union, decisions on human rights issues have become increasingly frequent, particularly in recent years in the field of asylum.[57]

6.4 The Role of Supermajority Laws as Safeguards of Fundamental Rights: General Considerations

After having outlined, in a nutshell, the ecosystem of safeguards for the protection of fundamental rights, the potential place of supermajority law within this structure could be assessed.

Supermajority laws usually focus on two main areas: the organizational structure of the state and the relationship between the state and the citizen, i.e. fundamental rights.[58] Nevertheless, political intentions may lead to the contention of further subject matters also within the scope of supermajority law.[59] The latest example of this came from Hungary, where the Fundamental Law adopted in 2011 added a greater number of public policy subjects to the list of supermajority laws,[60] in addition to fundamental and institutional subjects.

Fundamental rights serve as the undeniable pillars of a democratic and constitutional social order based on rule of law. They impose essential limits on the powers of a government, and their protection guarantees the well-being and freedom of citizens. For these reasons, fundamental rights might be regulated as supermajority subject matters, defining the position of the individual in the constitutional system and outlining their rights and obligations. However, one cannot ignore the fact that the institutional framework of the State determines the requirements of law-making, including the possibilities for enacting and amending legislation and all other lower-ranked legal norms. These constitute the formal limits on exercising public power. In contrast, acts on fundamental rights regulate the substantial restrictions on the exercise of public power.[61]

---

[56] von Bogdandy (2012).

[57] Boswell (2003), pp. 619–638.

[58] Szentgáli-Tóth (2020), pp. 210–228.

[59] Cowan (2024).

[60] Art. 40 of the Fundamental Law of Hungary (April 25, 2011).

[61] Szentgáli-Tóth (2017).

Accordingly, an elevated majority requirement can help in holding a political community together by creating a broad political consensus on the main institutional design and on the formal limits on exercising public power. However, the same logic does not apply to fundamental rights, where one would raise the question of whether the necessary guarantees are envisaged for the exercise of fundamental rights rather than whether the constitution stipulates a supermajority consensus on these matters. For this reason, a less convincing legal justification could support a supermajority on fundamental rights than a supermajority on paramount institutional fields.

Despite a clear distinction between the institutional and fundamental right aspects of legislative supermajority, there may be an overlap between these two categories. Several institutions that are subject to the supermajority requirement may play a crucial role in safeguarding fundamental rights. Therefore, the indirect role of supermajority as a safeguard for protecting rights should also be conceptualized through these institutional fields.

Besides this, in the aforementioned case of public policy matters, it is difficult to explain the increased majority requirement, as no compelling arguments would justify the application of this guarantee. Proponents of this approach usually point out that public policy matters directly affect fundamental rights legislation and should therefore be subject to supermajority voting. The flaw in this approach, in my view, is that, following its logic, almost all laws should be regarded as supermajority subjects.[62] In addition, public policy matters fall within the scope of inherent governmental competences in a parliamentary system; the government may implement its priorities through the regulation of these legislative fields.[63]

All forms of supermajority contradict the basic logic of parliamentarism. However, the level of malfunctioning may differ depending on the various groups of supermajority subject matters. In the case of fundamental rights, I believe that we must look in a different direction for substantive guarantees of legal protection. The price paid for the possible guarantee function of supermajority voting shall not be commensurate with the benefits to be gained. The perception of this balance can vary in space and time, as will be demonstrated below.

The form of supermajority required would also influence the protection of fundamental rights. The two-thirds solution used in a small number of Central- and East-European, African and Latin-American countries aims at strengthening the safeguarding role of the supermajority in its stricter form, but it also highlights its restrictive function. By contrast, the absolute majority requirement affects the basic logic of parliamentarianism less, and does not make as much difference to the ordinary legislative procedure. Given these differences, requiring an absolute parliamentary majority to pass laws covering fundamental rights instead of a two-thirds majority might be more plausible; however, the argument remains in both cases that the real guarantees of legal protection must be sought elsewhere.

---

[62] Arato and Miklósi (2010), pp. 67–368.

[63] Cameron and Evans (2024), pp. 110–141.

Mandatory ex ante constitutional review constitutes, at least in principle, the most effective legal tool to enact supermajority laws protecting fundamental rights. Constitutional courts usually deal with possible restrictions of fundamental rights on the basis of predetermined tests.[64] Therefore, in case of such a challenge, a law that excessively restricts fundamental rights can be filtered out of the legal system before it enters into force, but it has already been pointed out that the effectiveness of mandatory ex ante constitutional review depends mainly on the opening of the possibility to file a detailed petition.

6.5 The Role of Supermajority Laws as Safeguards of Fundamental Rights: A Comparison Between Different National Legal Systems

The role of supermajority laws as fundamental rights protection instruments varies from one national legal system to another. In the original French model, the catalogue of fundamental rights was not included in the constitutional text. De Gaulle and his entourage did not consider the fundamental rights approach important. Instead of explicit enumeration, the French Constitution of 1958 referred in its preamble to a number of documents guaranteeing the protection of fundamental rights. This pragmatic approach of the French Constitution explains why the original system of the Fifth Republic was dominated mainly by institutional issues. As a consequence, apart from the constitutional text, the original scope of organic law also did not cover fundamental rights. It focused almost exclusively on the institutional aspect.[65] However, as a function of indirect safeguard, organic law regulates the status and competence of certain constitutional actors who play crucial roles in the protection of fundamental rights. Thus, the detailed rules on the French ombudsperson or the Constitutional Council are provided by organic laws.[66]

It has been conceptualized earlier that the Constitutional Council, in a series of decisions from 1971 onwards, has developed the aforementioned system of constitutional block. This framework aimed primarily to replace the missing catalogue of fundamental rights and thus create a guarantee system for effective legal protection. The Constitutional Council has ruled on several occasions that organic laws fall outside of the constitutional block, so the extension of the constitutional concept did not directly affect the French organic laws. However, during the constitutional review of organic laws, the extended constitutional concept will be referred to as a standard of compliance; therefore, organic laws should not undermine fundamental rights anymore. This statement is further underlined by the opening of the detailed possibility of ex-post review in 2008. Therefore, the French model preserves its

[64] Bobić (2022), pp. 175–238.

[65] Troper (2008), pp. 30–31.

[66] Sales (2022), pp. 366–369.

specialty: organic laws have not been implemented for the protection of fundamental rights, but the conditions have had to be created to enable the constitutionality of organic and ordinary laws to be reviewed in the light of fundamental rights.[67]

The Spanish development has been reflected by various means on the interdependence between a legislative supermajority and the protection of fundamental rights. Similarly to the Hungarian model, Spanish organic laws have been introduced as a result of an evolution from a dictatorship. Whereas in France, organic law aimed primarily at rationalizing parliamentarism and creating stability, both in Spain and in Hungary the newly established democratic institutions had to be safeguarded.[68] As a result, the function of protecting fundamental rights was viewed as a key element of legislative supermajority. In Spain, Article 81(1) of the Constitution stipulates that the domain of supermajority voting relies on three main branches: institutional aspects, fundamental rights, and additional subjects beyond the first two subcategories. In principle, this would have meant that either the Spanish or the Hungarian approach would have required that all statutory provisions affecting fundamental rights should be enacted by a supermajority. However, in both countries, the long - term feasibility of such a solution was contested. Therefore, the circle of fundamental rights subject to a supermajority requirement should have been narrowed. Unlike in Hungary, however, in Spain, this step was not taken through a constitutional amendment resulting from a compromise between political parties, but through the evolution of the Constitutional Court practice.[69] The Spanish Constitutional Tribunal has stated that only the fundamental rights covered by Articles 15–29 of the Spanish Constitution fall within the scope of organic law. With this decision, the role of a supermajority in the protection of fundamental rights in Spain became more predictable. However, we have seen that Spain follows the absolute majority model, so it has a very limited impact in comparison with the two-thirds majority regime.

Once again, Hungary represents an exceptional model, as we have witnessed a variety of approaches to the role of supermajority voting in the protection of fundamental rights over the past 35 years. Initially, the interpretation close to the Spanish one and also impacted by the Austrian model dominated the discourse, and the developments of the 1990s followed this logic. By contrast, two decades later, the Fundamental Law has shifted the Hungarian system towards the French concept, pushing the rights protection approach into the background, although one probably cannot speak of a conscious constitutional transplant.[70]

Shortly after the implementation of modern supermajority law, the dictatorial experience led to all legislation affecting fundamental rights being subject to supermajority voting. Hoverer, this made it impossible to govern the country in the short term. Recognizing this, the political parties agreed to provide an enumerated

---

[67] Ardant and Mathieu (2014), pp. 344–345.

[68] Szentgáli-Tóth (2018), pp. 419–435.

[69] SJCC 76/1983, of 5 August, LC 2; 160/1987, of 27 October LC 2.

[70] Elkins et al. (2009), p. 38.

list of fundamental rights subject to a two-thirds majority, so as not to tie the hands of governments too tightly.[71] Two decades later, the drafters of the Fundamental Law considered that supermajority might be replaced with other means for the protection of fundamental rights. Therefore, these subjects were almost completely removed from the list of supermajority legislative matters.[72] We have seen how this narrowing of the supermajority legislative domain differed from the Spanish step towards the same direction.

Can it raise constitutional implications if the scope of supermajority is significantly narrowed, and fundamental rights are removed from supermajority legislative subject matters? The elements of the answer illustrate excellently that functions of supermajority law may be reasonably reconsidered in light of changing circumstances.

We must place the removal of the two-thirds majority from the safeguards of fundamental rights in the context of a broader constitutional revision. Overall, we can speak of a slight decline in safeguarding fundamental rights in light of abolishing action popularis;[73] centralizing the ombudsperson model of the country,[74] and limiting the competence of the Constitutional Court to review laws on public finances.[75] However, one should also take into account the fact that the level of fundamental rights protection that emerged after the democratic transition was far above international expectations. Given the distorting effects of supermajority voting on parliamentarianism, the decision not to use supermajority voting as a legal protection mechanism can be justified by convincing arguments, even if weighty counterarguments might also be listed. Furthermore, no satisfactory explanation has been provided as to why fundamental rights have been replaced with public policy matters amongst the fields of supermajority legislation. All in all, strong arguments could support the reintroduction of legislative supermajority on fundamental rights, but other instruments of fundamental rights protection seem more appropriate to address the potentially existing inadequacies in this regard.

It should be stressed that similarly to the Spanish development, the constitutional revision only affects the direct role of supermajority in the protection of fundamental rights. However, similarly to the French model, the indirect aspect remained untouched. Among the institutional subjects directly related to fundamental rights, the freedom of the press,[76] the functioning and management of political parties,[77] the status of religious communities and established churches,[78] the status of the judiciary, the status and competences of the Constitutional Court, as well as the status

[71] Kilényi (1994), pp. 201–209.

[72] Kukorelli (1994), pp. 449–456.

[73] Gárdos-Orosz (2012), pp. 302–315.

[74] Szabó (2012), pp. 112–120.

[75] Chronowski and Gárdos-Orosz (2017), pp. 139–154.

[76] Art. IX (6) of the Fundamental Law of Hungary (April 25, 2011).

[77] Art. VIII (4) of the Fundamental Law of Hungary (April 25, 2011).

[78] Art. VII (5) of the Fundamental Law of Hungary (April 25, 2011).

and competences of the commissioner of fundamental rights, are still classified as supermajority legislative matters.

The other relevant Central and Eastern European constitutional systems operate only in a very narrow circle with supermajority law as a direct instrument for the protection of fundamental rights, except in Croatia and Montenegro where, according to the general clause, the statutory rules on fundamental rights should be covered by organic laws. Nevertheless, freedom of religion[79] and the right to citizenship are classified as a supermajority field of legislation in most of the relevant constitutional frameworks.[80] The requirement of a supermajority shall not only concern the fundamental rights themselves, but also those institutions which safeguard the protection of these rights. Most of the relevant constitutions contain three such institutions amongst the supermajority legislative subjects: the constitutional court, the ombudsperson, and the judicial system. Additionally, the role of supermajority laws is even more complex with regard to the indirect protection of fundamental rights: for instance, the education system also, as a public policy matter has been acknowledged as an organic field of legislation in Romania and Moldova.[81]

The reference in the Croatian Constitution to fundamental rights and freedoms as organic legislative fields makes this list open-ended. It would be the task of the Parliament, and, on the final instance, the Constitutional Court to interpret which statutes or statutory provisions related to fundamental rights fall within the coverage of organic law.[82] Neither the Parliament nor the Constitutional Court has specified the scope of fundamental rights subject to two-thirds organic legislation.

Similarly, the Montenegrin Constitution mentions, in a general clause, the fundamental rights and freedoms provided by the Constitution as legislative fields that should be covered by an elevated majority requirement.[83] This regulatory method is very similar to the Hungarian solution, which was applied during the 1989 constitutional revision. It is based on a broad reference to fundamental rights and duties, as well as an exhaustive enumeration of institutional matters. However, unlike the aforementioned and short-lived Hungarian model, the domain of Montenegrin supermajority laws protecting fundamental rights has not been narrowed so far.

In Africa, following the French model, the indirect aspect of human rights protection received more attention when the circle of supermajority laws was outlined. In most of the relevant countries, the organization, functioning, and competences of the judiciary, as well as the detailed rules on the highest judicial bodies (the supreme court, the constitutional court, judicial council, court of cassation, state audit office),

[79] Art. 73 (3) point S) of the Constitution of Romania (December 8, 1991); Art. 72 (3) point K) of the Constitution of Moldova (July 29, 1994); Art. 12 (3) of the Constitution of Georgia (August 24, 1995).

[80] Art. G) (4) of the Fundamental Law of Hungary (April 25, 2011); Art. 5 (1) of the Constitution of Romania; Art. 17 (1) of the Constitution of Moldova (July 29, 1994).

[81] Art. 73 (3) point N) of the Constitution of Romania (December 8, 1991); Art. 72 (3) point K) of the Constitution of Moldova (July 29, 1994).

[82] Art. 82 (1) of the Constitution of Croatia (December 22, 1990).

[83] Art. 91 of the Constitution of Montenegro (October 19, 2007).

fall within the coverage of organic law. Besides this, organic law may regulate the national electoral commission,[84] the Social and Economic Council,[85] the ombudsperson,[86] the media authority,[87] the municipalities,[88] as well as elections[89] and referendums[90] embodying direct democracy.

Therefore, the role of African organic laws indirectly protecting fundamental rights should be underlined; moreover, fundamental rights themselves also appear as organic legislative fields mainly in the Maghreb region. For instance, in Morocco, the right to petition[91] and the right to strike[92] are classified as organic matters. In addition, the Tunisian Constitution adopted in 2022 stipulates that fundamental rights and duties of the citizens should be regulated by organic laws.[93] This wording is almost equivalent to the concept of constitutional law introduced in Hungary during 1989–1990; however, the two frameworks should be clearly separated. In Hungary, the enactment or amendment of constitutional laws was subject to two-thirds parliamentary consent, which meant a too high threshold. By contrast, Tunisian organic laws on fundamental rights shall be passed by an absolute parliamentary majority. Thus, the Tunisian framework has been more flexible and easily adaptable; consequently, its lifespan has been significantly longer. As a consequence, the recent Tunisian constitutional reforms had only a limited impact on the concept of organic law, just the presidential veto and the three-fifth parliamentary majority required for overriding such a veto in the organic legislative process have been removed.

[84] Art. 211 of the Constitution of Democratic Republic of Congo (February 18, 2006).

[85] Art. 140 of the Constitution of Benin (February 2, 1990); Art. 141 and 160 of the Constitution of Burkina Faso (June 2, 1991); Art. 97 of the Constitution of Gabon (November 16, 2024); Art. 97 of the Constitution of Mauritania (July 12, 1991).

[86] Art. 169 of the Constitution of Côte d'Ivoire (November 8, 2016); Art. 154 of the Constitution of Togo (May 6, 2024).

[87] Art. 24 and 143 of the Constitution of Benin (December 2, 1990); Art. 212 of the Constitution of the Democratic Republic of Congo (February 18, 2006); Art. 97 of the Constitution of Gabon (November 16, 2024); Art. 91 of the Constitution of Guinea (March 22, 2020); Art. 163 of the Constitution of Niger (October 31, 2010); Art. 31 of the Constitution of Togo (May 6, 2024).

[88] Art. 143 of the Constitution of Central African Republic (August 30, 2023); Art. 87 of the Constitution of Djibouti (September 4, 1992); Art. 91 of the Constitution of Guinea (March 22, 2020); Art. 88 (4) of the Constitution of Madagascar (October 14, 2010); Art. 146 of the Constitution of Morocco (July 1, 2011); Art. 75 of the Constitution of Tunisia (July 25, 2022).

[89] Art. 79, 88 (3) and (10) of the Constitution of Madagascar (October 14, 2010); Art. 48 (1) of the Constitution of Mauritania (July 12, 1991); Art. 35 of the Constitution of Senegal (January 7, 2001).

[90] Art. 164 g) of the Constitution of Angola (January 21, 2010); Art. 187 (1) c) of the Constitution of Cape Verde (September 5, 1980); Art. 151 of the Constitution of Republic of Congo (October 25, 2015).

[91] Art. 15 of the Constitution of Morocco (July 1, 2011).

[92] Art. 29 of the Constitution of Morocco (July 1, 2011).

[93] Art. 75 of the Constitution of Tunisia (July 25, 2022).

Organic law also covers the direct safeguard of fundamental rights in certain Latin-American countries, such as the Dominican Republic,[94] Ecuador[95] and Venezuela.[96] Nevertheless, protected fundamental rights are not expressly enumerated by these constitutions. A general clause confers any role on organic law in the protection of fundamental rights, and it might be complemented by additional exemplificative constitutional references.

As a concluding remark, one may find that meaningful arguments could underline the necessity of a supermajority as a safeguard of fundamental rights. However, such considerations do not outweigh the great number of relevant concerns. Effective constitutional review and systematic monitoring may contribute more valuably to the protection of fundamental rights vis-à-vis elevated levels of legislative consent behind the respective statutes. Supermajority law as a guarantee of fundamental rights is always brought to the forefront by political transitions: within unforeseeable circumstances, supermajority law may be seen as a safeguard; however, in the long run, it gradually becomes a burden instead of a guarantee. Supermajorities can have a place in the legal protection system to the extent that the institutions responsible for their protection can be enshrined in supermajority laws. It is therefore justifiable from a constitutional perspective to include the acts on the organization and functioning of the constitutional court, the judiciary, and the ombudsperson within the scope of supermajority law. However, in my view, the protection of fundamental rights can only arise indirectly through the aforementioned institutions. It may be worth looking for additional guarantees of fundamental rights, but in my opinion, legislative supermajority probably does not constitute the appropriate direction of these valuable endeavors.

After analysing the potential role of supermajority legislation in the protection of fundamental rights, I proceed with the issues of the relationship between the separation of powers and supermajority laws as a final justificatory argument.

References

Arato A, Miklósi Z (2010) Transitional politics in Hungary. In: Miller LE, Aucoin L (eds) Framing the state in times of transition. US Institute of Peace, pp 350–390

Ardant P, Mathieu B (2014) Droit constitutionnel et institutions politiques. 26e. LGDJ, Paris

Barak A (2012) Constitutional rights and their limitations. CUP, Cambridge

Bedau H (1968) The right to life. The Monist 52(4):550–572

Bobić A (2022) Fundamental rights review. The jurisprudence of constitutional conflict in the European Union. Oxford Studies in European Law, Oxford

Bódig M (2020) Human rights protection and state capacity: the doctrinal implications of the statist character of international human rights law. In: Kasey McCall-Smith et al (eds) Human rights in times of transition. Edward Elgar, pp 64–88

[94] Art. 112 of the Constitution of Dominican Republic (June 13, 2015).

[95] Art. 133 (2) of the Constitution of Ecuador (September 28, 2008).

[96] Art. 203 of the Constitution of Venezuela (December 20, 1999).

Boli J, Thomas GM (1997) World culture in the world polity: a century of international non-governmental organization. Am Sociol Rev 62(2):171–190

Boswell C (2003) The 'external dimension' of EU immigration and asylum policy. Int Aff 79(3): 619–638

Brewer-Carias AR (2011) Constitutional courts as positive legislators. CUP

Cameron BT, Evans B (2024) Policy capacity research: an overview and bibliography of the international literature, 1978 to 2023. Int Rev Public Policy 6(1):110–141

Carozza P, Shelton D (2013) Regional protection of human rights. OUP, New York

Chakim ML (2019) A comparative perspective on constitutional complaint: discussing models, procedures, and decisions. Const Rev 5(1):96–133

Chronowski N, Gárdos-Orosz F (2017) The Hungarian constitutional court and the financial crisis. Hung J Leg Stud 58(2):139–154

Clapham A (2016) Human rights and international criminal law. In: Schabas WA (ed) The Cambridge companion to international criminal law. Cambridge Companions to Law; CUP, pp 11–33

Corder HA (2020) Right to administrative justice: 'new' or just repackaging the old? In: von Arnauld A et al (eds) The Cambridge handbook of new human rights: recognition, novelty, rhetoric. CUP, pp 493–506

Cowan D (2024) What does a super-majority mean and is it something we should worry about? June 18. 2024. https://www.electoral-reform.org.uk/what-does-a-super-majority-mean-and-is-it-something-we-should-worry-about/

Creutzfeldt N (2020) The role of ombuds - a comparative perspective. In: Palmer M et al (eds) Research handbook in comparative law: comparative dispute resolution. Edward Elgar, pp 380–393

de Cecco F (2014) Fundamental freedoms, fundamental rights, and the scope of free movement law. German Law J 15(3):383–406

Dijkstra H, Debre MJ (2022) The death of major international organizations: when institutional stickiness is not enough. Global Stud Q 2.4, ksac048

Domaradzki S et al (2019) Karel Vasak's generations of rights and the contemporary human rights discourse. Hum Rights Rev 20(4):423–443

Donnelly J (2003) Universal human rights in theory and practice, 2nd edn. Cornell University Press, Ithaca

Donnelly J (2011) Human rights. In: Baylis J et al (eds) Globalisation of world politics: introduction to international relations. OUP, Oxford, pp 496–508

Edelenbos J et al (2018) The evolution of community self-organization in interaction with government institutions: cross-case insights from three countries. Am Rev Public Adm 48(1):52–66

Elkins Z et al (2009) Identifying risks to constitutional life. In: Elkins Z et al (eds) The endurance of national constitutions. CUP, Cambridge, pp 6–30

Fariss CJ (2018) The changing standard of accountability and the positive relationship between human rights treaty ratification and compliance. Br J Polit Sci 48(1):239–271

Ferrone V (2017) The rights of history: enlightenment and human rights. Hum Rights Q 39(1):130–141

Flogaitis S et al (eds) (2013) The European Court of Human Rights and its discontents: turning criticism into strength. Edward Elgar Publishing, Cheltenham-Northampton

Follesdal A (2021) International human rights courts and the (international) rule of law: part of the solution, part of the problem, or both? Global Const 10(1):118–138

Gardbaum S (2003) The "horizontal effect" of constitutional rights. Mich Law Rev 102(3):387–459

Gardbaum S (2008) Human rights as international constitutional rights. EJIL 19(4):749–768

Gárdos-Orosz F (2012) The Hungarian constitutional court in transition – from actio popularis to constitutional complaint. Acta Juridica Hungarica 53(4):302–315

Grimm D (2015) The role of fundamental rights after sixty-five years of constitutional jurisprudence in Germany. IJCL 13(1):9–29

Harris D et al (2014) The Law of the European Convention on Human Rights. OUP, Oxford, pp 7–24

Jayawickrama N (2017) The judicial application of human rights law: national, regional and international jurisprudence. CUP, pp 70–101
Joyner DH, Roscini M (2015) Is there any room for the doctrine of fundamental rights of states in today's international law? Introduction. CJI Comp Law 4(3):467–481
Keith LC (2002) Judicial independence and human rights protection around the world. Judicature 85(4):194–200
Keller H et al (2010) Debating the future of the European Court of Human Rights after the Interlaken Conference: two innovative proposals. EJIL 21(4):1025–1048
Kilényi G (1994) Az alkotmányozás és a "kétharmados" törvények. Jogtudományi Közlöny 49(5):201–209
Kukorelli I (1994) Az alkotmányozás néhány koncepcionális kérdése. Magyar Közigazgatás 44(8): 449–456
Marcinkutė L (2011) The role of human rights ngo's: human rights defenders or state sovereignty destroyers? Baltic J Law Polit 4(2):52–77
Munoz P (2012) The possible contribution of international civil society to the protection of human rights. In: Cassese A (ed) Realizing Utopia: the future of international law. OUP, Oxford, pp 75–88
Nederman C, Pasnau R (2009) Individual autonomy. In: Pasnau R (ed) The Cambridge history of Medieval philosophy. CUP, Cambridge, pp 551–564
Oppong RF, Niro LC (2014) Enforcing judgments of international courts in national courts. J Int Dispute Settlement 5(2):344–371
Pasqualucci JM (2003) Introduction. In: The practice and procedure of the Inter-American Court of Human Rights. CUP, pp 1–26
Rauchegger C (2020) National constitutional courts as guardians of the charter: a comparative appraisal of the German Federal Constitutional Court's right to be forgotten judgments. Camb Yearb Eur Leg Stud 22:258–278
Reif LC (2004) The Ombudsman, good governance and the international human rights system. Nijhoff Martinus, Leiden
Rödl F (2013) Fundamental rights, private law, and societal constitution: on the logic of the so-called horizontal effect. Indiana J Global Leg Stud 20(2):1015–1034
Sadurski W (2001) Rights-based constitutional review in Central and Eastern Europe. In: Campbell T et al (eds) Sceptical essays on human rights, Oxford, pp 315–334
Sales É (2022) Le droit constitutionnel de la Ve Republique. 2e Ellipses, Paris
Shaw MN (2008) The international protection of human rights. In: International law. CUP, pp 265–344
Sinani B (2024) Global patterns of constitutional judicial review systems: two major models of constitutional judicial review in the world. Jurid Trib - Rev Comp Int Law 14(1):156–173
Sripati V (2005) National human rights institutions: the ombudsman and its hybrid versions: the emerging actors on the constitutionalism scene. Hum Rights Q 27(3):1137–1142
Szabó M (2012) Changes in the institutional context of the ombudsman system in the Republic of Hungary in 2012. Beijing Law Rev 3(3):112–120
Szentgáli-Tóth B (2017) Qualified law as an instrument for the protection of fundamental right. 125th Book of Abstracts. Romanian Association of Young Scholars (RAYS). Manolache C, Gheorghe A (eds) International Interdisciplinary Doctoral Conference (Bucharest) 29–30 September 2017
Szentgáli-Tóth B (2018) ¿Puede la mayoría cualificada socavar la democracia? El caso de Hungría. Teoría y Realidad Constitucional, Madrid 41(1):419–431
Szentgáli-Tóth B (2020) Supermajority laws as actors of the separation of powers. Hung J Leg Stud 61(2):210–228
Troper M (2008) Constitutional law. In: Berman GA, Etienne P (eds) Introduction to French law. Wolters Kluwer, Netherlands, pp 1–34
Váradi Á (2022) Access to constitutional complaint procedures: a real chance? Hung J Leg Stud 61(4):372–385

Vasak K (1977) Human rights: a thirty-year struggle: the sustained efforts to give force of law to the Universal Declaration of Human Rights. UNESCO Courier 30:11, United Nations Educational, Scientific, and Cultural Organization, Paris

Vašek M (2023) Constitutional jurisdiction and protection of fundamental rights in Europe. In: von Bogdandy A et al (eds) The Max Planck Handbooks in European Public Law: Volume IV: constitutional adjudication: common themes and challenges, Max Planck Handbooks in European Public Law, Oxford, pp 325–382

von Bogdandy A (2012) Reverse solange - protecting the essence of fundamental rights against EU member states. Common Mark Law Rev 49:489–519

Woodiwiss A (2006) The law cannot be enough. Human rights and the limits of legalism. In: Meckled-Garcia S, Cali B (eds) The legalisation of human rights: multidisciplinary perspectives on human rights and human rights law. Routledge, London, pp 30–58

Zysset A, Çalı B (2023) Exhausting domestic remedies or exhausting the rule of law? Revisiting the normative basis of procedural subsidiarity in the European Human Rights System. Transnatl Leg Theory 14(2):157–177

Chapter 7
Supermajority Laws as Factors of Separation of Powers

7.1 The Doctrinal Bases of Separation of Powers

The dogmatic and pragmatic frameworks of separation of powers have determined the development of constitutional and state theory during the last three centuries. Without their conceptualization, a deeper understanding of any modern constitutional design should not be provided.

Prior to the Enlightenment, the unity and transcendent origin of state power served as general views,[1] although ideas that could be evaluated as precursors to the separation of powers had emerged much earlier (for example, Plato divided society into philosophers, soldiers, and workers in his philosophy of the ideal state).[2] In the ancient democratic city-states, such as the Roman Republic and later in the feudal monarchies, strong limits were imposed on executive power. Hoverer, the system of checks and balances did not yet exist in its entirety. At the end of the Middle Ages and in the early modern period, the institutions of the privileged orders often acted against the monarch. In some countries, they even had the right of legal resistance, which is still provided nowadays for all citizens by the constitutions of 42 countries around Latin America, West Europe, and Africa.[3] The right to approve taxes and military recruiting became the strong competence of the privileged orders, and this often proved to be a useful means of thwarting or at least modifying the will of the monarch.[4]

---

[1] Robertson (2015).

[2] Bluck (1959), pp. 166–168.

[3] Ginsburg (2013), pp. 1184–1260.

[4] Bachrach (2022), pp. 1–26.

B. A. Szentgáli-Tóth, *The Past, Present, and Future of Legislation with Supermajority*, Ius Gentium: Comparative Perspectives on Law and Justice 126,
https://doi.org/10.1007/978-3-031-99324-4_7

The idea behind the social limitation of the power of the monarchy was further exacerbated during the Enlightenment in the eighteenth century with regards to the structure of state power. By this time, the theory of unified supreme power of a transcendent origin had become outdated, and thinkers sought to construct a new political structure based on rational considerations that would best serve the interests of the governed. This demand gave rise in France, first with Montesquieu,[5] and then in North America, to the multipolar concept of state power, in which the various factors of power mutually check and constrain each other. Therefore, none of the constitutional actors should gain unilateral power.[6] Almost from the outset, the discussion on the separation of powers was split into two main schools: one that emphasized the separation of powers and the other that highlighted a system of checks and balances. As a result of the last decades, today's theories go beyond the three traditionally elaborated branches of power and open up additional perspectives[7] (for example, with the inclusion of the constitutional court, the media or civil society).

The first idea of the modern separation of powers was developed by Montesquieu in France and was first elaborated and put into practice by the founding fathers of the United States of America.[8] Later, the two aforementioned versions of the theory have been crystallized. One possible interpretation focuses on the separation of powers, which traditionally relies on the combination of three branches of power: the legislative, the executive, and the judicial. These three branches of power are organizationally and personally independent of each other and cannot interact with each other's activities. Safeguards for the separation of powers aim to ensure and underpin the independence of the three branches.

Once again, it should be noted that the system of the legislature, the executive, and the judiciary reflects an approach that has been regularly contested but is still often quoted in academic discourse. Contestants of this theory generally consider several constitutional actors (for example, the head of state, the constitutional court, or the media are mentioned as potential additional branches of power). However, this concept does not take into account the phenomena of the inevitable interaction between the branches of power and describes the organization of the state as the overlapping conducts of several coexisting but almost entirely isolated branches of power.[9] Furthermore, this interpretation cannot comprehend the possible interlocking personalities where the same person is involved in several branches of power (for example, members of parliament also fill a ministerial position).

---

[5] de Montesquieu (1899), pp. 151–162.

[6] The Federalist Papers. No. 51.

[7] Ackermann (2000), pp. 633–729.

[8] Laski (1919).

[9] Gargarella (2022), pp. 124–135.

In my view, the idea of checks and balances might be more suitable to describe the interdependence of various constitutional actors. According to this theory, the branches of power are not entirely independent of each other, since they necessarily mutually affect each other's territory in the performance of their own constitutional functions. Neither branch should enjoy a predominant position vis-á-vis other constitutional stakeholders, the constitutional design should stipulate the interdependent relationships of constitutional players.

Each branch is vested with certain competences to influence the personal composition of the other branches; to approve or review their decisions, to shape the regulatory surroundings and possibly, to outline the organizational structure of other state authorities. Relevant constitutional provisions aim to establish a balance among the competing constitutional actors.[10] This approach therefore highlights the balanced nature of the allocation of competences rather than the autonomy of each constitutional stakeholder. The operation of the State is illustrated by the scope for maneuver of the various constitutional bodies, a system of relations which, according to this logic, should be based on reciprocity. Instead of providing taxonomy of the divided powers, one should focus on the principle of balance between the factors of power that pervades the entire organization of the State.[11]

7.2 The Distinction Between the Two-Thirds and Absolute Majority Models

Regarding the separation of powers, it is paramount to make a clear distinction between the absolute majority and the two-thirds model of supermajority voting. The requirement of a legislative two-thirds majority profoundly alters the relationship between constitutional actors in three main respects.

Firstly, the coexistence of a two-thirds majority and a simple majority provides an additional opportunity for the constitutional court to exercise its power of constitutional review: laws adopted without respecting the supermajority requirement can be annulled by the constitutional court.[12] This aspect of the separation of powers is particularly evident when supermajority laws are subject to mandatory ex ante control. However, the constitutional court would not be able to prevent the disregard of the supermajority requirement unless each law adopted by a simple majority in parliament is also subject to prior constitutional review.

Two-thirds majority legislation also modifies the interlocking nature of government and parliament: pro-governmental majority support could not regulate crucial legislative matters without oppositional votes, so the legislature may even block the will of the executive. In principle, this may also come up in the case of a simple

[10] Holcombe (2018), pp. 1–12.

[11] Vanoni (2019).

[12] Blacher (2021).

majority requirement, but this rarely happens because of the predominance of the pro-government majority in parliaments.[13]

With a two-thirds majority in parliament, the government can unilaterally enforce its intentions and even prevent future governments from changing the laws passed by the initial government. This phenomenon might be described as a temporal aspect of the separation of powers: the room for maneuver of future governments may be considerably narrower as a result of the decisions of the current majority.[14] One can experience such recent tendencies in Hungary, where a two-thirds parliamentary majority has been almost constant since 2010.

The phenomena discussed above should be less significant in the case of an absolute majority model. The less stringent supermajority requirement usually coincides with a pro-government parliamentary majority, so it does not imply a substantive change in the relationship between the government and parliament and, consequently, between the government and parliamentary opposition.[15] The incumbent government could simply rely on limited instruments to narrow the margin of movement of future governments, since supermajority laws should not be amended without oppositional cooperation. The absolute majority model would also concern less the position of the constitutional court, however, the presence of two different legislative proceedings would itself extend the potential grounds of constitutional review.

7.3 The Role of Supermajority Laws in the Relationship Between the Government and the Parliament

In the foregoing, these three main aspects will be investigated, focusing on how supermajority laws, particularly the two-thirds model significantly, affect the separation of powers. Firstly, supermajority law reassesses the relationship between the government and the parliament. Parliament shall constantly control the executive through various means: questions, interpellations, parliamentary reports, and hearings by parliamentary committees.[16] However, their effectiveness is limited when used by pro-government members of parliament who do not intend to criticize governmental actions.[17] Therefore, parliamentary review competences shall be exercised primarily by the opposition, who would really focus on the government's failings and malfunctions. Supermajority always enhances the role of the opposition within parliament, which in turn changes the relationship between government and parliament, and consequently, between government and parliamentary opposition.

---

[13] Laver and Shepsle (1996), pp. 277–288.

[14] Möllers (2013), p. 80.

[15] Szentgáli-Tóth (2020), pp. 210–228.

[16] Aaskoven and Martin (2024), pp. 695–720.

[17] Bateman (2020), pp. 199–226.

As the role of the opposition comes to the fore, the government has to pay more attention to managing the parliamentary stages of legislation and to address the implications caused by the exercise of parliamentary scrutiny. In the case of a strong supermajority requirement, the opposition would be able to influence the work of the government, use parliamentary obstruction more extensively, and even undermine the feasibility of parliamentary work. The means of parliamentary scrutiny allows for the gradual contestation of certain governmental policies, while the means of parliamentary publicity enable perceived or alleged governmental wrongdoing to be brought to the attention of the wider political community.

In the traditional system of Westminster parliamentarianism, parliament may occasionally overrule the actions of the executive by its decisions. However, such conflicts are counted as extraordinary, and this framework could not function effectively without strong cooperation between the government and the legislature. In France (albeit under a semi-presidential system rather than a parliamentary one), the case of cohabitation illustrates the complications that might arise once the president of the republic and the legislative majority rely on different political values. In such a case, the government's endeavors should primarily not be devoted to the implementation of its ideas, but to the political and constitutional struggle with the legislature.

As the other side of the coin, if the legislature does not unreservedly support the government's policies, the government's proposals may be significantly revised in the course of the parliamentary debates (and behind-the-scenes of inter-party negotiations). Supermajority law may also feature the reallocation of substantial debates from the internal forums of parliamentary parties to inter-party consultations. These special informal forums may easily conclude more inclusive compromises on the one hand, or may overturn well-founded professional arguments for the sake of wider political consent on the other hand.[18]

If separation of powers functions properly, the government's task during its term is to put its plans into practice, while the opposition seeks to change or even prevent the government's intentions, and to win the voters' trust in order to receive a greater number of votes in the forthcoming elections. Obviously, either the government or the opposition constitutes dynamic components of the framework: these positions might be easily altered depending on the election results.

The implementation of supermajority reconsiders this hypothetical model: the opposition can become a substantive factor in the legislation on supermajority subjects, without its agreement these statutes cannot be amended. This reconsideration may lead to controversial consequences as follows. On the one hand, the most important statutes should not be amended unilaterally by the governmental majority, which underlines the role of this requirement as a safeguard. On the other hand, two-thirds majority legislation makes it impossible to govern the country by elevating the major opposition forces to quasi-legislative status.

[18] Poppe et al. (2019), pp. 759–776.

Supermajority voting therefore limits the government's room for maneuver in terms of the separation of powers. The government must be given a wide margin of discretion to shape the legislative environment and policy orientations during its term of office. This margin of movement shall not be unlimited; however, the competences of constitutional actors should not prevent the government from making the necessary decisions to tackle the current challenges. Each model of supermajority voting was originally designed to reflect on this context: its aim is to ensure that the government does not have a free hand in key legislative matters, and that other political forces shall also be involved in decision-making.

In the meantime, one should also raise the question of whether the theory of separation of powers which limits the government's ability to maneuver, could justify depriving the government of the possibility to make decisions on crucial legislative issues. If an affirmative answer were given to this question, the prolongement theory would provide the main argument: constitutional rules should be detailed by a set of statutory rules on the most important legislative subjects, thus supermajority requirement would ensure the broadest possible consent behind these provisions. From the other side of the question, the governmental mandate received from the voters would be undermined if the incumbent government were denied access to the most impactful laws.[19] Arguments and counterarguments outline a complex issue, the only certain statement that can be made is that supermajority voting weakens the position of the government in relation to parliament and strengthens the role of the latter. However, we should also be aware that these trends could be reversed if the government were to obtain stable two-thirds parliamentary backing.

Supermajorities also generate a significant impact on the political surrounding of legislation. As a consequence, the government is constantly forced to negotiate with other political parties in order to enforce its will. Therefore, supermajority laws should be understood in the context of the relationship between the government and the opposition, rather than the government and the parliament. This context distinguishes modern supermajority laws from their historical predecessors.[20] For instance, from a separation of powers perspective, the current cardinal laws in Hungary show fewer meaningful similarities compared to a historical legal institution with the same name but significantly different content.[21]

[19] Debbasch (2021), pp. 136–137; 166–168; 277–289;

[20] Küpper (2014), p. 3.

[21] Küpper (2014), p. 4.

7.4 The Role of Supermajority Laws on the Relationship Between the Government and the Constitutional Court

Supermajority laws always extend the margin of movement of constitutional courts vis-á-vis governments and parliaments. In addition to examining other aspects, Constitutional Courts also take into account a further potential ground of constitutional review, whether the law in question has been adopted by the parliament with the appropriate majority.

Several constitutional courts have stated that the requirement of a supermajority does not constitute a question of form but of substance,[22] but we are not aware of any country where a Constitutional Court decision has annulled a law adopted with a supermajority on the ground that the law has been adopted exclusively with the votes of one political formation. In the practice of constitutional courts, therefore, a supermajority as a substantive constitutionality criterion primarily sets a numerical, not a substantive category. Consequently, the involvement of the opposition amounts to a political, rather than a constitutional requirement.[23]

In the meantime, the role of the constitutional court increases when scrutinizing supermajority laws. However, at the same time, its politicization would also be strengthened, as the constitutional court should issue politically sensitive rulings on the constitutionality of supermajority laws. The weight of constitutional review would emerge due to the stricter demands set for amending or repealing supermajority provisions by the parliament. Therefore, the constitutional court would bear additional responsibility to enforce constitutional standards within the domain of supermajority law, since other potential mechanisms to redress unconstitutional supermajority legislation would require a long series of negotiations with unpredictable outcomes.

As a further aspect of constitutional review, the depth of supermajority legislation in the enumerated supermajority legislative fields may be surrounded by additional uncertainties, even if separate clauses specify exactly the supermajority provisions in each law, as is currently the case in Austria and Hungary.[24] The question also arises regarding such aforementioned clauses: are they in accordance with the constitutional rules? Has the legislator not exceeded its constitutional space of maneuver by imposing the supermajority requirement for the enactment of certain statutory provisions?[25] These questions must be answered by Constitutional Courts as the main bodies of constitutional review and their decisions would be binding on all interested parties.

A prior constitutional review on supermajority laws, especially the mandatory prior constitutional review would also influence the position of constitutional courts

---

[22] To set some examples: 4/1993. (II. 12.) AB decision, ABH 1993, 48; JCC no. 236-2007; n° 84-177 DC du 30 aout 1984.

[23] Pozsár-Szentmiklósy (2017), pp. 281–290.

[24] Szente (2017), pp. 456–475.

[25] Jacqué (2022), p. 246.

among the constitutional actors. Constitutional courts would be forced to be involved in the political discourse more actively, as a clear position would have to be taken on each supermajority law before promulgation. Constitutional courts might thus become a truly negative legislator: not only the parliament but also the constitutional court should decide in favor of a supermajority law to enter into force.[26]

Thus, through the mandatory ex ante constitutional review, constitutional courts quasi become legislators (similar to what we have already observed in the relationship between the parliamentary opposition and the supermajority requirement). The constitutional court would not only participate in the legislative process occasionally, but its affirmative ruling would be required for the validity of each supermajority law. On the one hand, this partial and quasi-legislative status significantly strengthens the position of the constitutional court; while on the other hand, it calls into question its independence, since such a body would permanently participate in an inherently political process.

If the supermajority law has been implemented and the constitutional court is also vested with the competence to review the content of constitutional amendments, further points should complete the analysis. The substantial review of constitutional amendments presupposes the existence of legal norms above the constitution or the identification of principles that the constitution cannot undermine.[27] If these assumptions were accepted, the constitutional review of supermajority laws would play only a secondary role behind the competence of the constitutional court to examine the constitutional amendments. If supermajority laws should be interpreted as extensions of the constitution, amendments to supermajority laws might also be understood as quasi-constitutional amendments.

In the absence of substantive review of constitutional amendments, the constitutional court may be able to intervene in issues of constitutional significance through the review of supermajority laws. As a consequence, the constitutional court's space of maneuver would be largely limited to quasi-constitutional supermajority legislation, since the crucial rules setting out the basic framework would be included in the constitution, inaccessible to the constitutional court.

If a substantive review of constitutional amendments is provided, supermajority laws shall comply with at least two levels of norms above them. Substantive review of constitutional amendments would serve as the primary vehicle to assess paramount issues. The constitutional review of supermajority laws would also refer to that constitutional text, which might also be influenced by the constitutional court. The decisions taken in the review of supermajority laws cannot be in conflict with those taken in the review of constitutional amendments. In the relationship between the constitutional court and the government, the constitutional review of supermajority laws could therefore be of only secondary importance.[28]

---

[26] Chabrier and Haudrechy (2020), p. 89.

[27] Garlicki and Garlicka-Sowers (2018), pp. 307–317.

[28] Pardo-Álvarez (2023), pp. 1–28.

One may conclude that supermajority voting increases the weight of the constitutional court vis-à-vis other constitutional actors. However, some further pieces shall be added to complete this complex puzzle. The constitutional court may review supermajority laws considering a formal standing: if the supermajority requirement has not been met, the supermajority law would be nullified as void.[29] In addition to the exclusively formal ground, substantial points might also be examined during the constitutional review: the Constitutional Court investigates whether the supermajority legislation complies in all respects with constitutional requirements.

Obviously, one can easily experience the excessive entanglement of the two levels of the review as follows. Under the formal prong, the sufficient parliamentary consent behind the legislation shall be checked. Moreover, partly within the framework of the substantive approach, the constitutional court will focus on whether the legislator applied the broad consensus requirement in accordance with the constitutionally provided scope of supermajority. This step of the review assumes the joint reading of constitutional provisions establishing a supermajority requirement and the wording of statutory rules adopted with heightened consent.[30] In several cases, supermajority and ordinary provisions would appear within the same act, forming an almost indivisible unity; constitutional courts have the duty to provide orientation for the proper distinction of these mixed provisions.[31] Finally, supermajority laws might also be examined from a fully substantive point of view: these norms must be as consistent with the substantive constitutional provisions as ordinary laws. For instance, the same standards shall be respected under either majority scheme for the restrictions of fundamental rights.[32]

Turning back to the inevitable politicization of constitutional courts, this stems from the elections of the constitutional judges, which are usually governed by actors with clear political engagement.[33] Moreover, constitutional rulings affecting legislation would be reflected by all political stakeholders who would deepen the obvious link between constitutional courts and political actors.[34]

Apart from this, in making their decisions, constitutional judges cannot ignore the social and political constellation of their rulings. As a consequence, instead of independence, the terminology of the autonomy of the constitutional court—according to which it cannot be instructed or directly influenced by external actors—may be more plausible.[35] Evidently, the connection between the constitutional court and the political sphere should not be rejected but should be considered as an inherent

---

[29] 75-62 DC du 28 janvier 1976, 87-228 DC du 26 juin 1987, 88-242 DC du 10 mars 1988; 86-217 DC du 18 septembre 1986; 1/2017. (I. 17.) AB decision, ABH 2017, 3.

[30] Szentgáli-Tóth (2022).

[31] N° 86-217, DC du 18 septembre 1986; 4/1993. (II. 12.) AB decision, ABH 1993, 48; 1/1999. (II. 24.) AB decision, ABH 1999, 25.
Camby (1998), p. 1695.

[32] Caviedes (2022), pp. 1162–1187.

[33] Tiede (2020), pp. 1092–1123.

[34] Huber (2023), pp. 547–590.

[35] Castillo-Ortiz (2020), pp. 617–655.

necessity in the specific features of modern constitutional functioning. Tension may arise when political actors attempt to take over the role of the constitutional court or seek to circumvent it, thereby undermining its authority as recently happened in populist regimes such as Poland and Hungary.[36]

The presence of supermajority law would invigorate governmental efforts to gain dominance over the constitutional court, while the coexistence of supermajority law and mandatory a priori review would amplify such governmental ambitions. In principle, mandatory a priori constitutional review strengthens the position of constitutional courts, but in reality its impact very much depends on (1) the dominant strands of constitutional interpretation, (2) the constitutional court's perception of its own role and (3) the applicable procedural rules. It might therefore not be objectionable in itself that supermajority legislation reinforces the relationship between the constitutional court and the political sphere. However, if this entanglement evolves too excessively, or is even unilaterally controlled by the political actors, it may hinder the proper functioning of constitutional courts.

In the following, the distinction between the formal and substantial aspects of supermajority laws' constitutional review shall be revisited. The formal aspect intends to enable the constitutional court to enforce the supermajority in practice. If the constitutional court were not able to review the compliance with the supermajority requirement, the implementation of the supermajority law would result in simply a facade concept and the appreciation would depend on the governmental will. Since the supermajority requirement makes broad consensus a paramount element of the legislative process, adequate safeguards should be provided to ensure compliance with this demand.

In the following, the distinction between the formal and substantial aspects of Constitutional Courts may therefore be examined in order to determine the fulfillment of broad consent in specific cases, or to interpret the scope of supermajority legislation within a particular act in light of the constitutional clauses establishing an enhanced majority. In the latter case, formal and substantial arguments should be combined, as the specific application of a supermajority should not be justified unless the content of the reviewed norms is taken into account as well.

To demonstrate this, the Fundamental Law of Hungary differentiates between prescribing a supermajority for the detailed rules of a particular subject, or and simply limiting the scope of heightened consent requirement to the fundamental principles of the pension system or taxation.[37] As an additional example, Spanish and Hungarian case law only cover the essential safeguards of fundamental rights falling under the scope of a supermajority. To clarify these issues, in my view, constitutional courts should elaborate a so-called depth-test to orient legislation and also constitutional interpretation in outlining the constitutional standards for establishing the exact scope of the supermajority requirement.

[36] Szente (2023), pp. 127–155.

[37] Art. I (4) and 40 of the Fundamental Law of Hungary (April 25, 2011).

The structure of each supermajority legislative field would determine the distinction between a supermajority and ordinary provisions. Once the constitutional background of the supermajority requirement is considered, examining the content of a provision would not aim to enforce the complete set of constitutional standards, but only to determine whether certain rules fall beyond the constitutionally stipulated scope of a supermajority. However, a complete substantial constitutional review of supermajority laws relies on much broader constitutional and legal bases; all rules that are above the supermajority law in the hierarchy of legal sources must be taken into account. These can usually be identified with the Constitution, but further complications might also arise. One case would be the aforementioned hierarchy within the constitution, when several levels of norms may stand above the supermajority law.

What is more, supermajority laws do not form a homogeneous category either; certain hierarchy might also be established between them. An example from Azerbaijan, Hungary, and Montenegro has constitutionally distinguished multiple forms of supermajority. In France and also in several Francophone African countries, the organic law on public finances has quasi-constitutional character either explicitly by the constitution, or the case law of the constitutional courts. Therefore, these laws might supersede other organic laws. Additionally, in France, Spain and Hungary, a separate group of supermajority laws that limit the sovereignty of the State is constituted.[38] Apart from this, in Spain, organic laws regulating the status of autonomous communities are distinguished from other supermajority laws and subject to mandatory a priori constitutional review.[39] When conducting a substantial constitutional review of supermajority laws, all of these specificities should be taken into consideration.

7.5 Supermajority Laws as Limits on the Margin of Movement of Future Governments

Supermajority laws affect not only the horizontal but also the temporal dimension of the separation of powers originally conceptualized in the judicial context.[40] I have previously mentioned the potential constellation where a government enjoys the confidence of a two-thirds majority in parliament and could unilaterally amend supermajority laws. This configuration illustrates that the separation of powers should not be described as a static concept that applies to a particular moment in time, but also has to be considered in terms of its temporal extension both in the

[38] Art. E (4) of the Fundamental Law of Hungary (April 25, 2011); 1260/B/1997. (II. 09.) AB decision, ABH 1998, 816; Art. 88 (3) of the Constitution of France (October 4, 1958); Art. 104 (1) of the Constitution of Spain (January 4, 1978).

[39] Chofre Sirvent (1994), pp. 215–224.

[40] Beck (2012), pp. 1405–1464.

legislative and executive context. If the incumbent government were to revise supermajority laws, and forthcoming governments would not have a realistic chance to reconsider them, the room for maneuver for future executive power would be remarkably restricted.[41]

Supermajority would therefore reconsider the operation of parliamentarism, not only temporarily but also in the longer term.[42] The temporal dimension of the separation of powers highlights the fact that the widespread presence of supermajority laws can be detrimental to all political actors in the long term, especially in light of the changing political landscape. Most efforts that run counter to the separation of powers tend to distress the system of checks and balances on a temporary basis. However, supermajority laws misused by a two-thirds parliamentary majority could then preserve the pillars of the legal system for decades, pushing reform attempts beyond the limits of legality. As a consequence, behind the seemingly stable legal system, tensions arise on behalf of the opponents of the incumbent constitutional regime. Groups of interest that are excluded from unilateral legislation will seize every opportunity to assert their positions which will widen the distance between the government and the opposition.[43] The logic of parliamentarianism implies that a government has limited but extensive powers to implement its plans during its term of office. However, the powers it receives can only last until the end of the government's political term. In fact, unilateral changes to supermajority laws can be interpreted as an overreach of the government's authority. Obviously, from the government's point of view, such a move constitutes a matter of necessity, justified by the opposition's lack of or limited willingness to cooperate.

The two-thirds majority path has recently had an effect, primarily in Hungary,[44] but certain elements have also been experienced in Romania and Austria. Due to the overwhelming dominance of the absolute majority model among the constitutions operating with supermajority, these concerns are irrelevant for most of the constitutional frameworks. If the absolute majority is applied, the exact proportion of parliamentary majority would be less weighty. The simple parliamentary majority would be able to revise all statutes without exceptions. The risk factors entailed by the two-thirds requirement would not appear under the absolute majority demand: either the incumbent or the forthcoming governments could revise supermajority laws. Thus, the absolute majority would downplay the temporal dimension of the separation of powers.

An absolute majority is therefore less far-reaching in this regard, as the incumbent government, regardless of its majority, could not limit the room for maneuver of future governments to a large extent.

---

[41] Möllers (2013), p. 80.

[42] Forteza et al. (2024).

[43] Forteza et al. (2024).

[44] Halmai (2018), pp. 323–339.

By contrast, if both constitutional amendments and supermajority laws were subject to various forms of two-thirds majority support,[45] an overly rigid constitutional framework might be constructed. As I have pointed out before, stability of the constitutional order might be seen as an imperative value in itself, but to rule out any reasonable possibility of amendment might be a risky perspective: the overarching aim of the opposition will be evidently to overthrow the entire constitutional order instead of revising it.

The significance of temporal separation of powers also depends heavily on the exact scope of supermajority law. The institutional framework and the catalogue as well as safeguards of fundamental rights outline the main values of a political community. Therefore, broad consent may secure the agreement of at least most of the political stakeholders participating in the drafting on these features. However, for public policy matters, the same demand might be more difficult to justify. To set an example, the current Hungarian Fundamental Law classifies the basic regulation of the tax system, the pension system, and the system for acquiring ownership of agricultural land as supermajority subjects.[46] By contrast, in Romania and Moldova, the criminal code and the criminal procedure code are also subject to supermajority,[47] which has rarely been experienced when major codes have been concerned. If, in addition to the key institutions and fundamental rights, public policy issues and the main legal codes were at least partly removed from the inalienable elements of governance, very little room for navigation would be left for the government.

In modern constitutional arrangements, it is important to have a clear separation between the rules that underpin the defining social/political subjects and governmental policies. For these paramount rules, a supermajority would rely on compelling arguments, but weaker justification might be found when a supermajority is applied to regulate less significant issues. Political parties elaborate on various ideas concerning the tax and pension system, healthcare, education, and many other sectors that serve the daily functioning of society and are discussed intensely during electoral campaign periods.[48] It should be noted that even in these areas, the coverage of key principles by the supermajority requirement would be hardly objectionable. Nevertheless, one should recall, as a counterargument, the lack of an objective standard to delimit the scope of broad consent. Significance appears as a potential ground for classification, but without sufficient content to establish a predictable scale. My final point here, however, is that the rules implementing public policy, or at least the basic principles thereof as well as the main legal codes shall be left to the discretion of the incumbent government. Without amendment, the relevant codes

---

[45] Two-thirds majority of all deputies; or the two-thirds vote of parliamentarians who are present.

[46] Art. P (2) and Art. 40 of the Fundamental Law of Hungary (April 11, 2011).

[47] Art. 72 (3) f of the Constitution of Romania (December 21, 1991); Art. 72 (3) n. of the Constitution of Moldova (July 29, 1994).

[48] Ahrens (2024), pp. 77–100.

regulating a wide range of societal relations, such as the aforementioned criminal codes in Romania and Moldova, may lose their living instrument character.[49]

Despite the differences between countries of varying degrees, the subject areas covered all aspects of the separation of powers. Supermajority law usually regulates the functioning of Parliament, the status of courts and judges, the status of constitutional courts and constitutional judges, the legal status of the Ombudsperson and the State Audit Office. The basic contours of separation of powers shall be outlined in the constitution, but should have been implemented as supermajority law; the details would be incorporated into supermajority laws. Vertical separation of powers might also be relevant: in states with federal or autonomous communities, the legal status of these entities usually falls beyond the terrain of supermajority law. Spain and the Latin American countries that are transplanting the Spanish model assign this function to supermajority law. The relations between the central government and the autonomous communities are governed in these countries by organic laws.[50]

7.6 Supermajority Laws as an Actor of Separation of Powers: Additional Remarks to the Comparison Between National Constitutional Systems

Several concrete examples have already been mentioned to demonstrate the comparative insights analyzing the role of legislative supermajority in formulating the contours of separation of powers. To summarize these findings, three highly relevant legal systems in my topic, France, Spain, and Hungary, will be examined presenting different models from the perspective of how the presence of supermajority voting affects the separation of powers.

In France, one of the leading considerations behind the introduction of organic law was the rebalancing of the separation of powers. De Gaulle and his supporters accused the misconceptualized rules of the 1946 Constitution establishing the Fourth Republic of providing overbroad competences for the Parliament, making stable government impossible due to the lack of a permanent parliamentary majority behind the government. In practice, the legislative branch has been the dominant constitutional actor during the Fourth Republic rather than the executive power. De Gaulle considered this overbearing position of the Parliament as the primary reason for the instability experienced during the Fourth Republic. Therefore, his constitutional reforms aimed at restricting parliamentary supremacy. Organic law played an important role in this context with the establishment of an absolute parliamentary

[49] Anghel (2022), pp. 86–107.

[50] Art. 81 (1) of the Constitution of Spain (January 4, 1978); Art. 195 of the Constitution of the Dominican Republic (June 13, 2015); Art. 133 (3) of the Constitution of Ecuador (September 28, 2008); Art. 16 and 169 of the Constitution of Venezuela (December 20, 1999).

majority behind crucial decisions and providing mandatory, prior constitutional review over organic laws.[51]

In France, therefore, organic laws increase the role of the Constitutional Council, although since 2008, the limited possibility of ex post review has also been introduced. However, ex post review shall not contest the disregard of the required legislative majority; the organic law should be in conflict as regards its content with any constitutional section.[52] French Organic laws determine the status of the President of the Republic, the way in which members of the legislature are elected, and the framework of the judiciary, so their scope would imply the constitutional spectrum. While the two-thirds model of supermajority laws seeks to tie the hands of the government, the French absolute majority model introduces checks and balances into the legislative process. The presence of mandatory prior constitutional review and the exclusion of a vote of confidence linked to the adoption of an organic law illustrate this difference excellently.

In Spain, organic laws are contextualized in the light of the vertical separation of powers. Organic laws that regulate the status of autonomous communities and the relationship between the central government and territorial units should be clearly distinguished from other fields of supermajority legislation. The several autonomous communities of Spain represent enormous territory, population, and economic potential. Therefore, this function of organic laws should not be underestimated. Note that Spain relies on an absolute majority model of supermajority in a bicameral parliamentary structure, and that mandatory prior constitutional review has also been implemented, but only for organic laws regulating the status of autonomous communities. In addition, organic laws in Spain also lay down the succession of the throne, framework for the functioning of the judiciary and the legislature, and provide for the status and competences of the Constitutional Court. Spanish organic laws therefore mainly influence the vertical and horizontal separation of powers by means of direct regulation. Other aspects outlined in Sects. 7.3–7.5 have less relevance due to the less demanding form of supermajority required.

In Hungary, one faces various implications of successive supermajority law models. Constitutional laws have overestimated the protection of political minorities as the primary value and have considered broad consensus as the main tool of decision-making. It has been analyzed that due to its inconsistency with parliamentarism, this approach was not feasible in the long run. Laws adopted with a two-thirds majority continued to focus on protecting parliamentary opposition but did so within a rationalized framework. The opposition could still participate in paramount parliamentary decisions, but the scope of such supermajority legislation was outlined by more precise terms.[53] This relative balance was disrupted after 1994, when over two thirds of the MPs supported the left-wing government. This marked the first Hungarian experience of a two-thirds parliamentary "steamroller", although

[51] Le Divellec and de Villiers (2022), pp. 236–237.

[52] Décision en 2012. 278 QPC du 5 Octobre 2012; CC, 25 mars 2014, 2014-386 QPC.

[53] Smuk (2007), pp. 62–73.

the parliamentary supermajority showed some restraint in unilateral legislation and constitution-making partly due to internal tensions within the governmental coalition.[54] Over the course of two decades having two-thirds laws, several advantages and disadvantages of the supermajority requirement were observed in the relationship of the government and the parliament, as well as the constitutional court.

During 2010–2011, the adoption of the Fundamental Law resulted in the reconsideration of several constitutional relations. Apart from the changing regulatory and institutional landscape, the stable two-thirds pro-governmental parliamentary majority backing of FIDESZ governments also put cardinal laws in a completely new perspective: rules included in these acts would be very demanding to be revised within the foreseeable future. In the list of cardinal laws, fundamental rights have been replaced by public policy issues, so the Fundamental Law contains stronger restrictions on a simple governmental majority than the previous Constitution of Hungary.[55]

As for conclusion, supermajority law may affect the separation of powers by either tying the hand of the government or the parliament. The absolute majority model weakens the position of the parliament, while the two-thirds majority requirement—where the governing party does not have a two-thirds parliamentary majority—serves as a means of limiting the governmental margin of movement. Supermajority shall not only be interpreted in the context of the relationship between the government and parliament but also significantly impacts the position of the constitutional court. As a result of these considerations, one may draw the conclusion that supermajority law may have a limited contribution to developing a rational model of checks and balances; it may give some actors excessive power and exclude others from decision-making. It leads us to conclude, once more, that the disadvantages of supermajority law would outweigh its potential advantages if its scope is overbroad. Therefore, its coverage should be severely limited.

References

Aaskoven L, Martin S (2024) Parliamentary control of the executive and the duration of government formation. Legis Stud Q 49(3):695–720

Ackermann B (2000) The new separation of powers. Harv Law Rev 113(2):633–729

Ahrens L (2024) The impact of public opinion on voting and policymaking. Zeitschrift für Politikwissenschaft 34(1):77–100

Anghel V (2022) Minority governments in Romania: a case of stable instability. In: Field B, Martin S (eds) Minority governments in comparative perspective. OUP, pp 86–107

Bachrach DS (2022) Introduction. In: The foundations of royal power in early medieval Germany: material resources and governmental administration in a Carolingian successor state. Boydell & Brewer, pp 1–26

[54] Kukorelli (1994), pp. 449–456.

[55] Smuk (2016), pp. 75–82.

Bateman W (2020) Failure of parliamentary control. In: Public finance and parliamentary constitutionalism. CUP, pp 199–226
Beck R (2012) Transtemporal separation of powers in the law of precedent. Notre Dame Law Rev 87(4):1405–1464
Blacher P (2021) Droit constitutionell. 8e. Hachette Supérieur, Livre, Paris
Bluck RS (1959) Plato's 'ideal' state. Class Q 9(2):166–168
Camby JP (1998) Quarante ans de lois organiques. Revue de droit publique 5-6:1686–1698
Castillo-Ortiz P (2020) The dilemmas of constitutional courts and the case for a new design of Kelsenian institutions. Law Philos 39(6):617–655
Caviedes C (2022) A core case for supermajority rules in constitutional adjudication. IJCL 20(3):1162–1187
Chabrier L, Haudrechy B (2020) Droit constitutionnel de la Ve republique. Ellipses Édition Marketing S A, Paris
Chofre Sirvent JF (1994) Significado y función de las leyes orgánicas. Tecnos, Madrid
de Montesquieu CS (1899) The spirit of laws (trans: Nugent T). 2 vols. The Colonial Press, New York 1, pp 151–162
Debbasch R (2021) Droit constitutionnel. 13e Lexis Nexis, Paris
Forteza A et al (2024) Can political gridlock undermine checks and balances? A lab experiment. J Behav Exp Econ 108(3):102–128
Gargarella R (2022) Checks and balances: combining "institutional means and personal motives." In: The law as a conversation among equals. Cambridge studies in constitutional law. CUP, pp 124–135
Garlicki L, Garlicka-Sowers ZA (2018) Unconstitutional constitutional amendments. Vienna J Int Constitutional Law 12(3):307–317
Ginsburg T et al (2013) The right to resist in the world's constitutions. UCLA Law Rev 60(5):1184–1260
Halmai G (2018) Is there such thing as 'populist constitutionalism'? The case of Hungary. Fudan J Humanit Soc Sci 11(3):323–339
Holcombe RG (2018) Checks and balances: enforcing constitutional constraints. Economies 6(4):1–12
Huber PM (2023) Constitutional courts and politics in the European legal space. In: von Bogdandy A et al (eds) The Max Planck handbooks in European public law: Volume IV: Constitutional adjudication: common themes and challenges, Max Planck handbooks in European public law. Oxford, pp 547–590
Jacqué JP (2022) Droit constitutionnel et institutions politiques. 14é Dalloz, Paris, p 246
Kukorelli I (1994) Az alkotmányozás néhány koncepcionális kérdése. Magyar Közigazgatás 44(8):449–456
Küpper H (2014) A kétharmados/sarkalatos törvények jelensége a magyar jogrendszerben. MTA law working papers 46:2–5
Laski HJ (1919) Authority in modern state. YUP, New Haven
Laver M, Shepsle KA (1996) (eds) Governments and parliaments. In: Making and breaking governments: cabinets and legislatures in parliamentary democracies. Political economy of institutions and decisions. CUP, pp 277–288
Le Divellec A, de Villiers M (2022) Dictionnaire du droit constitutionnel. 13é Dalloz, Paris
Möllers C (2013) The three branches: a comparative model of separation of powers. OUP, Oxford, p 80
Pardo-Álvarez D (2023) The sovereign minority: the supermajority rule for constitutional amendments. Revista de Investigações Constitucionais 10(3):1–28
Poppe AE et al (2019) Introduction: negotiating the promotion of democracy. Democratization 26(5):759–776
Pozsár-Szentmiklósy Z (2017) Supermajority in parliamentary systems – a concept of substantive legislative supermajority: lessons from Hungary. Hung J Leg Stud 58(3):281–290

Robertson J (2015) The enlightenment. A very short introduction (Very short introductions). OUP, Oxford

Smuk P (2007) Ellenzéki jogok a parlamentben, különös tekintettel a parlament ellenőrzési tevékenységére. Jogtudományi Közlöny 62(2):62–73

Smuk P (2016) Az Országgyűlés hatáskörgyakorlása az Alaptörvény hatalommegosztási rendszerében. Iustum Aequum Salutare 12(4):75–82

Szente Z (2017) Challenging the basic values–problems in the rule of law in Hungary and the failure of the EU to tackle them. In: Jakab A, Kochenov D (eds) The enforcement of EU law and values: ensuring Member States' compliance. Oxford Academic, pp 456–475

Szente Z (2023) The myth of populist constitutionalism in Hungary and Poland: populist or authoritarian constitutionalism? IJCL 21(1):127–155

Szentgáli-Tóth B (2020) Supermajority laws as actors of the separation of powers. Hung J Leg Stud 61(2):210–228

Szentgáli-Tóth B (2022) Organic/cardinal laws. In: Grote R et al (eds) Max Planck Encyclopedia of Comparative Constitutional Law (MPECCoL) OUP, Oxford, Paper e302

Tiede LB (2020) Mixed judicial selection and constitutional review. Comp Polit Stud 53(7):1092–1123

Vanoni LP (2019) Checks and balances. Max Planck Encyclopedia of Comparative Constitutional Law [MPECCoL] 220. https://oxcon.ouplaw.com/display/10.1093/law-mpeccol/law-mpeccol-e220

Part III
The Perspectives of Supermajority Law

Chapter 8
Proposals for Future Constitution-Making Processes

8.1 The Possible Main Directions of Reconsidering Current Supermajority Law Concepts

In the previous chapters, I have discussed in detail the arguments that underpin the existence of supermajority laws. Based on these analyses, it can be concluded that the disadvantages of the current supermajority law concepts outweigh the advantages. Therefore, alternatives should be sought to maintain the benefits while being able to eliminate the unwanted externalities. Several possible ways of future development might be outlined.

Firstly, in the context of the hierarchy of legal sources, the relationship between the statutory and regulatory levels could be revisited. In parliamentary systems, statutes have traditionally covered a very broad range of legal relations, whereas in many semi-presidential constitutional frameworks, governance through regulations based on parliamentary authorization has been widely accepted. Taking this model into account, a shift in this direction may be feasible in parliamentary systems as well.

Secondly, certain stages of the legislative process might be reconsidered, for example, by introducing a longer preparatory period, institutionalizing a moratorium on the adoption of legislation, or establishing additional parliamentary commissions to discuss supermajority bills. In the final stage of the legislative process, the guarantee of mandatory prior constitutional review could also be an inevitable part of the legislative process for supermajority laws.

Furthermore, some experts argue that any existing requirement for an elevated majority in legislation should be eliminated from constitutions without any corrective measures.[1] The introduction of a second chamber, or vesting the existing

[1] Szente (2017), pp. 456–475.

B. A. Szentgáli-Tóth, *The Past, Present, and Future of Legislation with Supermajority*, Ius Gentium: Comparative Perspectives on Law and Justice 126,
https://doi.org/10.1007/978-3-031-99324-4_8

second parliamentary chamber with additional competences concerning supermajority legislation, could also be investigated. However, the consequences of such steps would go far beyond the issue of supermajority legislation. For this reason, the potential replacement of supermajority law with bicameral legislation has not been discussed in depth by this volume. However, this possibility should also be kept in mind for potential future references.

Thirdly, the constitution would explicitly specify the scope of legislative fields. In matters falling beyond this exhaustive enumeration, the government may regulate by decree, subject to parliamentary approval and review. In my opinion, the concept of supermajority law should have a limited scope, focusing only on a few subjects that are crucial for the organization of the state.

8.2 The Possible Reconsideration of the Hierarchy of Norms

Supermajority law could be mentioned explicitly among the main categories of legal sources and should be placed clearly under the constitutional level but above ordinary laws. This would remove several sources of dogmatic disputes from the constitutional framework: it would be beyond doubt what role supermajority laws play in the constitutional review, as well as the fact that supermajority laws fall outside the constitution, even in the broadest sense of this term.[2]

As a consequence, no supermajority and ordinary provisions could be placed in the same law, and each law shall explicitly provide its character as a supermajority or ordinary statute. If a rule is placed in an inappropriate law (for example, a supermajority provision in an ordinary law or vice versa), the constitutional court would annul the rule in question. Supermajority laws would not necessarily be distinguished from ordinary laws by virtue of a supermajority. Instead, additional guarantees could be provided by mandatory prior constitutional review or partial rethinking of the legislative process.

It would not be permissible to incorporate supermajority and ordinary provisions into the same law, as this practice features controversial doctrinal concepts over supermajority laws. While a perfect separation would be hardly imaginable for the current large number of supermajority laws, it may be a more feasible objective for a narrower range of those. If parliamentary intentions were to remain to enact the abrogated provisions, those should be adopted again by the legislature in accordance with each formal requirement set by the constitution, including the appropriate choice between supermajority and ordinary legislation.

In such a scenario, not only should the substantive constitutional requirements be complied with, but also if an ordinary statutory provision was included in a supermajority law or vice versa, the constitutional court could still annul it on the grounds of

[2] La décision du CC, n° 84-177 DC du 30 aout 1984; JCC no. 11/1981, 8 April 1981; 1/1999. (II. 24.) AB decision, ABH 1999, 25.

the rule of law and legal certainty. Similar mechanisms have already been in place for the enactment of annual budget laws: the adoption or amendment of an annual budget law, although not a supermajority law, cannot be merged in certain countries with the adoption or amendment of any other statute.[3]

8.3 The Reconsideration of the Procedural Rules

The legislative process can be an important arena for seeking safeguards that potentially replace elevated majority voting. At this point, the potential guarantee mechanisms should be divided into two main subgroups: one need to distinguish between the parliamentary stage of the legislative process and the stage between the adoption of a bill and its promulgation. In the parliamentary phase, three possible solutions shall be highlighted. On the one hand, additional parliamentary commissions could be incorporated into the current legislative mechanism, which would deal exclusively with supermajority laws. This model may increase the depth of legislation, but it could also be easily reduced to a mechanical component.

The extension of the timeframe for parliamentary debate could also distinguish between supermajority and ordinary laws. The limit of this method is set by its inherently quantitative character; the substantive discussion cannot be measured with qualitative indicators. The third alternative may reconsider the role of public participation in the legislative process. Professional organizations, international observers, experts, practitioners, and individuals may contribute to the consultation with valuable inputs and suggestions. In the case of supermajority laws, specific forums or electronic platforms may be set up even by the exploitation of recently emerging democratic innovations, where anyone can express their views on the draft of the new law.

In the post-parliamentary stage, the implementation of mandatory prior constitutional review might also be taken into account as a prerequisite for valid legislation. However, the idea of mandatory a priori constitutional review goes far beyond the traditional framework of the legislative process and could therefore be seen as a completely separate alternative falling between the adoption of a bill and its promulgation.

8.3.1 The Permanent Parliamentary Commissions

Among the elements of the legislative process, I will first turn to the idea of extending the circle of permanent parliamentary commissions. Such commissions currently also play a crucial role in parliamentary work: proposals that do not receive

[3] Briffault (2021), pp. 169–193.

meaningful support from the competent commission cannot go forward to the plenary stage.[4] To replace the supermajority, a special parliamentary standing commission could be established to focus solely on supermajority laws. This commission could employ various methods to promote the stabilizing functions of supermajority voting. On the one hand, the government and the opposition could have equal representation on this commission, with decisions requiring a simple majority. On the other hand, a supermajority requirement could be imposed within the commission, taking into account the proportion of parliamentary groups.

External experts may also be invited to attend the commission's sessions and express their views. However, these external experts would not have the right to vote, as they lack democratic legitimacy.[5] However, the involvement of experts might be indispensable to analyze the substantive details of each supermajority legislative matter. Moreover, during the selection of the commission members, parliamentarians with relevant professional experience might be favored.

Such a move would also imply that the scope of supermajority laws would be significantly narrowed.[6] The presumably narrowed scope of supermajority laws lies behind all other alternative proposals, but it will be addressed separately as the most important, but not the only element of an alleged revision.

8.3.2 Determine the Minimum Time Limit of Parliamentary Debates on a Supermajority Bill

Nowadays, parliaments face an unprecedented workload. As a consequence, with rare exceptions, neither time nor energy can be devoted to the in-depth discussion of the issues at stake.[7] This phenomenon can be explained by several factors.[8] On the one hand, the majority of parliamentary members do not have the necessary expertise on a particular piece of legislation and are therefore unable to contribute to the debates in any meaningful way. On the other hand, the number of enacted laws also constantly increases, as I will come back to later. In this situation, Parliament has neither the time nor the capacity to conduct more in-depth debates, and the opposition's obstructionist policies may further undermine the effectiveness and prestige of parliamentary debates.[9]

These factors underline that extending the timeframe for debating supermajority laws constitutes a very risky instrument; no guarantee has been provided that the quality of the debates will be improved and that their content will be linked to the

[4] Sebők et al. (2023), pp. 1–22.

[5] Yamamoto (2007), pp. 29–34.

[6] Vincze (2014), pp. 86–97.

[7] Sohoni (2012), pp. 1585–1634.

[8] Palonen and Rosales (2015), pp. 11–30.

[9] Bell (2018), pp. 499–525.

proposal on the table. An extended timeframe gives the political groups more opportunity to express their views, but it also provides a powerful blocking power in the hands of the opposition. Furthermore, extending the timeframe would not result in increasing the depth of supermajority voting unless it is accompanied by quality guarantees.

According to a similar logic, a minimum period of time might be required between the final debate and the final vote on supermajority laws, as some current constitutions also provide a required minimum timeframe between the two readings of a supermajority bill, such as in Azerbaijan and Italy. In this case, stakeholders have the opportunity to reconsider their positions. It may be asked, of course, whether the time thus gained would actually be used for this purpose, as it could easily become an additional instrument of obstruction. Slowing down the legislative process would run counter to current trends in parliamentary work, but at least in principle, it could also contribute remarkably to the development of legislative culture.[10] However, a quantitative approach in itself should be combined with qualitative aspects to further such ambitions.

8.3.3 Strengthening Social Participation

Public participation as a legislative prerequisite has grown steadily during the last few decades. Recently, various democratic innovations aim to promote such means and enhance their effectiveness.[11] Recent constitutional amendment processes in Ireland and Iceland[12] have demonstrated that inclusiveness should be a crucial concept in a modern constitutional process. In legislation, the importance of such requirements may be less strict, but they cannot be disregarded here either. In most democratic countries, referendums and direct democracy are considered exceptional forms of popular participation. However, softer forms of citizen involvement are becoming more prevalent.[13] Social consultation occurs during the process of drafting laws, and occasionally citizens are given the chance to express their opinions on specific issues through different types of plebiscites.

Supermajority laws might also be distinguished from ordinary laws by stricter requirements for public participation. This could take several forms: deliberative workshops, forums, roundtables, and assemblies open to all interested stakeholders can be organized, where whoever is entitled to comment on the proposed legislation orally or at least in writing. The establishment of deliberative virtual platforms

[10] Neumann (2016), pp. 396–467.

[11] Smith (2010), pp. 8–29.

[12] Landemore (2014), pp. 166–191.

[13] But et al. (2022), pp. 52–82.

represents another option, where everyone has the opportunity to express their comments and discuss the draft for a longer period of time.[14] For this purpose, electronic platforms could be set up, and a sufficiently long period of time would be available to channel social input.[15]

The in-person form of inclusiveness would provide more opportunity for dialogue for the stakeholders with closer expertise, while virtual platforms would allow for a broader circle of individuals to contribute with their inputs to the legislative process. In the case of supermajority laws, both forms of public participation could be fostered, thus broadening the embeddedness of legislation. However, overbroad requirements of public participation for all supermajority legislative processes shall be avoided, as this would again make the legislation extremely rigid

8.4 Mandatory Prior Constitutional Review

Mandatory ex ante constitutional review could also be an appropriate tool to distinguish supermajority laws from ordinary ones. This has already been implemented in France, Portugal, Venezuela, several African countries; and also in Spain for the statutes of autonomous communities. If this instrument were implemented, all adopted supermajority laws must be sent to the constitutional court in advance, so that the court can give its opinion on the constitutionality of the text before it enters into force. This concept would entail far-reaching consequences: the legislative process would be prolonged and sophisticated, leading to a more careful consideration of the constitutional issues. Mandatory a priori review eliminates, at least in principle, unconstitutional supermajority laws from the legal system. However, it may be argued that supermajority laws primarily serve a legitimization function. Therefore, the substantive constitutionality of the adopted supermajority laws should not be enforced by institutionalizing such demanding requirements as mandatory prior constitutional review.

It should also be borne in mind that mandatory ex ante constitutional review is not sufficient in itself, and can only really fulfill its function if it is accompanied by a number of additional instruments. One of these elements would open up the possibility of a detailed motion at the same time as the supermajority law has been sent for scrutiny.[16] The constitution should also set a strict and enforceable deadline for the examination of laws sent for prior scrutiny; otherwise the legislative process would suffer extreme and unforeseeable delays.[17] Ex ante scrutiny shall not be

[14] Valentini (2022).

[15] Aichholzer and Allhutter (2011).

[16] Troper (2006), pp. 33–44.

[17] Thomas (2010), pp. 108–109.

necessarily imposed on all laws, but only on certain categories of such laws (e.g. in Spain, on organic laws regulating the status of autonomous communities).[18]

Ex ante constitutional scrutiny can only be truly effective if it can be enforced. This might be ensured if ex-post review of the supermajority legislative process can be initiated within a short period of time after promulgation. Mandatory ex ante scrutiny, as mentioned above, always leads to a massive increase in the caseload of the constitutional court, which may jeopardize the quality of the work carried out. I have already pointed out that mandatory ex ante constitutional review may also increase political pressure on the Constitutional Court, which could undermine public confidence in the body.

In the following, I will discuss the possibility of submitting a specific motion before constitutional courts in the case of mandatory ex ante review. Constitutional courts would often have a short period of time to examine significant and voluminous laws from a constitutional point of view, and in the absence of orientation, the substantive review of supermajority laws would be highly questionable. These shortcomings of mandatory ex ante review could be remedied by the selection of at least a narrow group of constitutional actors vested with the power to submit detailed motions completing the mandatory referral of the law to the constitutional court.

Actio popularis shall not be recommended for the submission of motions. Instead, such competence should be given to the constitutional actors dominating the political process and/or leading the public institutions involved in the protection of fundamental rights. The selection of potential initiators shall rely on the relevant professional/political knowledge of supermajority legislative subject matters, especially because the time available for tabling a motion would be limited to a maximum of a few days. Furthermore, due to the short time limit, no such authorization could be given to bodies comprised of several members, but only to the constitutional actors chaired by one particular person. Just to give a list of potential initiators for further consideration, in my view, the head of state, the Members of Parliament (possibly a certain number of Members), Commissioners for Fundamental Rights (ombudspersons), the Prosecutor General, and the President of the Supreme Court could be entitled to submit a detailed motion in the case of a mandatory preliminary constitutional review to assist the work of the Constitutional Court.

The motion could point out any potential constitutional problems that might arise from the adopted supermajority law, which constitutional courts could focus on during the review. The submission of a motion would be an option, not a duty, and the motion would not be binding for constitutional courts. The content of the motion would not restrict the unlimited nature of the review. It should be noted that the exhaustive list of persons entitled to submit a motion would not exclude anyone else, including individuals, from expressing their views to the constitutional court as amicus curiae within the short timeframe for submitting motions.

In the case of mandatory ex ante control, we shall define the scope of this obligation. Mandatory ex ante control may apply to all supermajority laws or to a specific

[18] Art. 81 (1) of the Constitution of Spain (January 4, 1978).

group of supermajority laws. France serves as an example of the first model, where the Constitutional Council examines the constitutionality of all adopted organic laws.[19] However, the French model must be understood in light of the fact that ex post constitutional review was excluded until 2008 and has been slow to gain ground in France in recent years. In legal systems that prioritize a posterior review, prior review is applied just sporadically. In Spain, mandatory ex ante review, which initially existed, was abolished and later reinstated only for organic laws governing the status of autonomous communities. Spain provides an example of how mandatory prior constitutional review can be applied to only a well-defined group of supermajority laws. The Portuguese Constitution opens up the possibility of prior constitutional review for all organic laws; however, this should be requested explicitly by the president of the republic, the prime minister, or any parliamentary group within 8 days of the enactment of the particular organic law. In this constellation, oppositional parliamentary groups would show more willingness to initiate prior constitutional review; such motions would come with less probability on behalf of the head of state or the head of government.

Mandatory prior review would, in my opinion, be appropriately applied if it were made mandatory in some of the most important areas of state organization (those already mentioned: supermajority law on the constitutional court, parliament, president of the republic, commissioner for Fundamental Rights (ombudsperson), judicial independence, elections, Limitation of Sovereignty). Mandatory prior constitutional review can be an effective guarantee if surrounded by the additional elements discussed, but its proliferation could jeopardize the proper exercise of the other powers of the constitutional court due to the excessive additional workload caused. Therefore, in the envisaged new model of supermajority law, the introduction of mandatory prior constitutional review shall go hand in hand with a significantly reduced scope of supermajority law.

It should also be noted that after the mandatory ex ante control, the head of state would no longer be able to veto the constitutionality of a supermajority law. In other words, after the enactment of a supermajority bill, the presidential referral to the constitutional court shall potentially be preceded by the presidential veto, but the reverse of this order should be prohibited.

The mandatory requirement of prior constitutional review will only be enforceable if the failure to do so would be accompanied by a substantive and enforceable sanction. Such a legal consequence might be applied after the law has entered into force, when it can be assessed whether all constitutional requirements have been respected during the legislative process. A special form of ex-post control may therefore be necessary, which could only be initiated within a short period (e.g. 30 days) after the promulgation of the supermajority law. It would be inappropriate to leave open for a longer period for the possibility of an exclusively formal ex-post review, as this would create unnecessarily long uncertainty in the legal system.

[19] Art. 46 of the Constitution of France (October 4, 1958).

The option of initiating ex-post review for a declaration of invalidity could therefore be opened up to the above-mentioned group of petitioners for a period of 30 days after the promulgation of the supermajority law. If the adopted supermajority law is deemed by the constitutional court to be contrary to the constitution on formal grounds, this would not necessarily entail the removal of the matter from the agenda and the loss of the effect of the adopted supermajority law, but the parliament could re-negotiate the bill on the basis of the observations of the constitutional court. The law adopted by the parliament in this stage should be sent back to the constitutional court to ensure full compliance with formal and substantive constitutional requirements. If the constitutional court declares the unconstitutionality of the re-negotiated version of the supermajority law, the bill will be removed from the agenda and would lose its effect.

Therefore, once the law has been adopted and promulgated, the legislative process would not end, as the 30-day deadline would be open for requesting a posterior review on formal grounds. This motion could be submitted by the same group of constitutional actors who are entitled to initiate prior constitutional review. After the termination of the 30-day deadline, constitutional review could not be initiated on formal grounds, but the possibility of substantive review would remain open according to the general rules of initiating ex post constitutional review. This relatively complex system would of course only apply to a narrow range of supermajority laws, not to the huge groups of ordinary laws.

8.5 Reconsidering the Scope: Limiting the Number of Supermajority Legislative Subject Matters

Above, I have listed the possibilities where we may seek to transform the concept of supermajority law and its terrain. However, several arguments support the position that does not rely on the future role of supermajority laws and argue for a homogeneous category of ordinary law. In my view, however, the option of implementing supermajority laws would seem to be more convincing if the scope of supermajority laws were not defined in an unreasonably broad way. Supermajority law contributes significantly to ensuring the stability of certain essential legislative subjects and, if used properly, can be a meaningful constitutional guarantee. Most of the countries admittedly operate feasibly without introducing any model of supermajority law. Therefore, one could draw the conclusion that a homogeneous concept of ordinary law could be verified with weighty arguments. However, completely abolishing a still existing model of supermajority law might be evaluated as a waste of a valuable possibility with significant perspectives.

In the absence of supermajority laws, the constitution might be dismantled by ordinary statutory rules while several technical norms would be converted into regulations. Many dogmatic disputes would undoubtedly be eliminated, but the perspective of establishing a broad consensus requirement for the basic rules of political life and main state authorities would be lost. The elimination of supermajority laws from the legal system constitutes therefore a defensible position, but I do not share this view. When narrowing the scope of supermajority laws, we must be mindful of which legal institutions will take over or continue the guarantee role of supermajority laws. Until the identification of such institutional safeguards, the most important statutory rules of the constitutional framework could be incorporated into supermajority laws expanding the content of the constitution, while the less important ones could be grouped together into ordinary laws.[20]

As regards fundamental rights, supermajority law must concentrate on strengthening the institutional system of legal protection, although I have already pointed out that despite various shortcomings, the number and effectiveness of available legal remedies is constantly emerging. As a consequence, no public policy matters would be included among supermajority subjects, and in the case of fundamental rights, it would be sufficient to provide for their protection at this level in an indirect way.

Narrowing the scope of supermajority laws, but keeping them in the legal system, would not resolve the dogmatic and legal-theoretical debates that are currently ongoing in the countries concerned on the legal nature and scope of supermajority laws. In my opinion, the right solution to tackle this challenge would be to designate supermajority laws rather than supermajority subjects. The subjects already mentioned could be considered as supermajority laws: the laws on the electoral system, the parliament, the constitutional court, and the head of state, the independence of the judiciary, the ombudsperson, and the voluntary restriction of state sovereignty, i.e. a total of about eight subjects. The inclusion of the voluntary limitation of sovereignty would, of course, make the list of supermajority laws open-ended.

The constitutional court would be responsible for monitoring, upon request, that the domains of supermajority and ordinary law are properly separated. If the legislator has acted improperly, if ordinary provisions have been inserted in supermajority laws, or vice versa, the constitutional court would not only identify the wrongly categorized provisions, but also annul the rules that have been placed at the incorrect level. The annulment would apply both where a supermajority provision is inserted in an ordinary law and where the reverse has been conducted.

Obviously, neither constitutional amendment would operate with the combination of a change in the hierarchy of legal sources; mandatory prior constitutional review; as well as a bicameral parliament and a revamped legislative process simultaneously. These ideas just constitute possible elements of any potential constitutional reform, building on which a supermajority concept could be developed as a more effective guarantee in the long term. I have already indicated on several occasions my views on the possible directions of such a reform, but I have not yet set out in full what I consider to be an ideal concept of supermajority law. In the concluding section, I will show how the supermajority law model, that I consider most appropriate, would work. Based on the considerations so far, I should already make it

[20] Szentgáli-Tóth (2020), pp. 61–76.

clear that I do not see this model as a final or an exclusive concept, but only as a stage in a thought process that opens up the possibility of moving forward. The de lege ferenda proposals outlined above are intended primarily to provide an impulse for further scientific dialogue.

In examining the prospects for the concept of supermajority law, I have relied on two basic assumptions: first, that the idea of supermajority legislation shall not be rejected in general terms, and second, that the current scope of supermajority laws would need to be revisited as regard its legal rank and procedural rules; and significantly narrowed as regard its scope.

8.6 Summarizing the Main Outcomes of My Analyses

The last section of this chapter briefly reviews the considerations discussed in each of the major chapters, on the basis of which I have drawn my conclusions. Building on this, I conclude my work in Chap. 9 by outlining in detail the model that I personally consider to be the best one to follow in relation to supermajority laws and to be a point of reference for further scientific debate. Finally, the volume will be closed with some concluding thoughts. This concept aims to stimulate further scientific reflections on the perspectives and disadvantages as well as the comparative insights of operating with supermajority laws.

In the first phase of my book, I focused on a comprehensive outline of the possible arguments supporting the implementation of supermajority laws. So far, no interdisciplinary analysis of supermajority laws has been carried out, taking into account comparative insights, the main existing models, and the perspectives of different disciplines. In the present volume, I have attempted to do so by proposing five theories justifying the existence of supermajority laws: the prolongation of the constitution, an instrument for the stability of the constitution, a political instrument, a guarantee of fundamental rights, and a factor influencing the separation of powers.

I have demonstrated the contrast between the various approaches and outlined the competing lines of argumentation. My work might be separated from previous studies in this area in two respects. Firstly, I have sought to identify and weigh up systematically the advantages and disadvantages of current supermajority law concepts by taking into account the various implications caused by the introduction of this subcategory of statutes. Some justifying arguments have already been addressed by several authors, but a comprehensive analysis of them has been lacking. The range of selected justifying theories shall be obviously open to debate and can never be absolutely complete and exhaustive: I have selected the five sets of argumentation whose literature seemed to have a considerable background.

My other novelty combines the primary and secondary sources dealing with supermajority law written in different languages (English, French, German, Hungarian, Romanian, and Spanish). A significant part of these studies has not been analyzed in this integrated manner so far. Therefore, their structured assessment may give a new impulse to the professional dialogue on supermajority laws.

The historical references were needed following the introductory remarks at the beginning of the second chapter because without knowledge of the relevant legal historical tradition, the development of modern supermajority law cannot be understood. The legal-historical approach could even be a separate justificatory argument, but because of its function, it seems to be more of a fundamental premise underlying all theories than a concept suitable for justifying the supermajority laws in it.

The comparative insight was highlighted in the context of constitutional migration, when participants in constitutional-drafting processes sought to apply models of supermajority law by analyzing foreign constitutional experience. The idea of supermajority legislation was born in Europe, but today one should look at supermajority laws from a broader perspective: we must also take into account that for the sample of France and Spain in particular, we are talking about around 50 countries that have transplanted elevated majority legislation on all continents around the world. Supermajority law is no longer just an isolated feature of a few major Western European countries. It must be taken seriously considering the weight of the countries that apply it. Furthermore, it has become a constitutional instrument that is widespread from Madagascar to Ecuador, from Chile to Moldova, and Papua New Guinea.

The academic study of supermajority law usually focuses on the functioning of this concept in practice, and its potential analysis in the relevant Constitutional Court case law, while fewer efforts have been devoted to elaborating the theoretical and dogmatic bases behind these doctrines. In the third chapter, emphasis has been given to the considerations of constitutional theory, which also entail far-reaching practical implications.

In academic discourse and constitutional case law, supermajority laws are often considered as part of the constitution, describing the broader sense of the constitution as a set of the constitutional text and supermajority laws.[21] This overly broad and vague definition of the constitution gives rise to the general deficit of legal certainty.[22] Supermajority laws can only be considered part of the constitution as quasi-constitutional norms if their scope is outlined sufficiently narrowly. However, under the current extensive supermajority law regimes, this approach would relativize the authority of constitutions and make it difficult to fulfill their function in practice. The clear hierarchical relationship between quasi-constitutional and constitutional rules would disappear, while supermajority laws would undoubtedly be placed above ordinary laws in the hierarchy of legal sources. Constitutional courts would not have to take into account a single constitutional document during constitutional review, but a great number of laws falling under the scope of the supermajority requirement.

Supermajority laws can only be considered part of the constitution as quasi-constitutional norms if their scope is outlined sufficiently narrowly. However, under the current extensive supermajority law regimes, this approach would relativize the

[21] Formery (2020), pp. 101–103.

[22] Genevois (1996), p. 324.

authority of constitutions and make it difficult to fulfill their function in practice. The clear hierarchical relationship between quasi-constitutional and constitutional rules would disappear, while supermajority laws would undoubtedly be placed above ordinary laws in the hierarchy of legal sources.[23] Constitutional courts would not have to take into account a single constitutional document during constitutional review, but a great number of laws falling under the scope of the supermajority requirement.

The role of supermajority laws in stabilizing the constitution shall also be contextualized among the instruments that ensure the constitution's durability. Supermajority laws have usually been left out from the main safeguards of constitutional stability; however, their indirect effects in this regard are worth contemplating. The extension of the constitution, the strong emphasis on the constitution as a fundamental norm, and the broad application of the elevated consensus requirement all work against the frequent amendment of the constitutional document. In spite of these considerations, legislation with a supermajority does not appear to be an appropriate means of promoting constitutional stability. Keeping in mind its undoubted role as a guarantee during transitional periods, this could not outweigh its significant impact on undermining constitutional endurance by generating constant constitutional disputes, increasing political tensions, and blurring the boundaries of the constitution. In my view, the introduction of a supermajority requirement or a referendum for amending the Constitution, the unamendable provisions, and the power of the Constitutional Court to review the substance of constitutional amendments are more effective and appropriate means of preventing frequent amendments to the Constitution. Instead of its current versions, the reconsidered supermajority law models could reduce the huge uncertainty around the legal rank of supermajority laws.

Strengthening the stability of the constitution may be a reasonable need in the constitutional system, but the means to achieve this should not be provided by supermajority laws. Looking for additional safeguards of constitutional stability might be a reasonable demand; however, I would prefer other constitutional instruments to fulfill this task. What supermajority law gives in this respect on the one hand, it takes away on the other, and so from the two constitutional justifications of supermajority law, the extension of the constitution, with all its self-contradictions, seems to be the more defensible concept. Supermajority laws may only have a secondary and incidental role in strengthening constitutional endurance. Therefore, it is crucial to fully clarify the rank of supermajority laws in the legal system. However, achieving this seems almost impossible due to the frequent excessive entanglement of supermajority and ordinary laws.

Turning to the procedural requirements attached to supermajority legislation in the context of political impact, four key issues shall be highlighted: the protection of minorities, the distortion of parliamentarianism, the link with the electoral system, and the two-thirds pro-governmental parliamentary majority. The political role

---

[23] Barak (2011), pp. 329–330; Juhász (2022), pp. 573–602.

of supermajority laws cannot be understood unless these four elements are read together with the various elevated majority requirements and also with the additional procedural safeguards.

Supermajority laws under the two-thirds model might not easily comply with the basic logic of parliamentarianism. In the case of a two-thirds governmental majority, supermajority voting can easily become a means of centralizing political power in the long term, which may exacerbate the already existing tensions.

Many instruments could safeguard the interests of political minorities in contemporary constitutional systems; however, supermajority voting could play, at most, a subsidiary role in this regard.

The complex link between the electoral system and supermajority legislation depends to a large extent on the difficulty of obtaining two-thirds or close to two-thirds parliamentary majority in a given electoral framework. One should assess supermajority differently in the case of majoritarian, proportional and mixed electoral systems; in unitary and federal states; and also in unicameral and bicameral parliamentary frameworks.

The political significance of supermajority voting increases in transitional periods when an authoritarian regime suddenly or gradually gives way to a democratic political and social order.[24] In such cases, all stakeholders are faced with various factors of uncertainty. Therefore, it is in everyone's interest that the constitution should include instruments to steer the transition process in a consolidated direction. The transitory element appears in each implementation of supermajority law, sometimes also in parallel with seeking long-term stability with the help of this mechanism.[25]

The role of the parliamentary opposition should be emphasized again: the parliamentary opposition might play a decisive role in the case of supermajority legislation, so that its function shall not be limited to monitoring and opposing government legislation. The supermajority requirement results in the confusion of traditional tasks between the government and the opposition; the legislative and control functions might not be separated clearly. This feature runs counter to the theoretical basis of parliamentarism, which a well-functioning parliamentary system needs a government with the necessary powers, supported by the parliamentary majority, and an opposition to the government's ambitions, acting within the limits of the law. The final decision rests with the government, while corrective or remedial mechanisms stand at the disposal of the opposition, such as constitutional review; initiating ombudsperson proceedings; or litigation in international judicial forums. However, these steps are not directly integrated into the parliamentary decision-making process itself, but rather emerge as follow-up possibilities to be addressed against statutes enacted by the parliamentary majority.

[24] Ginsburg (2009), pp. 201–223.

[25] Saunders (2019), pp. 330–351.

Despite the weighty counterarguments already presented, supermajority laws have been regularly used in a broader extent, including the protection of fundamental rights. Furthermore, the effectiveness of guarantee mechanisms for fundamental rights relies on the expertise and commitment of both individuals and bodies operating them. Supermajority laws, as legislative guarantees, can support the protection of direct substantive regulation of fundamental rights, as well as the structure and competences of the institutions responsible for safeguarding them. While increased legislative protection of fundamental rights may be justified, involving a supermajority in enacting laws on fundamental rights could jeopardize the adaptability of the legal system to constantly changing needs, due to the broad scope of legislation concerning the catalogue of fundamental rights.[26] Furthermore, excluding or significantly limiting the government's discretion in these areas would easily lead to deadlock in the political process. In my view, instead of the direct aspect, supermajority legislation for the protection of fundamental rights shall be limited to safeguarding institutions as the indirect aspect, such as the ombudsperson and the constitutional court.

With the coverage of status, organisation and competences of main constitutional actors, supermajority laws generally restrict the government's room for maneuver, if we are talking about the two-thirds model.[27] By contrast, the absolute majority framework primarily reduces the role of the parliament.[28] In both cases, at the expense of the government, the position of the constitutional court would be strengthened, since the constitutional court would carry out constitutional review on more extensive grounds. In all cases, the task is conferred upon the constitutional court to consider the supermajority requirement as a substantive constitutional guarantee of legislation and to decide on the violations accordingly. The Constitutional Court shall also rule on doctrinal questions relating to supermajority laws. Such rulings do not necessarily mean the end of theoretical debates; however, the legal practice shall usually be in line with the theses laid down in the decisions of the constitutional court.

The question arises if the scope of supermajority laws would be narrowed, which subjects should continue to be regulated by supermajority laws? In my view, the new model of supermajority laws should focus on the main institutions of the state. By laying the foundations of the political system, the electoral system (both at national and local level) and the functioning of parliament would be covered by a supermajority law. Supermajority law would also regulate the functioning and status of the constitutional court and the election of constitutional judges, thus strengthening the most important guarantee of the protection of the constitution. Apart from this, it would also be appropriate to require broad consent for the enactment of detailed rules on the status and competences of the head of state. Moreover, the

[26] Kovács and Tóth (2011), pp. 183–203.

[27] Gardbaum (2017), pp. 229–264.

[28] Blacher (2021), p. 146.

ombudsperson, as a key factor of effective legal protection in a modern constitutional framework shall also be covered by a supermajority law. Finally, the independence of the judiciary constitutes a fundamental, though not inalienable, guarantee of the rule of law, the details of which would also need to be covered by legislative supermajority. In total, there would be seven permanent supermajority subjects, but in addition, any voluntary limitation of state sovereignty would also require the same level of supermajority.

Based on these discussions, I have identified three main avenues whose combination might help for the exploration of alternatives to current supermajority law concepts (redefining the legal rank of supermajority laws; revisiting the elements of the supermajority legislative process; and reconsidering restrictively the scope of this legal instrument). In my book, I have considered these three alternatives in more detail. I have interpreted them in a framework that does not call into question the very existence of supermajority laws, just anticipates a significant narrowing of their scope. However, rethinking the concept of supermajority laws cannot be launched as an isolated constitutional reform that addresses only the issue of supermajority voting. If the structure and scope of supermajority laws would be significantly changed, this will also affect other segments of the constitutional system, just as amendments serving other purposes may also affect supermajority laws. I have not yet attempted to outline my proposals in full, but have instead looked at each of the potential elements, listing the arguments for and against the various alternatives.

In my view, all five main theories described give meaningful arguments justifying the existence of supermajority laws; therefore, I have sought to rationalize supermajority laws rather than justify them. Meaningful considerations could question the uniformity of law as a category of legal sources; as a consequence, we must single out the very narrow circle of the most important fields of legislation and give them quasi-constitutional protection. This will unburden the constitution, while not unduly undermining the logic of parliamentarianism, and will give the government within the respective constitutional limits a free hand, except for the very foundations of the constitutional framework.

In the meantime, the constitutional court would be given an additional opportunity for constitutional review, but the narrow scope of supermajority laws would not lead to the involvement of the Court in day-to-day political debates. Supermajority laws would also have a function in the protection of fundamental rights, but this should be furthered without constituting an undue constraint on the current government. Political consensus on key issues should be ensured without imposing a day-to-day barrier to legislation.

References

Aichholzer G, Allhutter D (2011) Online forms of political participation and their impact on democracy. https://ideas.repec.org/p/ita/itaman/11_02.html

Barak A (2011) Unconstitutional constitutional amendments. Israel Law Rev 44(3):321–341
Bell LC (2018) Obstruction in parliaments: a cross-national perspective. J Legis Stud 24(4):499–525
Blacher P (2021) Droit constitutionell. 8e. Hachette Supérieur, Livre, Paris
Briffault R (2021) The single-subject rule: uncertain solution for Omnibus Legislation. In: Bar-Siman-Tov I (ed) Comparative multidisciplinary perspectives on Omnibus Legislation. Springer International Publishing, pp 169–193
But JJ et al (2022) Direct democracy in the constitution: good or bad for democracy? Theory Pract Legis 11(1):52–82
Formery S-L (2020) La Constitution commentée. Article par article. 23e Hachette Livre, Vanves cedex
Gardbaum S (2017) Political parties, voting systems, and the separation of powers. Am J Comp Law 65(2):229–264
Genevois B (1996) Normes de références du contrôle de constitutionnalité et respect de la hiérarchie en leur sein. In: de Braibant G (ed) L'État de droit. Mélanges en l'honneur de Guy Braibant. Dalloz, Paris, p 324
Ginsburg T et al (2009) Does the process of constitution-making matter? Annu Rev Law Soc Sci 5(5):201–223
Juhász K (2022) Abusive constitutionalism in Hungary. Polit Central Europe 18(4):573–602
Kovács K, Tóth GA (2011) Hungary's constitutional transformation. Eur Constitutional Law Rev 7:183–203
Landemore H (2014) Inclusive constitution-making: the Icelandic experiment. J Polit Philos 23(2):166–191
Neumann RK (2016) Legislation's culture. West Virginia Law Rev 119(1):396–467
Palonen K, Rosales JM (eds) (2015) Parliamentarism and democratic theory: historical and contemporary perspectives, 1st edn. Verlag Barbara Budrich, pp 11–30
Saunders C (2019) Processes of constitutional transitions in the face of territorial cleavages. In: Anderson G, Choudhry S (eds) Territory and power in constitutional transitions. Oxford, pp 330–351
Sebők M et al (2023) Comparative European legislative research in the age of large-scale computational text analysis: a review article. Int Polit Sci Rev:1–22. https://doi.org/10.1177/01925121231199904
Smith G (2010) Democratic innovations: designing institutions for citizen participation. CUP, Cambridge, pp 8–29
Sohoni M (2012) The idea of "too much law". Fordham Law Rev 80(4):1585–1634
Szente Z (2017) Challenging the basic values–problems in the rule of law in Hungary and the failure of the EU to tackle them. In: Jakab A, Kochenov D (eds) The enforcement of EU law and values: ensuring Member States' compliance. Oxford Academic, pp 456–475
Szentgáli-Tóth B (2020) Organic laws and the principle of democracy in France and Spain. In: Miras AP et al (eds) Setenta años de Constitución Italiana y cuarenta años de Constitución Española, Retos en el siglo XXI, vol 4. Centro de Estudios Políticos y Constitucionales, Madrid, pp 61–76
Thomas J (2010) L'indépendance du Conseil Constitutionnel. PhD dissertation, Université libre de Bruxelles
Troper M (2006) La V Republique et la separation des pouvoirs. Droits 43(1):33–44
Valentini C (2022) Deliberative constitutionalism and judicial review: a systemic approach. Revus J Constitutional Theory Philos Law 47. https://doi.org/10.4000/revus.8030
Vincze A (2014) Wrestling with constitutionalism: the supermajority and the Hungarian Constitutional Court. Vienna J Int Constitutional Law 8(1):86–97
Yamamoto H (2007) Tools for parliamentary oversight: a comparative study of 88 national parliaments. Inter-Parliamentary Union

Chapter 9
The Proposed New Model of Supermajority Law

First and foremost, it should be stressed that a new model for supermajority laws can only be envisaged if the rules for amending the Constitution are simultaneously rethought. Since supermajority laws should be adopted under a less demanding procedural regime than the constitutional provisions, in order to be compatible with the hierarchy of legal sources, the new model should increase the distinction between constitutional norms and those placed in supermajority laws. As my book does not aim to develop a complete draft constitutional reform, but rather to formulate and elaborate recommendations for the future of supermajority laws, I do not discuss how the rules for amending the constitution could be rethought. This could be the subject of a separate volume. However, a major revision of the supermajority law concept would likely also prompt a reconsideration of the rules for amending the Constitution.

Moreover, a reform could and should also clarify the legal rank of the supermajority laws between the constitution and ordinary laws in order to eliminate uncertainty in this area. As I have explained in detail above, the supermajority laws fall clearly outside the framework of the Constitution, and it should therefore be established that they are below the Constitution in the hierarchy of legal sources and cannot contain provisions that conflict with the Constitution. At the same time, it should be made clear that supermajority voting does not constitute just a technical rule, and that such a distinction has far-reaching consequences. It would be justified to constitutionally reflect that supermajority laws are above ordinary laws in the hierarchy of legal sources, and that, contrary to the practice of most constitutional courts concerned, the relationship between supermajority and ordinary laws would be determined by the hierarchical principle rather than by the competence principle.[1]

A clear and unambiguous distinction between supermajority and ordinary laws would form an additional crucial element of the recommended framework. Only

[1] Troper and Chagnollaud (2012), pp. 344–345; la décision n° 96-386, DC du 30 décembre 1996.

B. A. Szentgáli-Tóth, *The Past, Present, and Future of Legislation with Supermajority*, Ius Gentium: Comparative Perspectives on Law and Justice 126,
https://doi.org/10.1007/978-3-031-99324-4_9

one supermajority law/subject matter would be needed, containing all the rules of the particular field relating to supermajority voting. A supermajority law would contain only supermajority rules, while an ordinary law would include only provisions subject to a simple parliamentary majority. The constitutional court would annul any provisions of a law that were unjustifiably and unconstitutionally included either in a supermajority or ordinary law, and Parliament would have to restore the proper hierarchy of legal sources by means of a new legislative act. Moreover, it would not be possible to combine supermajority and ordinary provisions within the same act, since supermajority would not be linked to statutory provisions but to specific legislative subject matters to be covered by one supermajority law.

The constitutional court would be equally responsible either for ensuring that the scope of supermajority voting does not extend beyond the constitutional mandate or that absolute majority consensus prevails within the scope defined by the Constitution. Supermajority laws would not be invoked during the constitutional review of ordinary laws, so their quasi-constitutional character would not arise. The constitutional court would therefore have even broader powers to review supermajority laws than at present, but most of the doctrinal and practical disputes that have arisen over the interpretation of supermajority law would be eliminated. In the meantime, the ex-ante review of the constitutional court would allow for a proper separation between supermajority and ordinary provisions in the legislative process. One should keep in mind that in total, around eight supermajority laws would have been enacted (the number could be slightly increased by the laws concerning the voluntary limitation of state sovereignty).

Turning to the details of the supermajority legislative process, my recommended model of supermajority would rely exclusively on absolute parliamentary majority of all deputies, as the potential drawbacks of current models stem from the excessive majority requirement in addition to the overly broad regulatory space. At the moment, only a small number of Central and Eastern European, African, and Latin American countries apply two-thirds, three-fifths or four-sevenths legislative majority as illustrated by Figs. 5.1 and 5.2, except for the voluntary limitation of sovereignty, where the elevated form of supermajority has been widespread. In contrast, the absolute majority has been implemented by several countries and seeks to ensure an adequate level of protection by incorporating other safeguards in addition to a lower voting ratio.[2]

In my opinion, an absolute majority could also reduce the difference between supermajority and ordinary laws, even in parliamentary practice and the political process. The boundary between the government and the opposition would not be relative; moreover, the legislative process would not be blocked by the lack of political consensus. The guarantee element would be shifted from the political level (broad consensus) to the professional one by strengthening the role of the constitutional court. In the case of an absolute majority model, the likelihood of the deadlocks that I have discussed in detail in connection with the two-thirds majority

[2] Troper (2008), pp. 1–34.

would be remarkably lower. From the four main political consequences discussed, only the lower probability of minority governance would be relevant in the case of an absolute majority model, while the political instrumental character of supermajority laws would be played down by their constitutional function. Moreover, in the case of an absolute majority, supermajority laws would not differ from ordinary laws primarily in terms of the majority required, since the government shall usually enjoy the reliable confidence of the absolute parliamentary majority. Instead of the consensus component, the distinction would focus on other guarantee elements attached to supermajority legislation. The decrease of the required parliamentary support would point to the need to implement additional pieces to the puzzle to duly replace the disappeared safeguards.

The relaxation of the supermajority requirement might be outweighed by two main instruments. On the one hand, Parliament could establish a standing commission to deal exclusively with supermajority laws. This commission would be set up on a parity basis, i.e. with equal representation from the government and the opposition. The specific distribution of seats on the commission would be determined by the number of parliamentarians from each political group; however, the parity principle should be maintained.

As a general rule, a majority decision in the commission would be required to support a bill, but if the bill received 50% support in the commission (i.e. just government or oppositional support), the speaker of the parliament could decide whether the bill will be put on the plenary parliamentary agenda. The speaker of the parliament would not have unlimited power to do this, as it would undermine the work of the commission. The role of the parliamentary speaker could be rationalized by maximizing the number of times per parliamentary session that he/she may exercise this right, or by specifying the number of times per parliamentary session that a political group may initiate a plenary debate on a bill that has received just 50% support in the commission of supermajority legislation. Usually, this option would presumably be used by the governmental side, but the opposition could also benefit from it if they receive 50% support from oppositional votes. Parliamentarian's independent from any faction would be counted as a separate oppositional parliamentary group in this special committee. As the number of supermajority laws would be reduced, relatively few laws would be dealt with by this body. Therefore, each supermajority bill would be expected to be debated more thoroughly. The commission would always be chaired by the government side, with one vice-chair from the government side and one from the opposition.

The reason for establishing such a complex arrangement in the decision-making process of the commission would be to ensure, as much as possible, that this body would provide any meaningful guarantee for supermajority legislation. At the same time, the opposition should also be prevented from using its position in the commission to gain abusive political advantage by making it impossible for the government to enact even reasonable amendments of supermajority laws. The commission would function as a standing commission but would not be a specialized commission, as it would not be set up to examine a single area of expertise, but to discuss a specific set of laws. Apart from the discussion in this new commission, the specialized commissions would also continue to deal with pieces of supermajority legislation that fall within their area of expertise.

Although this does not constitute a paramount issue in itself, the new commission could be called the "Commission on Supermajority Legislation." It would convene as and when deemed necessary, depending on the number of bills under its remit, with proposed bills coming before it after discussion in the specialized commissions.

A supermajority law that has been passed through the Commission of Supermajority Legislation should be adopted by an absolute majority in the plenary sitting and then shall be forwarded by the speaker of the Parliament to the constitutional court. Any supermajority law shall not be promulgated and shall not enter into force unless the constitutional court confirms its compliance with the constitution. Once the bill has been adopted by the parliament, within 5 days, apart from the constitutional court, it should also be sent by the speaker of the parliament to the head of the state for information. At the same time, the speaker of the parliament would also send the adopted bill to the ombudsperson, the president of the supreme court, and the chief prosecutor. Any (or a specified number of) Parliamentarians, the head of state, the ombudsperson, the president of the supreme court, and the chief prosecutor may, within 15 days of the final vote on the law, submit their views to the constitutional court on the constitutionality of the adopted text, and if deemed necessary, draw the attention of the constitutional court to any points of concern. The right to submit opinions and motions shall not confer any duty on the addressees but rather gives an opportunity to a narrow circle of constitutional actors to direct the attention of the constitutional court within the short period envisaged for conducting this special review process.

The constitutional court would have 30 days from the date on which the speaker of the parliament would send the adopted text of the law to the constitutional court to deliver its decision. If the constitutional court does not find any reasonable constitutional concern, it will record this in its decision and the law will be promulgated within 5 days of publishing the constitutional court ruling, after countersignature by the Head of State. However, if the constitutional court considers that the text of the adopted supermajority law violates the Constitution, the supermajority law will be sent back to parliament, which might put the draft back on its agenda within 30 days not taking into account the periods outside the parliamentary sessions. If Parliament fails to start the renegotiation within 30 days, the bill shall not be put back on the parliamentary agenda. In the case when a new version of the supermajority law has been adopted as a result of the renegotiation process, the review of the constitutional court must be repeated, and if the body again declares the unconstitutionality of the bill, it will not be sent back to Parliament for a second time. This structure shall be adapted accordingly to the needs of bicameral frameworks, where the necessary time for the negotiations of the two chambers shall also be duly considered.

Within 30 days of promulgating the supermajority law, those entitled to submit exact motions for a mandatory preliminary constitutional review may request the constitutional court to review, within a 30-day time limit, whether the legislative process has respected formal constitutional requirements, in particular the rules on required parliamentary majority and mandatory a priori constitutional review. If the answer to this question is in the negative, the constitutional court will annul the law as invalid.

Considering the scope, the main area of supermajority laws could be the organization of the state: the most important areas where additional guarantees are justified should be identified within this category. The political framework should be outlined by the electoral law, which determines the conditions under which political parties compete for parliamentary mandates and for the legislative and executive power. Therefore, electoral arrangements for parliamentary and local government representatives shall be enshrined in supermajority law. However, in the case of elections to the European Parliament, given the relatively limited room for manoeuvre of European parliamentarians, the justification of this guarantee might be highly dubious.

The constitutional court means the primary guardian of the constitution and plays an important role in the protection of fundamental rights, which justify its enhanced protection. Apart from this, the coverage of the ombudsperson could strengthen the indirect role of a supermajority to safeguard fundamental rights. Moreover, the Parliament embodies and expresses the will of the electorate. It serves as the scene of daily political battles; therefore, its rules of operation should be subject to broad political consensus. Besides this, supermajority laws could also include rules to safeguard the status of the head of state, the independence of the judiciary and voluntary restriction of state sovereignty. Beyond these fields, all other statutes would be enacted as ordinary laws. The envisaged list of supermajority legislative fields significantly overlaps with those topics, which are classified according to Fig. 9.1 by most countries under the supermajority legislative requirement.

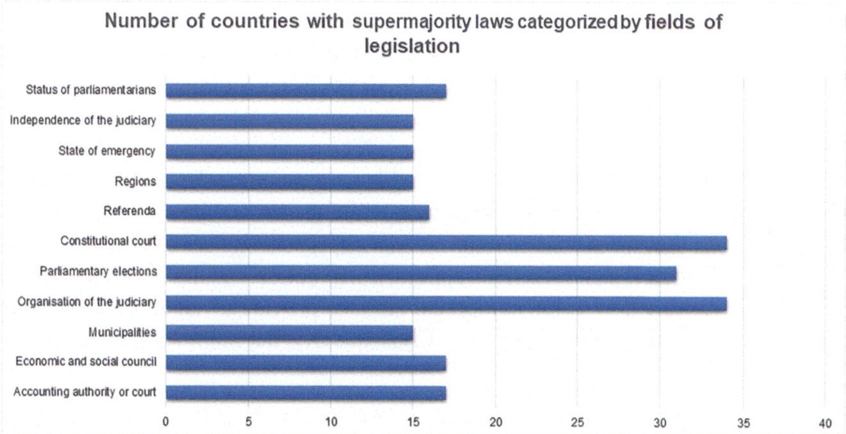

Fig. 9.1 The list of the most widespread supermajority legislative subject matters: displaying the Number of countries, where a topic is covered by the supermajority requirement (Source: desk research of the author)

In my view, the denomination of supermajority laws represents just an aspect of secondary importance. I have previously pointed out that the various terms already used to designate supermajority laws have different meanings, but this does not, in itself, make a substantial difference. The special procedural requirements and the scope of applicability, rather than the terminology, determine the true nature of a supermajority law concept. Disputes over terminology generally (including in the case of supermajority law) serve to distract attention from substantive issues, dividing stakeholders along formal fault lines. This would be inappropriate in the event of rethinking the current supermajority law concepts; therefore, the best solution would be to maintain the current names. Nevertheless, personally I would recommend the term "supermajority law" or "supermajority law" as outlined at the beginning of this volume and consistently used thereafter.

In addition to the introduction of a new supermajority law concept, the attitudes towards these legal instruments should also be revisited. The supermajority laws of different countries vary significantly, but what is common to all, except Hungary, is that the concept of a supermajority law, once introduced, has proved to be permanent. The scope of the supermajority law may have been extended or some elements of the concept changed (as in the case of Spain's mandatory prior constitutional review), but the conceptual framework of the supermajority law has remained unchanged. By contrast, in Hungary, we have seen at least four different versions of supermajority legislation, with each political formation shaping the theory and practice of supermajority legislation always adapted to their own objectives.[3] The scope of supermajority laws, the supermajority required for their adoption, and their legal rank have been constantly changing, so that no consistent legislative practice has been established in this area. A similar reform has also been experienced recently in Côte d'Ivoire, where organic laws were passed in a unicameral system with a two-thirds parliamentary majority until 2016,[4] while the current constitution has introduced a bicameral legislature, where organic laws should be enacted by the absolute majority of both chambers.[5] In case of conflicts between the two chambers, the first chamber should enact the final version of the organic law with a two-thirds majority. As the most recent development, both draft constitutions of Chile, which were rejected by referendums, would have abolished the already existing category of organic laws.

Frequent changes do not allow for a stable supermajority legislation practice. Therefore, it is important to establish a stable, time-tested, and predictable concept. To achieve this, the aim should be to reconsider supermajority laws through a broad political and academic dialogue. This approach will not only address the challenges of a specific historical or political moment but also provide a viable and beneficial constitutional solution in the long term. Consequently, the main ideas of my book

[3] Gárdos-Orosz (2024), pp. 225–244.

[4] Art. 71 of the Constitution of Cote d'Ivoire (July 24, 2000).

[5] Art. 102 of the Constitution of Côte d'Ivoire (November 8, 2016).

revolve around a consolidated and well-prepared reform, leading to a stable long-term concept for supermajority law.

References

Gárdos-Orosz F (2024) Confused constitutionalism in Hungary–New assessment criteria for recognising a populist constitutional court. Hague J Rule of Law 16(2):225–244
Troper M (2008) Constitutional law. In: Berman GA, Etienne P (eds) Introduction to French law. Wolters Kluwer, Netherlands, pp 1–34
Troper M, Chagnollaud D (eds) (2012) Traite international de droit constitutionnel. Dalloz, Paris

Chapter 10
Closing Remarks

In my work, I mainly aimed at laying down initial proposals to raise new perspectives that could serve to improve the concept of supermajority law. Profoundly tailored amendments require an inclusive academic and political dialogue with all stakeholders in the countries concerned on the future of supermajority laws in the coming years. Political parties, constitutional scholars and legal theorists, as well as legal practitioners and social organizations, can play a key role in this process. When considering the future of supermajority laws, it should be borne in mind that a combination of main constitutional principles, domestic traditions, comparative insights, and innovative solutions can lead to the elaboration of the most favorable solutions. My endeavors presented here make a modest contribution to this tough process.

B. A. Szentgáli-Tóth, *The Past, Present, and Future of Legislation with Supermajority*, Ius Gentium: Comparative Perspectives on Law and Justice 126,
https://doi.org/10.1007/978-3-031-99324-4_10

The manufacturer's authorised representative in the EU is Springer Nature Customer Service Centre GmbH, Europaplatz 3, 69115 Heidelberg, Germany. If you have any concerns regarding our products, please contact ProductSafety@springernature.com

Printed and bound by CPI Group (UK) Ltd, Croydon, CR0 4YY
01/10/2026
02225864-0001